AUTISTIC SPECTRUM DISORDER A NEW OUTLOOK

Paul A. Bensur Jr. PhD

Table of Contents

INTRODUCTION

WHY AUTISM?

In 2007 I was given the opportunity to go to a two-day seminar in Warren Pennsylvania. The whole idea of being out of the office for two days and going back to the area in which I started my mental health career was very inviting, and I went. The presenter was Dr. John McGonigle. I had not seen Dr. McGonigle since 1995 when he came to the state hospital and gave a talk. I talked to him back then at this point I walked up to him before the presentation and reintroduced myself. It seems as though although it had been 12 years it seems like we're picking up where we left off. Dr. McGonigle talked about what he was going to be presenting over the course of the next 13 hours, two days, and handed me a CD to take a look at and he indicated to me you might want to get involved in this. It seems that he was hinting at the fact that maybe this is something I might want to look into. Over the course of the next two days, I got to speak with him on the side on what he was doing and what I had been doing since last time we met. We seem to come to an understanding that he was handing something off to me that he felt that maybe I had the capability of doing something with.

At the time we were dealing with the DSM-IV and the boundaries and specifics the DSM-IV used to determine autism. It seemed that within the first hour or so of this presentation I started to get a very good understanding of what autism is, how to identify it and some ideas on how to work with. At that point my life I was dealing mostly with individuals with ADHD, anxiety, depression and some posttraumatic stress disorder issues. But he opened my eyes to the fact that I understood what autism is and how I had the awareness to start to identify it. Of all the seminars I've gone to since 2007, that seminar continues to be one of the most memorable I have ever gone to. In 2010 I attended another seminar that Dr. McGonigle was hosting and it was good to see him again.

Later in 2010 I started my own private practice and became acutely aware of the fact that a lot of individuals that were brought to me had

Asperger's Disorder. I noticed what deficits they had and came up with different treatment ideas to work with them on overcoming some of their deficits. Some of those techniques are in the back of this book. I started to compile different treatment modalities in which helping individuals with Asperger's disorder overcome their deficits and begin to excel in those things in which they were having problems in. It seemed to be quite successful some of the simpler things work the best when it comes to helping individuals with specific deficits. Working with the family's was another story. It always seems that one parent will take the time and understand and the other parent has problems even with trying to take the effort to understand. So I had to come up with a program for parents. When the DSM 5 came out in 2012, autistic spectrum disorder took on a whole new meaning with new parameters and new meanings. However, the public does not go out and buy a DSM 5 and try and understand the language in the DSM five to understand the new differentiation in autistic spectrum disorder. It doesn't seem like anybody is actually taken this to the point where anybody in public could sit down and read something and understand it. Now, it looks like everybody is trying to present things in their own way and it goes over the head of the average individual. To help the public start to understand what autism is in this modern century, I started to write articles on the different types of autism, behaviors and of course other associated topics when it comes directly to autism. After writing several articles, I realized that there was a lot more to try and inform the public about when it comes to autism. I then set about putting together other articles and pretty soon I had more than enough to put a book together. Over the course of putting this book together of the last 3+ years, this isn't the whole story; this is an excellent place to start, this book is an excellent generalized understanding of what I have been able to work with over the course of the last eight years in private practice. There's a lot of reasonable explanations in this book too many aspects of the autism spectrum. But this isn't all there is, there is more, and as autism becomes more prevalent, due to the awareness of autism, I'm sure there will be more to be written about. But at this time there is a lot of ignorance out there when it comes to autism. The old stereotypical thought process of autism was, you had an individual who is nonverbal, did not make eye contact, and played by themselves, had a

few people they would associate with, but they would not communicate, and if their needs were met they had a total meltdown. That is no longer the stereotypical individual with autism. That specific level of autism as explained in this book in great detail. With the initial question of "why autism"?, The answer is very simply this: this book was written to help the public understand that there are people out there with autism that need specific help to overcome their deficits or to help them to get to the highest level of their functioning. At this point, there isn't anything going on out there that is really beneficial to the individuals with autism. This book is kind of a guide to make parents, teachers, caregivers and other family members insight into their loved one who has autism. I am a firm advocate for individuals with autism, and they have a lot to offer society. This can happen if the right program, with the right person interacts with the autistic individual with patience, persistence, and awareness of what that individual is capable of. In reading this book be aware of the fact that there are things that may not be discussed in the greatest of detail, but you will have an understanding of autism by the time you finish this book.

Paul A. Bensur Jr. PhD-LPC

Best Wishes
Paul A. Bensur PhD

Autistic Spectrum Disorder (ASD)

LEVEL I **DYNAMIC**
STATIC

LEVEL II **HIGH LEVEL-RIGHT BRAIN DOMINANT**
LEFT BRAIN DOMINANT

MIDDLE LEVEL- RIGHT BRAIN DOMINANT

MIDDLE-MIDDLE LEVEL -PROGRESSIVE

-REGRESSIVE

MIDDLE LEVEL- LEFT BRAIN DOMINANT

LOW LEVEL- RIGHT BRAIN DOMINANT

LOW LEVEL- LEFT BRAIN DOMINANT

LEVEL III

DISCLAIMER

This book is a complete testament to my experiences with individuals with autism. It covers my experiences from the DSM-IV through the DSM-5. It is by no means all there is to Autism. Autism continues to evolve, but this book is a good place to start. There may be some controversial items throughout this book, but that may lead to, and I hope, that others will continue on with their work with Autism and add to or better the presentations in this book.

This book is the Authors Presentation or Authors cut. It is direct and to the point. It has not been altered or ghost written. This is the author's pure work. It has not been altered by any editors. It is the direct work of the author.

DEDICATION

This book is dedicated to my wife Lisa for enduring the last three plus years of this manuscript writing.

My son Paul III

My parents Paul Sr. and Dolores (In loving memory of PABSR)

Special thanks to Dr. McGonigle

TO: All individuals with Autistic Spectrum Disorder and the families involved.

Started: 2015

Completed: July 7, 2017

Edited and Bound: May 7, 2018

Final Editing: July 7, 2018

Copy Write: July 9, 2018

Paul A. Bensur Jr PhD-LPC

Biography

I am the sum total of family, friends and learning experiences that were to become the compassion of my contribution to the world.
I am the first and oldest son of the marriage of Paul A. Bensur Sr. and Dolores Ann McGaughey-Bensur. My father was the first generation of the Bensur clan born in America, and my mother's ancestry goes back into the 1700's. My father came from a family that valued hard work and farming, and my mother came from a historically strong academically minded and farming family. This is where I get my work ethics (father) and academics (mother) and combined is the hard-working professional that will work to help you find your way.
I was born on July 7, 1959. I like to recite this in the Irish language: I was born on the shore of Loch Eire, in the city of Eire in the county of Eire in the state of Pennsylvania. In other words, I am a born and educated Erieite. I did live in Erie at times and even in, but I was raised in the West County areas of Girard and Lake City.
Educationally, I started half-day kindergarten in 1964 in Lake City at the new school named Elk Valley, but after kindergarten, I went to another school. In 1965 I started first grade at Saint John the Evangelist school. It was a ten-room school under St. John's Church. I was there from 1965 till I graduated in 1973. It was a great experience at that school. We had one sport: Basketball and I played from 1971 to 1973. I was the starting center in 1972-73 seasons. We had some good times on the court playing schools from all over the county. I was also an altar boy from 1968 to 1977 for the church. I also ran the candy store in 1972-73 and also assisted the janitorial staff in cleaning the social center. I took the test to be accepted to Cathedral Preparatory School for Boys in 1972 and was admitted. After graduation at St. John's in 1973, where I was the biggest kid in the school, I started Cathedral Prep in 1973 where it was all business.
The eight years that I was at St. John's were the most important of my life. We learned a lot about respecting authority as well as learning that we all have a purpose in this life. I personally learned a lot of

responsibility as I was in charge of the candy store, clean-up of the lunch room, clean-up of the social hall, being an altar boy, running errands for the pastor and most of all looking after my brothers. In my last year at St. John's School, all four of us were in attendance, and I was responsible for my youngest brother getting home. They don't have grade schools like this anymore, and they are very much needed in this world. So I graduated from St. John's in June of 1973 and was given the Parent-Teacher Organization award. This was unexpected, but I accepted it. It seemed to be the topper of my eight years there. Then it was off to Cathedral Prep.

Cathedral Prep was very different than anything that I had experienced up to this point. There were a lot of codes at that school. There was a dress code: dress pants, shoes, ties or a turtleneck and the official Cathedral Prep Blazer with the official patch on the left pocket. The first three years you wore a black jacket and the seniors wore the gold jacket. You wore the jacket every day all day unless you were permitted to take it off. The class ring was not authorized to be purchased until the end of the junior year, and you could not take delivery of the ring until the beginning of the senior year. The school ring was a symbol that you made it to the senior year and that you were going to become an alumnus. The school was highly competitive, disciplined and sports/organization oriented. There were few people in the school, if any, that did not participate in sports or some extracurricular activity. And there I was, the Lake City Farm boy in the middle of all that. Most people in the school were somewhat well off. Most did not know that there was a world beyond the city limits and nobody knew where Lake City was. I used to go to the library and on the Erie County map, show them where I lived. For some reason, everybody that I showed had the idea that Lake City was to the east on the map. Always thought that this was interesting that people in the city did not know there were places to the west. So over the four years at Prep, I was on the wrestling team, the track team and participated in intermural sports and the spirit club. I also had three years of Art Class and learned jewelry design and a few other artworks. I learned to type and became proficient in working a manual typewriter. But mostly, I grew up and learned more about responsibility and planning a future. For the most part, most of us were college bound, and some were headed for military service. Either way,

you never heard the words: "I DON'T KNOW" at Prep. You always had a plan or two or three or more. There was no lack of thought, and the future was always in planning. We were being prepared to become someone and be leaders to some degree. It was a highly disciplined environment, and we all were forged by the efforts of the faculty to become men.

I didn't score real high on the SAT test I took Junior year, I only scored in 870, and therefore I had to retake it senior year. In the meantime, of course, I received all kinds of information from various small colleges that I'd never heard of before. However, the influence of going to Gannon College had been introduced to me early in childhood, as my mother's brothers attended that fine institution. I re-took the SAT and scored an 880, not much better. It was my desire to at least look into Gannon College as I aspired to become a medical doctor. Over the course of the summer of 1976, along with the bicentennial celebrations, I had filled out and sent in several postcards requesting a college catalog of Gannon College. I had sent in a postcard and received a brochure with another postcard which I had sent in and received another postcard. At this point, I had not received a college catalog but more requests for the college catalog. After the third postcard that I sent in, I finally received a college catalog from Gannon College. I was so excited to receive the college catalog that all I did was open the envelope and pull out the college catalog. The document that was enclosed with the college catalog was a certificate from the college saying I was accepted to the college for the fall of 1977. I was accepted to Gannon without applying. So destiny seems to be the teacher and the student was off to follow his destiny.

Gannon College is quite a big difference from Cathedral Prep. Cathedral Prep was a highly structured environment complete with a dress code, and hair code and homework and disciplinary policies. College, on the other hand, was more of a free and open environment that if you didn't want to attend classes, you didn't have to. This didn't make any sense to me, but I tried to follow suit the best they could. It seems that the lack of discipline in this environment caused me a lot of stress issues because at Cathedral Prep you are an individual and all individuals were accounted for at any given time. In the college situation, you are an individual who is a group of other individuals in

individual classes with instructors that did not have the disciplinary policy in which I was brought up on over the course of the previous 12 years. In other words, when you started college, you are just nobody just trying to find his way in an environment that had no real disciplinary policy or disciplinary code as compared to the previous 12 years. It was quite an adjustment for me. Up to this time I had never had problems with any type of courses I had taken in the past but, I was put in a calculus class and had no clue what was going on in there. I did my best but still failed. And putting all my time in trying to learn calculus my other grade suffered, such as biology and my writing class. I did not know you could drop a course if you are failing it. I failed calculus for the semester and decided to retake it in the spring semester, but it was apparent that even though I retook the same course, I still wasn't getting it and subsequently failed it again. And all my other courses faltered, and in the grand finale, I was expelled from day school. I was told I could take night classes till I got my grade-point average up. In the meantime I was not allowed to come back to Gannon College as a full-time student. It was the first time I ever failed in anything and the first time I was ever told by the Dean I was not allowed to attend the school full-time until that said time I had my grade-point average up again. So that seems to be the end of that dream.

I took a summer job working for a local borough as a street maintenance person. For the most part, I worked alone digging up old street signs, putting up new street signs, cleaning out ditches, and trimming branches. I also at this time took on a Little League team as the manager. Had an excellent relationship with the team and we went on to win the championship that year (1978). In the meantime, I took a night job as a janitor in an electronics company. A father of one of the boys that I coached was a human resources director at a particular global company. He sent me an application, and a few months later I was hired at that institution. I was told that I wasn't wanted because the person who filled the bill better than me but didn't want the job. So there I was working a job, in a facility, where my supervisor didn't want me, so I had to work harder, and this is a chemical facility and therefore I was doing my best to learn. I had switched my major per night school to chemistry. Through this company, I was able to take some day courses in chemistry and seemed to learn it quite well.

Difficulties continued between me and my supervisor, and then I was summarily discharged. I found another job within two months of that incident at a nether facility which I would be doing analytical chemistry work. In the meantime, I had switch focus and started to get into insurance and also real estate. I was taking real estate classes at Penn State the Behrend campus. It was a different school than what I was used to, but I seem to do well in that type of instruction. I took the test for life insurance and passed it, I passed both my real estate courses, but I did not sit for the examination. In the meantime, my day job in analytical chemistry was coming to an end. It seems the company was able to purchase a machine that would do 75% of my work. So the 25% of the work that could not be done by the machine, I still had to do manually. Most the time I was reading different books, and doing the manual work.

I knew I needed a change and I had kicked around the idea of enlisting in the Army. Being a member of a military fraternity, The Pershing Rifles, there was some influence of being duty-bound. Mostly individuals who graduated from Gannon who were in the Pershing rifles did do some term of military service as officers. And it seems that a few of us decided to enlist. I was one of them. I enlisted in the United States Army and chose to become part of the field artillery. Basic training in one stop training was at Fort Sill Oklahoma. After being part of a military fraternity for so many years, basic training was not as harsh because I already knew what could happen. After basic training, my first duty post was Fort Lewis Washington. After some significant difficulties in some legal matters, which had nothing to do with being in the military, I decided to get out, and I received an honorable discharge.

Civilian life became easy because if you could deal with the military, the civilian world is not at all that tough. However, finding a job was another issue. I worked three part-time jobs and thought that maybe I could go back to school. Filling out some paperwork and taking out a couple of loans I was able to go back to Gannon to finish. I struggled through the first year due to some personal problems, but after those were resolved, I was able to pass all my courses and bring up my grade-point average. Then came senior year which I planned out from start to finish and had all my books ahead of time. I developed calendar and organizational skills and everything that needed to be

done before it needed to be turned in. As a result, I was on the Dean's list my entire senior year. I went back to school with my focus on chemistry but also on secondary education. So not only did I have a degree in chemistry, I also have a secondary as a general science and chemistry teacher and received a certificate from the Commonwealth certifying that I was a teacher. So the family non-preferred who had been a failure up until this time found out that academia could be a source of inspiration and also a source to strengthen one's sense of self. It was an honor to be listed on the back of the graduation program within asterisk next to my name denoting that I was on the Dean's list the entire senior year. So I finally completed my undergraduate degree over the course of a nine-year period. If you look at the past, I'd failed a lot of things except for coaching baseball and graduating basic training and advanced training and being good at being a soldier, but this was different. Always said that farm boy from Lake City found out he could learn and that what he learned he could prove that he learned well. I was trying for a job as a teacher, but no one was hiring, and the only job available to me was a part-time job at Gannon, which was now a University, a security guard. It was a job, and it was a start, and this led to the idea of possibly continuing on with graduate work at Gannon University. I applied to the Master of Science degree program in counseling and was accepted. I was working as a security guard at Gannon, and I was also substitute teaching at local school districts. Although I was tired all the time, working two jobs and going to grad school, the goal in mind here was to graduate and in the meantime look for a real job.

I was hired for a three-quarter year position at my old high school, Cathedral Prep but, I kept my night job as a security guard. I was working around the clock and going to graduate school and slept 3 to 4 hours per day. It was a hard life but if you want some bad enough you will work hard to get it. Four years later from the start of my first graduate school course I graduated from Gannon University in 1990 with a Masters Degree in Counseling. I was able to take extra courses because I worked for the University and one of the fringe benefits was free education for you and your dependents. I took full advantage of this and graduated with more credits in what I needed. After graduation day it was on to the next level of trying to find some type of employment. I substitute taught for a while, but that wasn't making

enough money, so I took a temporary position working in a plastic injection molding facility. If I thought I had an education before this, I definitely got an education during the time I was at that facility. A short line of temporary jobs finally led to finding out about state civil service. I took the state civil service tests and was rated number one in a specific job category, and approximately one year later I was hired at the state hospital. It seemed like my education continued at that facility as I had many psychiatrists that I worked with. I was very eager to learn new things, and they were very keen to teach me. I learned a lot about medications, side effects, and drug interactions. I also learned a lot about human behavior and how to help people who sometimes don't really want to be helped. It was a great learning experience, and I realize I was very good at helping people. However, as my luck always runs, the state was downsizing, and I was going to be the first one to get furloughed. Instead of waiting to be furloughed I went into the Department of Corrections. Another learning experience as the Department of Corrections was a lot different than the Department of Mental Health. But I did learn things at the Department of Corrections. However, it was not the therapeutic environment that I was looking for. I resigned from my position and took on a position whereby I would be a district supervisor. I did do administrative duties as I had many people working for me. However, I was still tentative about what was going on around me. I left that position and came back to Erie County to regroup and to somewhat start over again. I took several positions for different agencies and found myself back in injection molding. Finally, as luck would have it, an agency responded to my resume, and I was hired working in the community again. That agency was sold after I was there for a year and I started to work under a licensed psychologist.

I continued work as a mobile therapist, and I lasted for just over four years. Things started to get interesting and applied for me and I was granted another position within a state institution. As time progressed, I found myself in a better situation and moved. In the process of moving, I picked up extra work on the side doing mobile therapy again. This then led to a full-time position within that organization, and I resign from the state institution.

As things would have it, a particular insurance organization took over the management of the funding, and therefore I was again looking for a

position. After working with a few more licensed psychologist, I found my way back to a state institution. This time I had a game plan scratched out on paper of how I was going to open my own private practice. So I rolled up some money and was actually going to go another couple of months but the situations there, it was time to move on.

I had an offer or rent office space from an individual that I worked with before and started my private practice. I had a game plan sketched out on paper, and I had learned several marketing and business things throughout the course of my lifetime. First business course I ever took was a correspondence course from some school back in 1978.

I started in private practice officially June 2010. It was a slow process, but once word-of-mouth got out plus some other advertising, the practice began to flourish. I bought one of the condos in 2013 and now had my own private practice in private practice space. The condo took a lot of work to get it to where it needed to be, to be the therapeutic environment which I strive to provide to any patient coming through the door. Many people are shocked and amazed at the waiting area which is unique. The waiting area has two couches, two televisions, a Jacuzzi foot bath, and a reading area with several books. I strive not to make my patients wait more than 20 minutes at most if I am running behind or if there is some type of emergency going on but, I make sure they get their full time that is allotted to them.

My practice specialties, as illustrated in this book, have to do with autistic spectrum disorder. I also do drug and alcohol counseling, anxiety, depression and posttraumatic stress disorder. With my background as a guidance counselor, I also try to help people find their way when it comes to possible employment, academics and of course educational facilities.

In all retrospect, I am still just a farm boy who through trial, tribulation and trial and error, found that he could use all these experiences to help other people to work through their experiences. Imagine if you let your experiences be your teacher and let your dreams be your guide what you may be able to do in this world. Apparently, it worked out for this farm boy from Lake City Pennsylvania.

CHAPTER 1

Autistic Spectrum Disorders

MISNOMERS

Autistic Spectrum Disorders-Misnomers

As the world changes, the rules in which we play by continue to change as well. Anyone not staying up with the changes in the rules and in the playbook needs to be educated and needs to stay out of the way of those that know the rules, rather than get in the way, and cause undue problems for others.

The sole purpose of this chapter is to bring people up to date on what the rules are regarding the diagnoses of autistic spectrum disorder. Over the course of this chapter, those who are not up to date will be given ample examples of why they need to get up to date with the diagnosis and treatment of autism.

The DSM-5 has now been a mandated diagnostic rulebook since 2014. It came into publication in the year 2012 and was then mandated to be used in 2014. When it comes to autism, it differs considerably from the previous DSMs. Many of the diagnostic names have been eliminated from the DSM-5 such as autism, pervasive developmental disorder, Asperger's disorder, Child Disintegrative Disorder and Rhett's disease. None of these will be found in the DSM-5 but were commonly found in the DSM-IV and the DSM-IV TR. Those previously mentioned diagnoses have now been eliminated from the DSM-5 and in place of them is Autistic Spectrum Disorder (ASD)-level I, level II and level III.

I find it very interesting since the DSM-5 has been available, it seems that there are people who were still using the DSM-IV (most recently) and misdiagnosed individuals with autism. I question why these individuals are allowed in the field and performing the diagnosis. It seems they are using criteria that were discontinued and eliminated in the DSM-5. I question why these people are allowed to even work in the field since the DSM-5 has now been out since 2012 and there have been countless workshops on the introduction of the DSM-5. It is very disgusting to me that there are people allowed to diagnose individuals with autism who do not know anything about it. If you are not up-to-

date on the criteria for autistic spectrum disorder, then consult with a person who is.

Misinterpretations of autism and the autistic spectrum disorder seem to be quite common with people who were not up to date with the DSM-5. One of the old criterions for autism was a lack of eye contact. This should no longer be used as a measurement as individuals with autistic spectrum disorder level I and level II show moderate to minimal eye contact whereas level III may show minimal to no eye contact. Therefore, this misnomer needs to be relearned and eliminated from the criterion to determine autism.

The Diagnostic statement of "High Asperger's" was never a diagnosis although it was used quite frequently. You will never find this diagnosis in any of the DSM's but it was used quite frequently, and it was even used as recently as 2017. This never existed but people still use it. In the DSM-5, this is probably a level I or a high level II. So if you hear someone give your individual this diagnosis, consider him or her to be outdated in his or her understanding of autism. Your best bet would ask them to leave, or, leave that clinic and find someone who is experienced in the diagnosis of autistic spectrum disorder.

One of the other major criteria that were removed, that was common in all the previous DSM's (II, III, III-R, IV, and IV-TR) was a specific age limit for the diagnosis of autism. This ranged from the earlier DSM's and the later DSM's from 30 months the 36 months (IV an IV-TR). This age was eliminated in the DSM-5. It was finally recognized that individuals who may have autistic spectrum disorder might have gone undiagnosed in that period that was designated by the previous DSM's. Therefore, if you hear that your child is too old to be diagnosed with autism, the person giving the diagnosis is wrong. They obviously know nothing about the new DSM-5. Avoid these diagnosticians because they are obviously behind the time and need to catch up. They will give you an incorrect diagnosis. Consulting with someone who is up to

date on autistic spectrum disorder and the DSM-5 is the best thing you can do for your individual and for your family.

Diagnosticians who are not up to date with the DSM-5 will give diagnoses of what they see, and behaviors are noted. They do not put the entire behavior picture together to come up with the correct diagnosis of autistic spectrum disorder. This has been noted on many occasions whereby several professionals evaluated the individual, and they ended up with a diagnosis that was what had been seen and not what was there. In other words, they saw behaviors, but they did not add all the behaviors up to come up with the diagnoses of autism. Rather they singled out each individual behavior and labeled each individual behavior under the DSM code. When it comes to looking at this from the diagnostic standpoint: you now have an individual with three or four diagnoses that all fall under the autism behavior patterns. However, since the diagnosticians who are doing the observation and final write-up may not know anything about the new autistic spectrum disorder, they may give them two, three, or more diagnoses based on the behaviors they saw and not an overall picture of what they see. This is poor training on the part of diagnosticians, and they need some major upgrading to the tenor of their knowledge base.

One of the more common mistakes when it comes to diagnosing individuals with autistic spectrum disorder is to label them with another diagnosis that may seem simple to treat but may actually exacerbate the problem. Some of the common misdiagnoses are as follows: any of the attention deficit hyperactivity disorder diagnoses, intermittent explosive disorder, obsessive-compulsive disorder, mood disorder and any related mood disorders, oppositional defiant disorder and even bipolar disorder. All these diagnoses may be relevant to others, but when it comes to individuals with autistic spectrum disorder, they may show elements of many of these diagnoses, but overall they may not totally meet the criteria for these disorders. However, mistakes will be made because some of the major criteria

for these disorders may be seen, but overall the criterion is not usually met. It may be close to any of these disorders, but usually, the number of criteria needed for that disorder is not met. (Nevertheless, since those previously mentioned diagnoses all have some sort of diagnostic protocol, which includes medication and possibly therapy and follows an already established path). However, if your individual really has autistic spectrum disorder, medication may be harmful to them, and the need for therapy with a qualified therapist that specializes in autistic spectrum disorders may be the answer to treating this problem in the most effective manner. This is not going to be easy, but helping individuals with autism is a very fulfilling role in life.

In summation, this chapter is a warning going out to parents who have autistic individuals. It is also a warning to autistic individuals who may actually be diagnosed with something else. The other factor here goes out to those diagnosticians whether they are a therapist, psychiatrist or someone who cares for individuals. Get up to date with the DSM-5. Failure to be up-to-date with what the new criteria for autistic spectrum disorder are unethical and could be considered a criminal offense. For those adults out there that have always question their diagnoses, there is a possibility that you have autistic spectrum disorder. It is possible that you have been misdiagnosed your entire life.

In closing, be cautious of individuals who talk in terms that are no longer in use when it comes to diagnoses, especially when it comes to autistic spectrum disorder. Seek out someone who specializes in autistic spectrum disorders and the situation will resolve into a better place to be.

CHAPTER 2

Autistic Spectrum Disorders

Autism-An Introduction

Autism-An Introduction

Autism is a condition that has been on the rise over the last two decades, and even though it is becoming more prevalent the question remains: what is it? In addition, why don't more people understand it?

Neither the following questions posed in the above statement have a clear-cut answer. It seems that in modern society the autistic spectrum disorders are being somewhat overlooked at the individual level and it seems at times that fewer people understand or even want to understand what autism is. However, before we get into the modern day understanding of this disorder, let us look back at a brief history of autism.

I was in graduate school at Gannon University during the latter part of the 1980s. At that time there was a transition going on between the old DSM-III and the DSM-IIIR. The textbook I had at the time was based on the DSM-III, and we were required to purchase a DSM-IIIR. The textbook had a section on autism, which covered an entire seven pages. It described individuals with autism and described one behavioral program, which was to help them to learn some skills. For the most part, an autistic person at this time was described as someone who was in his or her own world and made noises. For the most part, these individuals were either in institutions or and day programs and were heavily medicated. The behavioral program that was being introduced to them was a classical conditioning method of teaching them a reward system and getting them to follow through on it. They were rewarded for their behavior. That was the extent of what autism was during the days of the DSM-III. The following diagnostic criteria were taken from the DSM-III and the DSM III R.

DSM III (1980)

Diagnostic criteria for Infantile Autism were stated as such:

The onset was noted before 30 months of age, pervasive lack of responsiveness to other people (autism), and gross deficits in language development. It was also noted: If speech is present, peculiar speech patterns such as immediate and delayed echolalia, metaphorical language, and pronominal reversal. Also, the following was indicated: A bizarre responses to various aspects of the environment, e.g., resistance to change, peculiar interest in or attachments to animate or inanimate objects. Further noted behaviors were an absence of delusions, hallucinations, loosening of associations, and incoherence as in Schizophrenia. (DSM III, 1980, APA)

After 7 years, the DSM III-R replaced the DSM III

DSM III-R (1987)

Diagnostic Criteria for Autistic Disorder

It was indicated that at least eight of the following sixteen items are present, these to include at least two items from A, one from B, and one from C.

Section A. Qualitative impairment in reciprocal social interaction (the examples within parentheses are arranged so that those first listed are more likely to apply to younger or more disabled, and the later ones, to older or less disabled) as manifested by the following:

A marked lack of awareness of the existence or feelings of others (for example, treats a person as if that person were a piece of furniture. They do not notice another person's distress. Apparently has no concept of the need of others for privacy. None or abnormal seeking of comfort at times of distress (for example, does not come for comfort even when ill, hurt, or tired. They seek comfort in a stereotyped way,

for example, says "cheese, cheese, cheese" whenever hurt). They show none or impaired imitation (for example, does not wave bye-bye; does not copy parent's domestic activities. They display a mechanical imitation of others' actions out of context. They display none or abnormal social play (for example, does not actively participate in simple games; refers solitary play activities. They involve other children in play only as mechanical aids. They display gross impairment in the ability to make peer friendships (for example, no interest in making peer friendships despite interest in making friends, demonstrates lack of understanding of conventions of social interaction, for example, reads the phone book to uninterested peer.

Section B. Qualitative impairment in verbal and nonverbal communication and in imaginative activity, (the numbered items are arranged so that those first listed are more likely to apply to younger or more disabled, and the later ones, to older or less disabled) as manifested by the following:

No mode of communication, such as communicative babbling, facial expression, gesture, mime, or spoken language. They display markedly abnormal nonverbal communication, as in the use of eye-to-eye gaze, facial expression, body posture, or gestures to initiate or modulate social interaction (for example, does not anticipate being held, stiffens when held, does not look at the person or smile when making a social approach, does not greet parents or visitors, has a fixed stare in social situations). There is an absence of imaginative activity, such as play-acting of adult roles, fantasy character or animals. They show a lack of interest in stories about imaginary events; Marked abnormalities in the production of speech, including volume, pitch, stress, rate, rhythm, and intonation (for example, monotonous tone, question-like melody, or high pitch). There are marked abnormalities in the form or content of speech, including the stereotyped and repetitive use of speech (for example, immediate echolalia or mechanical repetition of a television commercial. The use of "you" when "I" is meant (for example, using

"You want a cookie?" to mean, "I want a cookie." Idiosyncratic use of words or phrases (for example, "Go on green riding" to mean, "I want to go on the swing." There are frequent irrelevant remarks (for example, starts talking about train schedules during a conversation about sports. There is marked impairment in the ability to initiate or sustain a conversation with others, despite adequate speech. For example, indulging in lengthy monologues on one subject regardless of interjections from others.

Section C. Markedly restricted repertoire of activities and interests as manifested by the following:

Stereotyped body movements (for example, hand flicking or twisting, spinning, and head-banging, complex whole-body movements). Persistent preoccupation with parts of objects (for example, sniffing or smelling objects, repetitive feeling of texture of materials, spinning wheels of toy cars. The attachment to unusual objects: for example, insists on carrying around a piece of string. Marked distress over changes in trivial aspects of the environment, for example, when a vase is moved from usual position. They display an unreasonable insistence on following routines in precise detail, for example: insisting that exactly the same route always be followed when shopping. They display a markedly restricted range of interests and a preoccupation with one narrow interest, e.g., interested only in lining up objects, in amassing facts about meteorology, or in pretending to be a fantasy character.

Section D. Onset during infancy or early childhood

Specify if childhood onset (after 36 months of age) (DCM III-R 1987, APA)

As one can see the difference between the two DSM's, it should be noted that the criterion for autistic disorder seems to have expanded and the criterion for the determination of autism changed in regards to

the expected outset of the problem which went from 30 months to 36 months of age. However if one was to look at all the criterion in the DSM IIIR, there seems to be a wide array of abilities, behaviors and other observable actions that do not appear in the DSM III. It should also be noted that many of these behaviors seem to cover a wider array of functioning levels extremely different from those described in the DSM III. This, of course, led the door open to other interpretations because some of these criteria were closely related to other mental health issues. So it seems that from the evolution of the DSM III to the DSM IIIR the idea of childhood autism which had very specific behaviors opened up to the possibility of other behaviors that were directly related to the autism diagnosis in the DSM IIIR. However, the major criterion minor changed was the time in which an individual had to be diagnosed with autism. It changed from 30 months of age to 36 months of age. This cutoff point seems to hold autism to a specific timeframe in which it could be determined. It is also during this time in history that the chronic condition for children at the time was attention deficit hyperactivity behavior. The use of Ritalin and its derivatives were widely prescribed to try to help children with some of the behavioral issues that also appear somewhat in autism but were not diagnosed prior to the 36-month cutoff. Therefore, the attention deficit hyperactivity disorder diagnosis was applied. In a facility, I was working at a time a statistic that was quoted to me by a counselor and a school, during this period, was that better than half the school district was on some form of Ritalin. However, looking back at this time in history, 1987, where these children really attention-deficit/hyperactivity disorder or did they actually have some form of autism to the 36 month cutoff in diagnoses? At this point in history when I look back, I would probably conclude that 50 to 70% of those children that were on Ritalin for attention-deficit/hyperactivity disorder probably had some form of autism. However, since the criterion cutoff was 36 months, it was determined that they had to have attention-deficit/hyperactivity disorder because they could not be autistic

because, for the most part, these children were school age and well beyond the 36 months, which was the cutoff. We cannot go back into history and try to correct the wrong, but what we can do in the present day is take more time, understanding and patience to understand what it is we can do with people who are diagnosed on the autistic spectrum disorder at this time. As you can see, the DSM IIIR, which was the guideline at the time from 1987 to 1994, did not open this up for more understanding instead it gave defined criteria and anyone who was not diagnosed before 36 months of age had to be something else. For the most part, individuals who are not diagnosed under these criteria at that time in history were for the most part given several interesting diagnoses such as attention-deficit/hyperactivity disorder, obsessive-compulsive disorder, oppositional defiant disorder, intermittent explosive disorder and selective mutism. Just think of what changes could have been made if that criterion of 36 months was not the gold standard at the time. As I stated I cannot go back and right the wrong but if we start today, we do start to correct things as they are.

The DSM-IV/IV-TR Criteria for Autism was listed as such:

DSM-IV (1994) and DSM-IV-TR (2000)

299.00 Autistic Disorder (was the diagnostic code) The Criteria was giving in the following:

A total of six (or more) items from (1), (2), and (3), with at least two from (1), and one each from (2) and (3):

Section 1:

Noted qualitative impairment in social interaction, as manifested by at least two of the following behaviors. Marked impairment in the use of multiple nonverbal behaviors such as eye-to-eye gaze, facial

expression, body postures, and gestures to regulate social interaction. They have a failure to develop peer relationships appropriate to developmental level. They have a lack of spontaneous seeking to share enjoyment, interests, or achievements with other people (e.g., by a lack of showing, bringing, or pointing out objects of interest). They have a lack of social or emotional reciprocity.

Section 2: Displays of qualitative impairments in communication as manifested by at least one of the following behaviors. A delay in, or total lack of, the development of spoken language (not accompanied by an attempt to compensate through alternative modes of communication such as gesture or mime). In individuals with adequate speech, marked impairment in the ability to initiate or sustain a conversation with others. They display the stereotyped and repetitive use of language or idiosyncratic language. They have a lack a varied, spontaneous make-believe play or imitative social play appropriate to developmental level.

Section 3: The display of restricted, repetitive, and stereotyped patterns of behavior, interests, and activities, as manifested by at least one of the following behaviors. They display an encompassing preoccupation with one or more stereotyped and restricted patterns of interest that is abnormal either in intensity or in focus. They display an apparently inflexible adherence to specific, nonfunctional routines or rituals. There are displays of stereotyped and repetitive motor mannerisms (e.g., hand or finger flapping or twisting, or complex whole-body movements). There is a persistent preoccupation with parts of objects.

The following criteria were also noted:

There are noted delays or abnormal functioning in at least one of the following areas, with onset prior to age 3 years: (1) social interaction, (2) language as used in social communication, or (3) symbolic or imaginative play.

This disturbance is not accounted for by Rett's disorder or childhood disintegrative disorder.

When one looks at the diagnostic criteria for autistic disorder, there was mention some other issues that seem to fall under the same general category. In the above quotation, it was noted other issues such as something called Rett's Disorder and Childhood Disintegrative Disorder. Also under this categorical section of the DSM-IV and also mentioned something called pervasive developmental disorder and another interesting item called Asperger's disorder. These criterions were placed in the part of a book that described childhood disorders. It should be noted at this time that pervasive developmental disorder was in the previous DSM going all way back to the DSM III, where it was referred to his childhood issues similar to autism. It should be noted that once again the cutoff point for the diagnosis of autistic disorder was at the 36-month mark of a person's life. So once again, autism was limited to the 36-month mark. Therefore, if an individual is not diagnosed prior to 36 months of age, they could not receive the autism disorder diagnosis. However, the DSM-IV and its revised edition the DSM-IV TR, had a section in the book referred to as disorders usually first diagnosed in infancy, childhood, or adolescents. This section of the book was attempting to help clinicians diagnose individuals that may have had long-standing problems going back to childhood that could not fit the diagnostic criteria for autism. Other diagnoses that were used were : Pervasive Developmental Disorder, Rett's Disorder, Childhood Disintegrative Disorder, Asperger's disorder. It was noted that these diagnoses were used extensively at times when the diagnoses were made after 36 months of age. It should also be noted that many of these diagnoses were not given attention since attention deficit-hyperactivity disorder and bipolar disorder was more popular to be used. This statement will render many an argument but, as it is, being aware of mental illness for the last 31 years may qualify me as knowing something of what was going on, but I will entertain all

academic discussions of this nature. During this time of the DSM-IV and the DSM IV-TR, which lasted 21 years, a term that continued to be repeatedly used which technically had very little merit, which was the diagnoses, which will not be found in either book, of high functioning Asperger's. This is another term that came from the semi-educated mind of someone who is trying to say that someone was beyond the Asperger's syndrome but had some issues. It was never valid, but it was extensively used.

One last footnote about the DSM-IV and the DSM-IV TR that should be noted was the expanse of the criteria in the form of different levels of functioning, behaviors and body language that went into the description of autism. It seemed too expanded even further than the DSM III-R. Nevertheless, in keeping the criteria of the 36 month cut off it would seem that the other diagnoses that were used in lieu of autism existed for the simple reason of giving someone with the criteria listed under autistic spectrum disorder and did not qualify due to the 36 month cut off, special notice and attention.

After almost 20 years, the DSM 5 replaced the DSM-IV and the DSM-IV TR. The DSM 5 officially came out in January 2012 but was not accepted and put into actual use until September 2014. The DSM 5 finally consolidated the criteria for autism and renamed it: Autistic Spectrum Disorder. As noted directly from the DSM 5 the diagnostic criteria for autism spectrum disorder are F84.0. Previously in the former DSM's the diagnostic code was 299.00.

Area 1:

Persistent deficits in social communication and social interaction across multiple contexts, as manifested by the following, currently or by history: Deficits in social-emotional reciprocity, ranging, for example, from abnormal social approach and failure of normal back-and-forth conversation; to reduced sharing of interests, emotions, or affect; to failure to initiate or respond to social interactions. Deficits in

nonverbal communicative behavior used for social interaction, ranging, for example, from poorly integrated verbal and nonverbal communication; to abnormalities in I contact and body language or deficits in understanding and use of gestures; to a total lack of facial expressions and nonverbal communication. Deficits in developing, maintaining, and understanding relationships, ranging, for example, from difficulties adjusting behavior to suit various social contexts; to difficulties in sharing imaginative play or in making friends; to the absence of interest in peers.

Specify current severity:

Severity is based on social communication impairments and restricted, repetitive patterns of behavior.

Area 2:

Restricted, repetitive patterns of behavior, interests, or activities, as manifested by at least two of the following, currently or by history. Stereotyped or repetitive motor movements, use of objects, or speech (e.g., simple motor stereotypes, lining up toys or flipping objects, echolalia, idiosyncratic phrases). Insistence on sameness, inflexible adherence to routines, or ritualized patterns of verbal or nonverbal behavior (e.g., extreme distress at small changes, difficulties with transitions, rigid thinking patterns, greeting rituals, need to take the same route or eat the same food every day). They display highly restricted, fixated interests that are abnormal in intensity or focus (e.g., strong attachment to or preoccupation with unusual objects, excessively circumscribed or perseverative interests). They display hyper-or hyporeactivity to sensory input or unusual interest in sensory aspects of the environment (e.g., apparent indifference to pain/temperature, adverse response to specific sounds or textures, excessive smelling or touching of objects, visual fascination with lights or movement). The overloading of any or a combination of the five senses or no over-reaction to sensory stimuli notes this.

Specify current severity.

Severity is based on social communication impairments and restricted, repetitive patterns of behavior.

The symptoms must be present in the early development. (They may not become fully manifest until social demands exceed the limit of capabilities, or may be masked by learning strategies in later life).

The symptoms cause clinically significant impairment in social, occupational, or other important areas of current functioning.

The disturbances are not better explained by intellectual disability (intellectual developmental disorder) or global developmental delay. Intellectual disability and autism spectrum disorder frequently co-occur. To make a comorbid diagnosis of autism spectrum disorder and intellectual disability social communication should be below that expected for the general developmental level.

Individuals with a well-established DSM-IV diagnosis of autistic disorder, Asperger's disorder or pervasive developmental disorder not otherwise specified, should be given the diagnosis of autism spectrum disorder. Those individuals who have marked deficits in social communication, but whose symptoms do not otherwise meet criteria for autism spectrum disorder, they should be evaluated for social (pragmatic) communication disorder.

Specifically if:

Noted: With or without accompanying intellectual impairment

Noted: With or without accompanying language impairment

There is an association with the known medical or genetic condition or environmental factor.

There is a possible association with another neurodevelopmental, mental, or behavioral disorder with catatonia. (DSM-5,2012/APA)

With the new DSM 5, the criterion of 36 months being the cut off was eliminated. It seems that it was finally recognized that individuals who may have autistic spectrum disorder their whole life and it was not recognized within the 36-month criteria. The current criterion for autistic spectrum disorder may be applied to adults at this time, as there is no longer the 36 months cut off point. The items that were eliminated in the DSM 5 such as Asperger's Disorder, Autism, Pervasive Developmental Disorder-not otherwise specified, Child Disintegrative Disorder, and Rett's Disorder. The DSM 5 has now denoted the diagnosis of Autism Spectrum Disorder(ASD) and has divided it up into 3 levels. To be perfectly clear on this I suggest that you buy the book (DSM 5) however; I will give a thumbnail sketch. The most severe of the autism spectrum disorders are referred to as ASD level III. This seems to be the new designation for the old autism diagnosis and may include Child Disintegrative Disorder. I did not write this, and therefore it would be under my clinical judgment that this is where these two items were categorized in ASD level III.

The next level is categorized as autism spectrum disorder level II: ASD level II has its own criteria. In my clinical practice, this is where many of my individuals with autism spectrum disorder fall.

The final level is referred to as autism spectrum disorder level I. ASD level I where I believe that Asperger's disorder was renamed. There are many interesting characteristics that the ASD level I possess, but this will be described in detail in a later chapter.

My professional advice to anyone who is working with children or adults with autistic spectrum disorder should become proficient in learning what the new criterions for autistic spectrum disorder are. Keep in mind that under the new DSM 5 criteria, anyone could be given the diagnoses of autistic spectrum disorder.

In closing, I would like to make the following statement: Many people with autistic spectrum disorder have been misdiagnosed with some other mental health issue. Only with understanding, compassion, and reasoning can anyone help an individual with Autistic Spectrum Disorder.

CHAPTER 3

Autistic Spectrum Disorders

Autism-The New Look

Autism-The New Look

In a previous Chapter "Autism- An Introduction, I basically gave you the evolution of Autism since 1987. Since that time, and a few years after, Autism diagnostics changed, and more individuals were placed under the Autistic Spectrum Disorder syndrome. This was in part due to the removal of the age restriction for autism but also due to the combining of the previously used syndromes such as Asperger's Disorder, Pervasive Developmental Disorder-Not Otherwise Specified, Child Disintegrative Disorder and Rhett's Disorder. In combining these syndromes under the heading of Autism Spectrum Disorder and removing the age limit, this opened up individuals to be understood, and hopefully, better treatment plans and opportunities are to be offered. However, how do we get the population (Parent, teachers, school districts and employers) to see the individual that has been diagnosed with ASD to see them as they are and not view them from the past diagnostic thoughts? In the past, when someone would talk about a child with autism there would be an immediate hush and then an apology for their "poor child" with autism. The child was already grouped as a lost cause in the minds who heard the word "AUTISM." This was due to the definition and misunderstanding that was in the minds of all. The thought that all autistic children were in their own world and that they were probably Intellectually Disabled (current definition of past syndrome known as Mental Retardation) the conversation would end and everyone would wonder about the individual but not ask any further questions. Autism was one of those words that caused people to back away and then count their blessing and be happy that it is not one of theirs. This type of thought process was quite common, and at times people shied away from families and parents that stated that they had an autistic child. For the most part, no one wanted to take the time to understand why his or her child was in his or her own world and the bizarre behavior at times, but some parents tried, and there was always a chance that his or her child

could learn some skills. They worked with the child the best they could. That was the past, and it seemed that those individuals that were diagnosed with autism had many issues and some did progress where others did not. But, this is the old definition and mindset of Autism. The adoption of the current Diagnostic and Statistical Criteria Manuel 5, (September 2014) changed the definition and renamed Autism as Autistic Spectrum Disorder. This contains the new definition and criteria for autism and what were the associated syndromes: Asperger's Disorder, Pervasive Developmental Disorder-Not Otherwise Specified, and Child Disintegrative Disorder. Now comes the problem, how do we help individuals to understand what the new definitions are when only a small population have the new DSM-5 in their possession? Well, my goal with this chapter and the entirety of this book is to help in passing on the message about Autistic Spectrum Disorder (ASD) as in: What it is, signs and symptoms, possible ways to deal with your child/adolescent/adult with ASD, and other much needed skills and understanding. This is my goal, and that is to help people with autistic spectrum disorder to be understood, given a chance to develop their strengths and have a chance for some level of independence and prosperity. The goal of this book is to: help the caregivers (parents, teachers, and support staff) in understanding and hopefully learn some tools to help change their methods and attitude so they can be more supportive and effective in helping the person with ASD to reach their goals.

Autistic Spectrum Disorder is currently classified into three levels such as ASD I, ASD II and ASD III. For the most part, I personally work with ASD I, and ASD II. The ASD III Level, for the most part, is treated in specialized centers, as there is the possibility/probability of the component of Intellectual Disability. There is a need for the specialized programs due to the level of intellectual functioning and their specific needs. I do not work with ASD III's at all in the outpatient setting; they are more suited for other treatment facilities

that provide day programming or even residential programming. That being stated, let me explain about the ASD I and II levels and why I work with them.

The focus of this chapter will be to describe the similarities and the uniqueness of ASD level I and II. In other chapters, I will discuss other topics such as communication problems and emotional issues. At this point, due to the complexity of the issues, I will stay with this specific topic of descriptions of the characteristics of ASD level I and II.

Similarities:

There are several similarities when it comes to ASD I and ASD II such as the following: they have average to above average IQ levels, they have a dominant side of the brain, they think in logical ideas, and they have problems understanding and expressing their own emotions and understanding or interpreting the emotions of others.

Intelligence level, from my experience, can be very high to average and with the test scores that I have been able, to acquire from the WISC intelligence test (WISC-R to V) it is noted that there are differences between the performance IQ and the verbal IQ scores for the most part. In some cases, it is not the overall score that should be compared but comparing the subtest scores that will help the therapist deal with how the person with ASD thinks and interprets the world. I have seen some overall IQ scores that were average, when the two divisions of the test are separated, the verbal or the performance IQ may be very high, and the other part of the IQ test may be much lower, and therefore the overall IQ score looks average. However, upon the separation between the verbal IQ and performance IQ, in some cases, there is a very notable difference of as much as three standard deviations. The full-scale IQ score then looks to be average due to the scaling of the two parts, verbal and performance tests, and this becomes somewhat deceiving. For example, a person who has ASD had an overall or full-scale IQ of 109, but his performance test

was 130, and his verbal test was 82. In this case, it can be seen that this person would be more of a performance individual, which then equates to having a right-brained dominance. It should also be noted in the WISC there is subtest that can be looked at individually with regard to possible strengths as well as weaknesses. Therefore it should be noted that individuals with ASD have strengths as well as weaknesses, but the issue is that the strengths should be identified and encourage where are the weaknesses should be taught in a remedial fashion. Weaknesses seemed to be stressed as being more important than the strengths, and they are not. It has been documented that in most educational systems when your strengths are identified, it is not emphasized as per se the weaknesses, which seem to be what is pushed to be learned. Even though individuals have an average to above average IQ it should be noted that if they are pushed to learn something that they feel is not logical, and is part of their deficit side, they will be resistive until someone can explain to them the importance, in a logical manner, of why he or she needs to be able to accomplish this task. If logic is not presented, then there is a possibility of some type of altercation or possibly a behavioral outburst. But it be known that people who have ASD level I and II are very intelligent, and with the use of logical explanations there is a good possibility that there will be better cooperation rather than someone trying to enforce or push their thought process upon the ASD person which will result in an altercation with the possibility of a meltdown. This is why individuals need to be specially trained and be very familiar with the clients they are working within an educational setting as well as in the behavioral settings. This is where one of the major problems of understanding and treating as well as educating individuals with ASD comes into play. Because people are not taking the time to understand all the parameters of ASD they become very ineffective in dealing with individuals who have ASD and therefore assume that by their own volition the individual is misbehaving. This is so far from the truth it is a very serious problem. Individuals with ASD

are intelligent, however, due to certain nuances or idiosyncrasies; it is assumed that they are deficits in their intelligence. They are very intelligent, but they have issues in dealing with what may be expected of them from other people when the instructions or the directions are not spelled out in a way that they are able to follow them and then follow through and of course, they must have some logical meaning. However, we will discuss communication issues in another chapter.

When the discussion about a dominant side of the brain comes into play one has to be aware of what each side of the brain functionally does. For the most part, I will keep this simple and to the point and therefore everyone can benefit from this tidbit of information. The left side of the brain is mainly the language side of the brain. In other words, this has to do with verbal communication and the deciphering and understanding of communication. Individuals who are dominant left brained are very good at writing, poetry, understanding the written word and some forms of art. They are able to explain in a very logical manner when it comes to their communication ability. They may overelaborate at times in their explanation to the point where the listener walks away or starts showing some negative body language or the speaker just interprets the situation as going nowhere and becomes frustrated. They have weaknesses in math, science, remembering numbers and to some extent understanding sequences that have to do with numbers. However, if the sequence has to do with letters or words, they have no problem in deciphering and putting it together.

The right-brained dominant individual has good mathematical skills, they have the ability to interpret and possibly even designs three-dimensional drawings, and they are very good at number sequences and interpretation of tone volume and inflection but not necessarily in interpreting the words that they hear. Their ability to explain things is in a very logical manner that has to do with some type of numbering sequence or sequence that involves numbers. At times, they will

become frustrated with the fact that they cannot explain what they are doing or what they are working on so that the listener can understand. They may become frustrated, quit speaking altogether, and start to have a minor meltdown. This is because there are so many things being dealt with at one time that the crossover between the left side of the brain and the right side of the brain may have the person frustrated and they may not be able to speak. However, if they are not questioned and left alone, they will complete the task in a very timely manner and afterward may be able to explain it in some form or another that may be decipherable by anyone. When things are explained the individual may use terminology that may not be commonplace and therefore the listener may not understand what is being said to them. This is quite common and what normally happens is that the individual tries to explain and the listener stops listening after the 2nd or 3rd word, forms an opinion, connects an emotion, shows certain body language and the ASD individual picks up on some of these things, sometimes, and becomes frustrated in the fact that there is a lack of communication going on between himself and listener. This will be covered in another chapter. However, at this time, this is a brief sketch about how the right and left-brain works. And with some minor differences both ASD, I's and ASD II's communicate and logically decipher information as well as trying to speak it.

That is a thumbnail sketch of the similarities.

Differences

The major difference between an ASD I and an ASD II are in their ability to implement adaptive skills. Both groups can learn adaptive skills. However, the implementation of the adaptive skills seems to be somewhat lacking with the ASD II group. This is one of the reasons how the ASD level I may have gone undetected for many years because they were able to develop adaptive skills and seems like they were just everyday people struggling with life. The ASD level II

probably have shown many problems struggling especially with social skills, commonsensical items, and common day abilities that many of us take for granted because we have been given the opportunity to learn. A person with ASD II was most probably not given the opportunity to learn certain skills because either they were marked as being unable to acquire said skills or no one took the time to teach them. This was possibly due to some behavioral issues that may have arisen or been in the persons past. It seems that once the behavioral issues occur, they are believed to be consistent and permanent, but this is far from the truth. It would be known that people with ASD II can adapt, but once they are marked as a behavioral problem, they are put in behavioral programming and do not learn adaptive skills and behaviors. ASD IIs have the ability to learn, but they may not implement the skill that is learned because it may not make logical sense even though it is practical. They may not be given the practice time to learn the practical side of the skill and therefore not adopt it. However, if the skill can be explained in a logical manner, it may become practical and learned. Nevertheless, this takes patience and someone who is willing to take the time and work with the individual with ASD II. The ASD level I can be difficult in picking up adaptive skills but, with a minimum explanation, they have a tendency to realize the logic and practicality of the skill that is being taught to them and may implement it rather quickly. In contrast, if an ASD II is taught an adaptive skill that they do not see as being logical or practical they may still learn it but they will not implement it, and they will back away from it. The ASD II's have developed what may be referred to as a comfort zone. This is a zone in which they do not feel any anxiety or the need to move away from. When they are pushed to try and learn a task or follow through on some activity or focus on something else, they may get close to learning or completing, and they may retreat into this comfort zone. It is best that when they retreat to this comfort zone just leave them alone. Any type of encouragement or pushing may lead to a meltdown, which may include an argument with

the possibility of some type of physical altercation. The ASD level II will retreat to this comfort zone when things do not go as planned and if they are pushed too hard to move beyond that comfort zone. The ASD II will resist and retreat and stay in that comfort zone for an indeterminate amount of time. They will focus on an item that is important to them but may have a minor detail that is unclear or illogical but will not progress to implement an adaptive skill or solution that may benefit them. In retrospect, the ASD level I does not retreat as quickly, however, they do go into a mode of hibernation for a set period of time. During this time, the ASD 1 goes through a phase of regrouping and planning whereas the ASD II just seems to retreat and fixate themselves on a minor/major problem in their life.

Overall, this is just a thumbnail sketch, and this chapter could go on and on, but that is what the rest of the book is for. I am going to divide this up into other major issues that plague people with autistic spectrum disorder over the course of this book. There are other problem areas that people see in individuals with autistic spectrum disorder, and hopefully, I can give an adequate explanation about these issues. However, It is my hope that working from this book, someone or a group use this information and move forward with the care and treatment of individuals with Autistic Spectrum Disorder.

CHAPTER 4

Autistic Spectrum Disorder

Level I

Autistic Spectrum Disorder-Level I

In the DSM 5 the Autistic Spectrum Disorder-Level I is defined by the following: under severity level: requires support. Under social communication: without supports in place, deficits in social communication cause noticeable impairments. Difficulty initiating social interactions and clear examples of atypical or unsuccessful responses to social overtures of others may appear to have decreased interest in social interactions. For example, a person who is able to speak in full sentences and engages in communication but who is to and fro conversation with others fails, and whose attempts to make friends are odd and typically unsuccessful. Restricted, repetitive behaviors: inflexibility of behavior causes significant interference with functioning in one or more contexts: Difficulty switching between activities. Problems of organization and planning hamper independence.

As defined by the DSM 5, the autistic spectrum disorder-level I individual has the best chance of independent living with minimal supervision. As compared to the level III, needing constant supervision, and the level II, supervision-mild to moderate, level I seem to have the best chance of achieving the highest level of their ability or minimizing all activities through the development of routines and boundaries. There are two specific types of level I's: Dynamic and Static (Chapter 4). There are noted strengths and weaknesses to some degree between the left and right brained individuals, but it seems that they have learned skills, specifically adaptive skills and learning skills that minimize the differences between an individual who is right brained dominant versus an individual that is left-brain dominant. There is some differentiation, but it seems to be more like a subject-by-subject matter that does not fit into the logical construct of the trivium and quadrivium. This may be a very accurate definition, and

they could be challenged, but for the most part, it is a guideline rather than something that is cast in stone. As the continuation of work with individuals with autistic spectrum disorder-level I continue the two groups fall into two basic categories: 1) individuals who have learned adaptive skills, dealt with society and decided on developing their own programs for dealing with life in general and live by a protocol they developed but will not change from that protocol (static). The second group has learned a lot of adaptive skills and learning other adaptive skills and making some changes (dynamic). The first group, levels I (static) are pretty much set in their ways, and learning of adaptive skills is minimal. This group seems to be shaped to some extent by the following: age, trauma, problems with people and negative experiences. They may have the co-occurrence of the following issues: depression, anxiety, mood swings and to some extent delusions or misinterpretations. Other items that already exist: obsessive-compulsive disorder, logical thought and some inflexibility, and rigid behavior patterns. They have lived long enough, experienced traumatic events and have come up with their own ways of dealing with these items in life that are logical to them. They have a rigid protocol, process, and procedure that will give them the expected product in the end. They seem to like predictable outcomes and routine. They seem to have issues with any type of change, and therefore in their construct, they have designed their existence with a lot of routine behaviors and predictable protocols that lead to predictable end products. They are highly resistant to change unless of course that change can be explained to them in such a way that it will be of benefit to them if they adapt to it. Henceforth they are static for the most part because they have figured out what they need to live and how to adapt to minimal change. Overall, they have a rigid protocol which they follow on a day-by-day basis. Any type of change could result in some type of loss of emotional control. This will be further explained in this chapter.

On the other hand, the other group of individuals with autistic spectrum disorder level I (dynamic) continues a learning process and continues to look for and enjoy learning, adaptive skills and dealing with people and problem-solving. Age is not a factor here, but it could be to some extent. Individuals who are younger may have a tendency to want to find more ways to fit in or learn things, but it is also dependent upon their experience or experiences with life. It may even be the case that individuals who were diagnosed in the level IIs have learned many adaptive skills and in a sense have been promoted to level I. This is not uncommon, and it has been noted that there are other recorded incidents of this occurring. It is logical that if the level II individual is paired with the correct therapeutic interventions and programming they can learn a lot of adaptive skills and become a Level I. The level II, at this phase in their life, is open to some direction and learning adaptive skills, work skills and also to some degree some communication and socialization skills. If the Level I individual has the proper instruction, they may become very successful and only have minimal issues that are of an autistic nature. They will not act like or display many of the outward behaviors of autism. They may be described as just a geek, a nerd or an intelligent person with no social skills or communication skills. However, even though they have intelligence and have the ability to problem solve and other academic qualities, they may not be able to express themselves or socialize with other people. Individuals like this in the past were called either arrogant or eccentric, but they actually had autism. This group of individuals with autistic spectrum disorder-level I (dynamic) can be very successful in the world around them, but they need some help with some of those details that they may not feel are important, or they feel they really did not need to pay attention to. Therefore, the deficit is not readily seen, but with enough contact with the individual, the issues brought about by autistic spectrum disorder are quite prevalent. In this area of level I-(dynamic), would be seen as someone who does not balance the checkbook, does not pay bills on

time, if at all, and has a tendency to miss minor details that they deem are not significant. This is where they need some minimal supervision or help in order to deal with these items that they feel are not that important but are important in the scheme of life.

As has just been presented there are two different groups in the autistic spectrum disorder-level I-(static and dynamic). Both groups will be compared and contrasted in chapter 4. The characteristics that were discussed in the autistic spectrum disorder-level II (Chapter 5) will be used as a guideline to show the adaptive qualities that an individual with autistic spectrum disorder level-one has achieved above and beyond what autistic spectrum disorder level II individual has. A brief review of those qualities/characteristics will be restated at this time.

<u>Comfort zone:</u> Also known as the safe zone or bubble is that environment or environments in which the individual prefers to be or seems to be most comfortable. For example the home, bedroom, school, and friend's home.

<u>Familiar individuals:</u> Those individuals that the person is most comfortable being around. For the most part, this is first-degree relatives and extended family. However, there are friends who have common interests that the individual will be comfortable being around. People allowed in the comfort zone.

<u>Adaptive skill:</u> The skills needed for activities of daily living, work, communication, social skills and any other skill that individual may need and utilize in order to live their life to the best of their ability.

<u>Meltdown:</u> The behavioral result when an individual with autistic spectrum disorder is pushed to their maximum limit of keeping their behavior under control. These can be as simple as shouting matches to the point of an all-out temper tantrum.

<u>Social etiquette:</u> Accepted or allowed social behavior in society displayed by any person.

<u>Social awareness:</u> The awareness that a person is expected to understand in modern society: this would include any and all systems that exist in the world. For example banking and money, the legal and judicial system, rights and responsibilities and social boundary issues.

<u>Consequences:</u> The final outcomes of one's actions or behaviors as dictated by society.

<u>Right brain dominance:</u> Thought processes that are dominated by the right side of the brain to include the following: mathematics, logic, and reasoning as dictated by mathematics and science, practical knowledge and the ability to use said qualities. This is modeled after the Quadrivium, which was a collection of academic studies to include the following: arithmetic, astronomy, geometry, music and to some extent logic that applies to mathematics. Music as it applies to the rhythms, and sounds of the music.

<u>Left-brain dominance:</u> Thought process that is dominated by the left side of the brain to include verbalization, verbalize logic and reasoning. This includes abilities as described in the Trivium: rhetoric, logic, and reading. Music on this side is not the tone and rhythm but rather only the words are heard.

<u>Brain-behavior and thought process:</u> The ability for a person to use both sides of their brain congruently and in conjunction with thought processes in decision-making and living.

<u>Jaded by Life:</u> Bad experiences, failures, and disappointments either by their own doing, trusting others or just did not succeeding due to not following through or trusting that something should happen that did not, causes them to give up easily, rationalize why they should not try again. This is a form of Conative Dissonance where their learning process and experiences cause them to choose to avoid similar

situations for fear that the same outcome will happen and cause them to feel the following: Anxiety followed by depression and hopelessness. This becomes their parameter for not moving forward and the "What If" thought process becomes the logic.

<u>Discrimination and Discretion:</u> An adaptive skill by which the individual learns to discriminate between those people who are their friends and those who want to be their friends. They can start to develop a sense that people want something from them and they have developed methods to avoid those types of individuals. This seems to be a very specific characteristic of self-survival and to personal and emotional preservation. This ability seems to be very specific to the level I autistic spectrum disorder. This is a learnable adaptive skill that can be well learned depending on the individual and their intellectual level. Individuals at the level I status usually have a very good working ability of this characteristic.

These characteristics will be examined in differentiation between the two different types of level I individuals. There will also be comparisons to the level II individuals that may also someday achieve a level I status.

<u>Comfort zone:</u> In regards to the comfort zone, for the most part, a level one individual has a specific place or places that they have found to feel comfortable in. For the most part, the level I (static), have very specific places where they feel comfortable. This is due to their experiences in life where they only feel that they can be comfortable, safe, in a specific environment. It seems that over time they have found that there is one or maybe two places they can go and feel comfortable about being themselves. This is usually a home that they will stay in for the rest of their lives or a specific apartment that they have lived in for quite a long time. It seems that once they have allowed the environment in which they live in to become comfortable

the comfort zone has been established. These individuals will go out into the real world, because they have mastered certain adaptive skills and need groceries, mingle in public for a period. The adaptive skills they may have mastered are driving, shopping, and going to specific preferred events. In addition, to be with individuals whom they have let into their comfort zone that they feel are part of their comfort zone. There is some social adaptability here, but for the most part, they have a tendency to stay in one place most of the time. It was noted that they feel comfortable in that environment and other than very specific reasons they will not leave it. They feel safe, and they feel they can be themselves in that environment. Any change in that environment/comfort zone may result in some problem that will be discussed later in this chapter. Individuals with autistic spectrum disorder-level I-static are very functional individuals, and they developed a comfort zone in which they will not leave except under specific circumstances. This has also been described as the bubble. Individuals at this level have a tendency to maintain their bubble and not expand it to any degree. Once their bubble has been established, it will be maintained to the best of their ability. There may be little room for growth, but there is always room to shrink this bubble. They can expand the bubble if there is a logical reason that may be of benefit to them if they have a good reason.

Autistic spectrum disorder-level I-dynamic continues to adapt and may develop other areas that they will associate with the comfort zone. This could be a function of age, but it seems to be a function of adaptability and their desire to have other places they may be comfortable. With the right intervention, a level I-dynamic may expand into different directions and different comfort zones if they are willing to try new things. This is why their comfort zone may also be called dynamic since it is a continuing process of adaptation to other external environments, which they may adopt into their comfort zone. They do not totally resist change but if someone takes time to explain

it to them and use logical reasoning, a level I will adapt to change. They will also apply it to their life as they continue to adapt and learn new adaptive skills along with changes in their life, which they understand is part of their life. They are more acceptable to change because they realize that change is a logical function of their activities and behaviors in life. Individuals at this level may not outwardly show any signs of autistic spectrum disorder. They learned many adaptive skills and had learned to deal with many of the issues that go along with autistic spectrum disorder. They have successfully been able to move away from many of those issues, but they still may have some of those issues that are not readily observed or noted. Individuals in this group seem to welcome some changes when they are ready for that change, or they have decided it is time for some changes. Their comfort zone can be very dynamic, and it can be more than one place. The dynamic individual has more than one bubble also known as an extension. It seems they continue to try to expand to some degree unless some issue, foreseen or unforeseen, happens and then they may not incorporate that bubble into their bubble system or their series of comfort zones. This may also be a function of learning and experiences and age over time. The level I-dynamic individual may reassess the necessity of different comfort zones and may have a tendency to choose the best while discarding those zones that may not be satisfying to them. Therefore, they use their best judgment in making the decision whether or not incorporating or rejecting a specific possible comfort zone that may or may not be beneficial to them.

This type of dynamic ability, depending on age and experiences in life, maybe a learning process for someone who is diagnosed with autistic spectrum disorder-level II. If the right individual works with an individual that is at a level II and has the support of family, friends, and environment, they may adapt and adopt a different comfort zone. This is possible because autistic spectrum disorder-level II-high level

has the intelligence to do this but may not unless they have the proper interventions and are taught the proper tools for moving forward. Not all level II-high level want to do this, but there is the capability there to basically learn adaptive skills to change one's comfort zone or add to an individual's comfort zone. This does take the proper therapeutic interventions in order to do so, but it can be done. One of the adaptive skills that will be discussed in regards to the level-I autistic spectrum disorder will be known as discrimination and discretion. Most level IIs do not have this or are in the process of developing it. It could possibly be one of the key adaptive skills that a level-II may learn in order to bring them up to a level-I

Familiar individuals:

In the level, I autistic spectrum disorder individual both the static and dynamic individuals have learned to discriminate a real friend from someone who is a designing person. However, there are exceptions as there are in any rule and it is always possible that they may not discriminate and could be taken advantage of. In contrast, the level II individuals that do not have that discrimination between a friend and a designing person may be taken advantage of. This is a big difference between the level I and level II when it comes to familiar individuals. Therefore, if a level II can learn discrimination between someone who is really a friend and someone who is trying to take advantage of them, a level II, in this case, could evolve to the level I designation. This will take a lot of work for someone who understands this and tries to help a level II to learn to discriminate between friend and someone who is just trying to take advantage of them. On the other hand, level I have learned discrimination over a period of time. They have a tendency to be more standoffish towards people because they are actually trying to determine whether they even want to speak to this individual, let alone have any type of relationship.

Level I-static individuals, have a very select group of individuals that they have let into their comfort zone. It is usually mostly family members, siblings and possibly first-degree relatives. For the most part, any type of relationship outside of that group may be for specific purposes, but it may not lead to any long-term friendship or relationship. These individuals have been known to get married and can be loving individuals towards their spouses, but have a tendency to be somewhat clingy at times, which can be a problem. When it comes to other people outside of their comfort zone, they may interact with them if they see that there is a good reason to do so. Otherwise, they may just be cordial and walk away. These groups of individuals are quite static in their relationships, as they seem to have a very strict protocol-program-procedure-final product when it comes to any type of specific relationship. They do recognize if another person is autistic and a have a tendency to relate to them at least superficially. They may not invite them into their comfort zone, but they will at least acknowledge an understanding. They are very resistant to change and any type of minor adjustment within their environment. These individuals have made their comfort zone very specific because of experiences that will be discussed later in this chapter. They have a tendency not to try new things but rather be happy with things the way they are. Minor changes may be adopted for a period of time, but there is a very good chance that things will go back to the way they were before the minor changes. They can be easily frustrated by the behavior of others if they try to extend some type of friendship and that person does not respond. When this happens, they may have a tendency to back up and rethink why they even bothered to try to become friends with someone. Encouragement at this point to try again is encouraged. However, they have had experiences with this before and maybe make their comfort zone a little smaller and change their protocol-program-process-product to a more stringent thought process that may actually push people away. They may have issues with eye contact with any new individual they may encounter. With the

familiar individuals, they do show good eye contact because those individuals are within their comfort zone. Static individuals have a tendency to be somewhat on the quiet side and will not speak until they are comfortable with that individual, for the most part. Other than superficial greetings, they may not talk about what they are actually thinking about. They have a tendency to be reserved and at times distant.

The level I-dynamic type of person has a tendency to have more interests than the static individual does. It seems that they will seek out other people who have the same interests as they do and not because they also can recognize other autistic individuals but they have a tendency to have some relationships with other people when it comes to common interests. This adaptability comes from years of trying different things and therefore relating to other people based on common interest at first and then, they may develop some type of friendship or social interaction. The level I dynamic is very close to their siblings and first-degree relatives as well as relationships with the opposite sex. This group has a tendency to continue to expand their comfort zone, and their protocol-program-process-product is specific, but it is open to change due to being open to new experiences. They are more adjustable to new things in their environment as well as specific changes within themselves. It seems that this group likes to challenge themselves to new things but also has an understanding that if they do not master that challenge they have a certain degree of satisfaction for trying. Individuals at this level also have a tendency to deal with rejection in a healthier protocol-program-procedure-process than do the individuals that are static. It seems that they have a tendency to try to understand the other person and why things are not going the way, they feel they should. The dynamic group is open to new encounters with new people. They can be very verbal, and after a time they may show more eye contact as they become more familiar with others. For the most part, eye contact

is not a problem with the dynamic individuals. Dynamic individuals have a tendency to make good friends, and they can be some of the most creative individuals that will ever be encountered. They also have a tendency to be open to new learning processes as well as good verbal discussion.

<u>Adaptive skill:</u>

In the level, I designation, both the dynamic and the static groups have learned a lot of adaptive skills. The dynamic group is still open to learning even though they have mastered a lot of adaptive skills. They will question the need to learn more adaptive skills, and it must be explained to them with logical reasoning for them to learn any new adaptive skill. If it is logical to them, they will more than likely adapt and master that skill to the point where they can use it in their lives.

In contrast, the level I-static group seems to be very resistive to learning any new adaptive skills. They have learned many adaptive skills, have mastered them, and have used them in their life. They are resistive to learning anything else new or any other skill that may benefit them unless they are totally convinced that it has some merit that they can put into their life. It is noted that the static individual may try new things over a period of time but when they feel it is no longer of benefit to them to change they will go back to the previous adaptation of that skill which they had already mastered. Sometimes these minor adjustments in the adaptive skill set may be tried by this group, depending on them, they will switch back to what they were doing previous because that is more comfortable for them and that is inside their specific protocol for life.

In retrospect, anybody with a level II-middle or high designation may be more apt to learning new adaptive skills and therefore they may even begin to present themselves more as looking like a level I. The level II can possibly become a level I through learning and mastering adaptive skills. The level II-H, need to learn many adaptive skills and

then be able to demonstrate them and incorporate them into their lifestyle in order to start to look like a level I. This is not impossible and with the right therapeutic interventions, a level II can possibly become a level I through the adaptation and mastery of adaptive skills. Not all level II can master those adaptive skills that they may need in order for living a more independent life and start to present themselves more like a level I than a level II. This is possible but will take a lot of work, patience and time.

In summation to this section, a level I-dynamic continues to learn adaptive skills but maybe a little resistive in mastering and incorporating them in their life until they realize there is some special quality that they may need in order to continue to adapt to the world around them. In retrospect, a level I-static may not want to learn any more adaptive skills as for the most part they feel they are doing well without any more skills needed as they have limited their environment to what they are comfortable with. A level I-static may pick up an adaptive skill for a period of time but if he doesn't see that it's worth the effort will drop it.

Meltdown:

The level I meltdown can be quite interesting as it can differ significantly from the other levels and their types of meltdowns. The level I dynamic group may have a tendency to be variable in their meltdowns. Their meltdowns can range from the possibility of stomping of feet to something as subtle as just walking away. Depending upon the age of the level I-dynamic individual, the meltdown may be a little more attention-getting as it may be anything from some whining and crying to the possibility of cussing and swearing, but after it's over with, the person may withdraw into their safe zone. Meltdowns can be very rare at this level because they have mastered a lot of adaptive skills and have experienced a lot of things in life. There may be something that they have never experienced

before and have no skill set to deal with it, and therefore the meltdown can occur. Meltdowns at this level are not always a given, but they can happen. The level I-static individual tries to avoid any type of situation where there could be a meltdown. It seems that avoidance is one of their tools in dealing with an event that they have no skill set for. If an incident does happen for a level I-static individual, there is a possibility of a minor meltdown, which may include the following: saying something under one's breath, possibly one or two select swear words and possibly the withdrawing from that environment in which the incident occurred that may cause a meltdown. They will retreat to their safe zone.

It seems that all level I have a tendency to be able to handle certain events that may cause a meltdown for any of the other levels. It seems they have developed a *skill set* that will help them to manage the situation until they can get to the safe zone whereby they can ponder the possibility of how they could have handled the situation better. Overall, for the most part, you will not see the fits, the rages, or temper tantrums that are somewhat of a characteristic of the emotionality of autistic spectrum disorder level II and even level III. The level ones have a tendency to have learned over the course of time: the temper tantrums, cussing and swearing, and other behaviors do not work in the world around them. They have over time developed specific adaptive skills, protocols and skill sets in order to deal with situations that could cause a meltdown. They have learned either through trial and error or through other means that the meltdowns of major behavioral disturbance do not work and they have corrected that problem over the course of time. For the most part, this could be used as a rule of thumb; however, there still may be an incident that could cause some type of emotional outburst that could be like the more severe emotional outbursts in a meltdown. For the most part individuals at the level, I have mastered several different adaptive skills, protocols and skill sets to help them handle any type of incident

that could possibly result in some type of emotional and behavioral meltdown.

<u>Social etiquette:</u>

Level I autistic spectrum disorder is quite polished when it comes to social etiquette, at least from the viewpoint that they dress appropriately and have good personal hygiene for the most part. Their ability to communicate can be somewhat restricted. They have a tendency not to ask a question but rather have a tendency to look at you as if you are going to ask them a question or say something to them. The opposite is true as well as they will start to talk to you and ask you questions directly whether they may know you or not. It seems that they have developed a certain discriminatory attitude towards people, but they do have the ability for spontaneous communication in a social environment especially if they feel that the person they are talking to is someone they can relate to. If an individual reaches, level one either static or dynamic they will have learned discrimination skills and do have a tendency to measure people before they start to talk to them if they start to talk to them.

For the most part, the level I-static and dynamic individuals have good social etiquette. They may be quiet, or they may talk without totally filtering what they are saying. It is noted that they are watching you to see your reaction and if they say something that you react to or respond to in a negative way, they may recant what they just said and restated it.

Level I-static individuals have good social etiquette. However, they choose not to be in the social environment and limit their contact outside their safe zone. If they do travel outside their safe zone and do encounter someone that they know, they will possibly start a spontaneous conversation. Although, if they are too focused on what they are doing, they may not totally recognize the individual and not stop and talk to them but rather continue on with whatever mission

they are on. They have developed good personal hygiene, proper attire (all items match including socks) and they can be very polite when they do speak. However, they will limit their social encounters to a minimum of what they can personally handle or what they must deal with or what they have scheduled themselves to do.

Level I-dynamics, on the other hand, can have some interesting social etiquette, as they can be very entertaining and amusing because they feel comfortable enough to be funny. They also continue to polish their skills in social situations, and they may even ask for advice on a myriad of items that to certain people may seem like nothing more than details, but to the level I dynamic, it will either be augmented to their skill sets or further questions will be asked. Level I-dynamics continue to evolve and to pick up social skills, skill sets, and social etiquette behaviors as it seems that they have adapted into their skill set the perception of body language and even emotion. They seem to be highly perceptive to the individual that they may be encountering as to their emotions and/or body language. This seems to be one of those mastered adaptive skills, but they do realize there are things they do not know. There is a possibility at times they will not pick up on someone else's emotions and/or body language especially if they're not interested in what that person is saying. If either the person they encountered they do not want to see or they do not want to listen to, they have a tendency to blank them out and possibly even act disinterested. Unless they are given instruction about this, they may or may not pick up on the fact that the person talking to them, who they are not interested in, may feel insulted because they are not listening and basically ignoring them. This further social etiquette training can be taught to individuals who are at this level I-dynamic because they are open to new training, especially if it can be explained to them how it can benefit them in a very logical and perceptive manner. If you do not explain it to them in a logical and perceptive manner, they will ignore you as well.

Overall, level I-static and dynamic individuals do have appropriate social etiquette although, the static one tries to avoid social situations and thereby not practicing his social etiquette, the dynamic individual may try out the skills that they have and also seek on how to improve them.

Consequences:

Both the static and dynamic individuals of level I have a pretty good understanding of consequences ; however, there still may be some issues to boundaries, especially social boundaries, that they may never have encountered before therefore they may step over the line and be handed consequences that they don't understand. Although the static individual has a tendency to avoid socialization and has a tendency to stay in their safe zone, things can happen in the safe zone, which could result in an event, which they do not have the skill set for and therefore end up with possible consequences. Hopefully, the consequences are not too dire, and a good counselor may help that individual along with the other individuals, who are imposing the consequence, understand what the individual understands. The static individual will limit the possibility of dealing with any consequences in their lives,especially accidents, by remaining in their safe zone. They stay in their safe zone for most of the time. They do not go out looking for trouble, but if trouble finds them, they have trouble understanding the consequences to some extent. They do understand the consequences of inappropriate behavior, and they never strive, for the most part, engage in behavior that has consequences. If they have, trouble is not usually of their own volition but rather by accident as something happens that they do not have the skill set to handle.

On the other hand, the dynamic individual tries to avoid consequences. When they are in learning and trial mode, social skills and social communication and a few other things, they may encounter some consequences, which they may not understand. As stated, they are

experimenting in trying to learn a new skill, that is what dynamics do, and they may step over a boundary or two in the process of learning or in mastering a skill, and there could be consequences. Hopefully, there is someone to perform some type of intervention in order to explain the situation thereby the consequences will be understood as well as others involved in understanding what happened. They do learn well what consequences are and from their learning experiences avoid situations whereby there are consequences. As they begin to learn new things, they may try new things on their own and thereby have issues that could lead to consequences.

Overall, both the static in the dynamic individuals try to avoid consequences at all costs. They do not want to be involved in something that could cause them issues of a negative nature they do not want. However, accidents do happen and there is a possibility that either group could get into some type of consequential situation. Hopefully, someone will intervene in the situation and explain it to the individuals as well as other people that are involved in the situation. It could happen that the individual may also have a diagnosis of posttraumatic stress disorder, and there is a possibility that if they are startled, they will respond in such a way that could cause issues followed by consequences. With the proper recognition of this disorder, the individual can be helped to understand what could happen to them and they can put it into their skill set, therefore avoiding the inappropriate reaction followed by the consequences.

Right brain dominance:

Both the static and dynamic individuals have the possibility of being right brain dominant. In other words, they have a great logic function, mathematical skills, engineering skills and probably decent musical ability especially when it comes to writing music. In some cases, they have these abilities, but they cannot always explain while they are

doing them and/or what they are actually doing unless the proper question is asked. If they are interrupted during one of their events where they are totally focused on whatever they are doing, an answer such as "not now can't you see I am working" or "in a minute let me finish this" or even a simple wave off of the hand. As the dynamic individual continues learning, they may be able to some extent explain what they are doing briefly, but they will not look at you when they speak. They are staying focused, and they will tell you whatever they tell you. Be satisfied with that because they are focused on what they are doing. They do have some left-brain function by this time. They continue to be able to work on that bridge between the right and the left-brain.

The static individual may stop what they are doing because they are usually in some type of routine. No extraneous thought process is going on, as they are mostly in the routine of the routine that they themselves have put together. They may stop what they are doing and talk to you because what they are doing is routine and they are used to it and can get back to it because they know exactly where they are going to stop and exactly where they are going to start. They also have mastered some skills that build a bridge between the right and left-brain; however, it seems that they refuse to use it, as they would rather not talk than possibly say the wrong thing. The static individual can be good at math, engineering and much of the same skills as a dynamic individual, only they stopped learning and retreated into their safe zone. They are fully functional and can work but they will not always communicate with coworkers, but they will communicate to some extent with supervisory staff. It seems that they reach a point in building a bridge between the right brain and the left-brain and stop because they feel they have good enough communication skills that go along with their technical abilities.

Overall, the static and dynamic individuals that have good right brain capabilities and have built some bridge to the left-brain. The static

individual may not engage in conversation about what they are doing but the dynamic individual will.

Left brain dominance:

Level I left-brain dominant individual has very good social skills through communication and arts, and crafts type work. They communicate very well, and they express themselves in a very eloquent manner. Some of them even have the ability to sing and follow along with the music tempo and beat. With this ability, they can tell when music is being played incorrectly, and they will let the person know what was wrong with what note in what stanza. They are very quick to point out flaws and give advice on how things should be done better. For the most part, this is the dynamic individual unless it occurs in the static individual safety zone.

Left brain dominant individuals have a tendency to build a bridge to the right side of the brain and start to use some of the capabilities of the right side of the brain. There are some possibilities of gaining some right brain skills, but there may be a limit to what can be learned, but still, that limit needs to be pushed until it is found. Many left-brain dominant individuals have the capacity to learn and master many right brain skills, but there are limitations especially when it comes to mathematics. It seems that they may have problems with math beyond algebra, but they seem to be able to do simple mathematics, which can be referred to as practical mathematics with proficiency.

The static individual has learned good communication skills and has learned skills from the right side of the brain. However, they only use what they want to use what they need to use in their safety zone and within the protocols of their ventures outside of the safety zone. The dynamic individual, on the other hand, may continue to try to develop some of the right brain functions to the point of their limitations.

This can be this can be considered a major adaptive skill and continuous practice can build good bridges between the right brain and left brain and the left brain and right brain. An individual that is of the level II-high can possibly achieve this crossover between the right-brained the left brain and left brain to the right brain and may be able to use it and even master it. This would be an adaptive skill that of the level II really mastered it may start to look more like a level I than a level II.

Brain-behavior and thought process:

level I individuals do have several thoughts going through there had any given time. However, they have mastered and have practiced the use of focus. Even though an individual of a level I group has many thoughts going through their head, they have learned over time to organize their thoughts and even though there may be several thoughts going at one time, they have developed several different protocols, skill sets, and organizational skills in order to control their flows of thoughts and to focus on the one thought at hand.

The level I-static individual may have several thoughts going through their head at any given time, however, since they do have a routine or a protocol or specific order of the way they do things, they focus on what they are doing to get it done even though the next task may already be in their thought process. However, since they can be very rigid and how they do things, they will stay focused on the task at hand. Even though there may be a preferred task, the level I-static has learned responsibility and the importance of following through on their specific protocol that they follow through on as it avoids any type of emotional or mental conflict. They still may have a preferred task however it may not be in their specific thought pattern at the time in which they are working on one task before they move on to another. The static individual likes to keep their safe zone in a specific order,

and any tampering with that order may cause a slight stop in the thought process to redo it or to put it back in order.

Level I-dynamic has a tendency to have many thoughts going at any given time, and when they are working on one specific task, they are thinking about others. They may stop that specific task in which they are focused upon and either engage in another task or take notes about what they want to do next. It seems they are always thinking about the next project and in contrast to the level I-static, they have a tendency to try new things and find new preferred tasks. If the preferred task is presented at the time, they may stop what they are doing and work on the preferred task instead. At times, they may need a short break from what they are doing but for the most part, they will go back to what they were working on or they will find another preferred task or another task that needs their attention and will focus on that next. They can look like they are scattered at times, however, do not get between them and their thought process or then they will be scattered. They have a protocol in which they are trying to organize things. It is noted that if they repeat certain tasks, over time, they will develop a new protocol each time in order to save time and actually developed a process in that protocol to make the task go smoother and more efficient. Since the dynamic individual is more creative in a more open manner, they can be extremely organized and continue to work upon their organizational skills to become very organized in the skills of total organization. They may become very organized in the less preferred tasks in order to participate in a more preferred task. In other words, they may find that there is a task they have to do and he will find ways to get that task completed to perfection in the least amount of time needed. After that, they will go on to the preferred task and actually take their time as they do enjoy preferred tasks or distractions. The dynamic individual is also thinking well air doing things and can think about not only the task that they are on but the following tasks following that and also how they can organize their

time in order to get done all their non-preferred tasks in order to make time for the preferred task. Even the preferred tasks have certain protocols and processes by which they will engage in them by which they have specific procedures in order to arrive at the specific product. (Protocol, process, procedures and the specific product will be explained in another chapter.)

The dynamic individual will have a set of procedures for a specific protocol and thereby follow the process to the specific product. This can be observed, as it seems they may go through a specific set of rituals or movements during the task. As a cautionary note, do not bother him while they are going through the specific movements are behaviors because it is part of how they will complete the task.

The static individual also has the same protocol, procedure, process and specific outcome product, however, since they are more focused on what at the time or overly focused on one thing at a time, they can be somewhat disrupted without any real problems because their entire protocol is very rigid, and they don't have a lot of them because they have learned over time that they don't need them or they don't want them and therefore they do not engage in them.

Jaded by Life:

The major issue with this situation is that anybody who has ever been diagnosed with autism, for the most part, has suffered from some type of trauma. Almost all individuals with autism report issues with problems in the home, problems with relationships with parents and siblings, being bullied in the school setting and also being bullied outside the school setting and also being taken advantage of in the workplace. Over the course of time, the amount of negative experiences builds up with every individual with autism. The interesting part of this is that the level I whether he is static or dynamic, have developed ways to deal with the negative experiences in life. In retrospect, a level I individual has learned to use adaptive

skills that he either has learned by observation or has been taught through therapeutic intervention to move beyond the trauma that was inflicted upon them by the world around them. Unfortunately, to some extent that trauma can reemerge in the form of posttraumatic stress disorder. The level to autistic spectrum disorder has problems in dealing and getting by their trauma, and therefore they may end up grounding themselves into a level II categorization due to the fact they cannot get past the trauma and continue to have severe emotionality. However, with therapeutic intervention and positive experiences they too can get past the trauma and possibly even start to achieve the abilities of the level one individual. However, this does take a lot of work, many interventions, and a lot of practice but it is possible.

In regards to the level I individual that is static, they have developed some major defense mechanisms to possibly avoid negative events that they have experienced in the past. They can be very rigid in their behavior patterns and in their protocols of life, skill sets and interaction with the world outside of their safety zone. This is one of the reasons they develop such a rigid pattern or protocol for adventures outside of their safety zone. Their motivation is to avoid any negative interactions or experiences by sticking to a rigid game plan. This is why they strive to keep their safety zone, and they strive to keep their boundaries rigid, as they do not want to experience any more negative interactions with the outside world. A negative interaction could actually trigger a startle response due to the fact they have posttraumatic stress disorder from their negative experiences throughout their life. However, they do have their own system of handling any type of negative response through avoidance and keeping to their rigid protocols on dealing with the public outside of their safety zone. They want to avoid any type of negative response or experience to the point where they will avoid the entire situation and get back to their safe zone as quickly as possible.

On the other hand, level I-dynamic individual seems at times to continue to test the water around them, seeks out more experiences, and then deals with the negative effects afterward. They seem to of developed openness to the possibility that there are positive experiences to be gained and possibly positive advantages to be learned. They are more flexible to the world around them as they realize their safe zone is not the only place in which they can feel good and be themselves. That is why the dynamic individual continues to learn, acquire new skills and develops other safe zones other than the major safe so in which they found themselves to be the safest. As the dynamic individual is more verbal about what he experiences, he may make comments upon any negative experience that he does encounter. It seems that the dynamic individual wants to learn more, wants to fit in, and will strive to do so through the acquisition of other adaptive skills, changing protocol and developing new skill sets. They still may experience some negative in their life but how they deal with it is much different from the static individual. The dynamic individual will try to assess what has happened, develop a skill set deal with it and/or get help to find a new adaptive skill or protocol to handle negative situations that they may encounter. For simply stating the dynamic individual as they continue to try to acquire new skills, find new safety zones, and develop new protocols, they find new ways to fit in as best they can in the world. It is indicated that they pay close attention to detail and therefore they can assimilate new things that they pay attention to. Therefore, they tried to go be on their possible limitations with the autistic spectrum disorder and assimilate new ways to handle situations in which they may not have had any training or intervention that would have to help them through it. In other words, they are more aware of their social surroundings and therefore pay closer attention to the details they may be able to use later than the static individual.

Paying attention to details in the social situation is a skill that level I individuals have. It is possible that they have learned them over time and through trial and error but either way, they have found a way to assimilate them, master them and incorporate them into their skill sets/protocol/social skills sets. This is one of the reasons why an individual who is of a level I-dynamic does not appear to have autism. However, if you're around the person long enough and you have a background in training with autistic spectrum disorders, you may find specific issues with the individual. As a therapeutic interventionist, I strive to find those little innuendos in order to help the individual gain the skills needed to eliminate those specific issues. It is a good possibility that it a level I-dynamic individual may even reach a stage in life that they no longer display any characteristics of an individual with autism. I believe this is possible because I have seen individuals that are level I-dynamic pick up new skills, acquire and master new skills and then use them in their skill set/protocol/adaptive skills. It is possible in a person who is a level I-dynamic may only have minor autistic issues over the course of time through the continued learning process. Nevertheless, as autism continues to emerge, it is hopeful that others will take note of the abilities of individuals with autistic spectrum disorder and help them to develop those skills rather than to criticize them and belittle them for their sometimes-notable deficits.

Discrimination and Discretion:

The ability to discriminate and be discreet is two conscious abilities that need to be mastered. Individuals with autistic spectrum disorder level I may have some experience, and even some of them may have mastered the ability to discriminate and be discreet. However, if they have never encountered a specific event or type of event, they may be taken advantage of. I believe it is possible for individuals who are of the level II to learn discrimination and discretion, however, it will take time and a lot of effort in order to help them to discriminate between friend and designing person and the ability to not to speak or say their

mind in public. However, it can be mastered over a period of time. The level I individual, on the other hand, seems to have developed certain protocols to handle situations and therefore has learned to discriminate and to be discreet. This does vary between the two types of level ones-the dynamic, and the static and will be discussed in the following paragraphs. Please be aware of the fact that to learn every and all-social or personal encounter that may need the ability to discriminate or to be discreet is a continuing learning process throughout the course of a lifetime. There is no finite amount of times when an individual will have all the skill set/protocols they need in order to handle life because life is a continuing experience. However, many of the skill set/protocols can be learned and developed for the most part with some generalities, which will assist, individuals with autistic spectrum disorder, in their quest for individualization and independence.

Level I-static individuals seem to of developed a skill set/protocol in their ability to discriminate by their ability to limit their activities and boundaries within their needed activities and in their safe zone. It seems that they have learned to avoid, for the most part, encounters with individuals that they may not know. It seems they use an effective method when they are in public such as ignoring the surrounding environment and only focus on what they are trying to accomplish in that specific environment. For example, an individual who is a level I-static goes into a supermarket in order to buy food. Before they leave their home, they already have mapped out the journey to the store and inside the store and which checkout counter they are going to go to, then back out to their car, and back home. It seems that this protocol follows a very strict guideline whereby in the process of going into the store their procedure is to focus on exactly what they need and where they are going in the final product is to get in and out of the store within a certain number of minutes. In doing so, they leave no opening for any possible encounters with other people

other than possibly if they run somebody they know they may say a greeting but then on with shopping. It seems that they have barriers up, so they do not have to deal with the possibility of having to discriminate. However, if they do and up in a situation where they have to discriminate between friend and some with an agenda, they seem to ignore them and just walk away.

When it comes to discretion, a level I-static individual can be very quiet. It seems that their ability to avoid problems is one of the strong points and their ability to be discreet. The verbalizations are for the most part at a minimum because they do not want any problems if they say anything and therefore they do not. This seems to be a skill set that works perfectly for them and ensures that they do what it is they have to do and return to their safe zone with relative ease. For the most part, conversations with individuals that are level I-static can be a few words and will be directed to the point. It seems they have learned this skill set/protocol as a way to cope with the world around them and avoid trouble at all cost.

This may also be an indication of some type of abuse or some type of trouble that may have happened in this person's past. In learning from that trouble or abusive engagement, they have learned to avoid at all possible cost those type of engagements or situations and have learned to walk away without saying anything. Some of the things that have been revealed over the course of time is that they were afraid to talk back, or they were afraid to state their mind so whether they had done once before and were rebuked or they have never done it, either way, a level I-static individual has learned to be discreet by being quiet and avoiding situations.

Individuals that are of a level I-dynamic seem to be more outgoing, and therefore they seem to be continuing to learn new abilities and developing new protocol/skill sets for dealing with the outside world. When it comes to discrimination, it seems that they are always willing

to learn a new skill set when it comes to being able to determine whether something is good or bad. It seems that they have mastered a great deal of these skill sets and are willing to go out into the real world and see if they can develop them further and master them as well as seeing whether or not they work. They continue to be very flexible in their environments, and they continue to look for social cues. However, they may come across a situation where they may not have developed a specific skill set/protocol and could possibly be taken advantage of. However, this will only ever happen once because they will learn from the experience. Therefore, they are still in the learning stages and are willing to adapt and develop new protocol/skill sets in order to handle situations in the world around them.

When it comes to discretion, a level I-dynamic individual, for the most part, has learned to be discreet in his behaviors and verbalizations in society. However, there may be a situation whereby they have not encountered that specific type of environment or encounter and may make a mistake and get into trouble. However, they will learn from that experience and develop a new protocol/skill set in order to handle that specific occurrence/environment in which they had a problem. They continue to learn, but sometimes they are taken advantage of and sometimes they can get into trouble for saying what they are thinking rather than using a social filter. Learning to develop a social filter is a skill that is needed by all level II and in some cases certain level ones to some degree. This social filter can be used in mastering to a high degree of success. This is another one of that benchmark by which the possibility is there for someone of a level II can possibly develop this type of skill as good as a level one has developed. Overall, level I individuals, both static and dynamic, have developed specific protocols/skill sets in order to be discreet and discriminatory. These two abilities can be learned and mastered especially by a level to the individual that still has need/desire to learn them.

In summation to the level I-autistic spectrum disorder individuals, they can be stated that if they master all the skills, develop skill set/protocols and have someone to help them continue to develop these type skills, it could be stated that their autistic spectrum disorder diagnosis may be undetectable. I believe it is possible with the right programs and therapists, individuals of a level I-autistic spectrum disorder may have very few if any signs of having autism. If they master all the skills and develop protocols, they may not look any different from anyone else. However, there will be some individual idiosyncrasies that may still resemble some autistic behavior. However, for the most part, they may not look any different from anyone else.

In my clinical experience, I enjoyed working with level I individuals as they have a lot of skills already in their possession and what they need is refinement and practice and encouragement to explore other things in the world around them. This especially goes for the level I-static individuals who seem to have developed their comfort zone and minor necessities of leaving the comfort zone and have a tendency to block everything else out of their environment especially when they are out of their comfort zone. The level I-dynamic individual is very open to suggestions and even has their own ideas. Moreover, working with them I like to work with them on their own ideas and see what we can do to set up protocols and skill sets in order for them to explore their new ideas. It is apparent after a while that individuals that are of the level I-dynamic seem to show little or no signs of any autistic traits whatsoever after a period of time. However, these individuals are few and far between however they do exist, and they can be very successful, very productive and very independent.

CHAPTER 5

Autistic Spectrum Disorder

Level II

Autistic Spectrum Disorder-Level II

In the new definition of autistic spectrum disorders as outlined in the Diagnostic and Statistical Manual of Mental Disorders fifth edition (DSM-5) there are three levels of autistic spectrum disorder. The focus of this article is on the autistic spectrum disorder-level II. In the DSM 5, the level II is categorized with the following issues: requiring substantial support, marked deficits in verbal and nonverbal social communication skills; social impairments apparent even with supports in place; limited initiation of social interactions; and reduced or abnormal responses to social overtures from others. For example, a person who speaks simple sentences whose interaction is limited to particular narrow interest, and has marked nonverbal communication. It further notes the following: inflexibility of behavior, difficulty coping with change or other restricted/repetitive behaviors frequently appears enough to be evident to the casual observer and interfere with functioning in a variety of context, distressed and/or difficulty changing focus or actions. Although these are the direct guidelines paraphrased from the DSM 5, there is some variability and flexibility within these guidelines. The focus of this chapter is to try to bring to the reader's attention that the level II autistic spectrum disorder is, for the most part, the most frequent of the autistic spectrum disorder levels that do have the ability to function and possibly even live a somewhat normal life in society. However, there are the specific issues that preclude them from being independent, and those issues do cause them to have some adjustments problems within normal society and therefore lead to legal as well as adaptive issues in society. Before we can get deeper into the construct of understanding the autistic spectrum disorder-level II, there is some terminology that needs to be understood and taken into consideration when encountering/caring for and dealing with an individual with autistic spectrum disorder level II.

Comfort zone: That environment or environments in which the individual prefers to be or seems to be most comfortable. For example, home, bedroom, school, and a friend's home.

Familiar individuals: Those individuals that the person is most comfortable being around. For the most part, this is first-degree relatives and extended family. However, some friends have shared interests that the individual will have comfortability being around.

Adaptive skill: The skills needed for activities of daily living, work, communication, social skills and any other skill that an individual may need and utilize to live their life to the best of their ability.

Meltdown: The behavioral result when an individual with autistic spectrum disorder is pushed to their maximum limit of keeping their behavior under control. These can be as simple as shouting matches to the point of an all-out temper tantrum.

Social etiquette: Accepted or allowed social behavior in society by any person.

Social awareness: The awareness that a person is expected to understand in modern society: this would include any and all systems that exist in the world. For example banking and money, the legal and judicial system, rights and responsibilities and social boundary issues.

Consequences: The outcomes of one's actions or behaviors as dictated by society.

Right brain dominance: Thought processes are dominated by the right side of the brain to include the following: mathematics, logic, and reasoning as dictated by mathematical thought and science, practical knowledge and the ability to use said qualities. This is modeled after the Quadrivium, which was a collection of academic studies to include the following: arithmetic, astronomy, geometry, music and to some extent logic that applies to mathematics and science.

Left-brain dominance: Thought process that is dominated by the left side of the brain to include verbalization, verbalize logic and reasoning. This includes abilities as described in the Trivium, which includes rhetoric, logic, and reading.

Brain-behavior and thought process: The ability for a person to use both sides their brain congruently and in conjunction with thought processes in decision-making.

Jaded by Life: Bad experiences, failures, and disappointments by their own doing. Trusting others or things did not succeed due to not following through or believing that something should happen that did not happen. This may cause them to give up easily and rationalize why they should not try again. This is a form of Conative Dissonance where their learning process and experiences cause them to choose to avoid similar situations for fear that the same outcome will happen and cause them to feel the following: Anxiety followed by depression and hopelessness. This becomes their parameter for not moving forward and the "What If" thought process becomes the logic.

Vulnerability: Webster defines this in the following way: capable of being wounded, susceptible to wounds, open to attack, liable to increase penalties in contract bridges. Individuals can be very susceptible to the influence of others and can be taken advantage of, duped or even severely hurt due to their inability at times to determine good people from bad people and trusting people who try or say that they are their friends.

The key: an item that opens up a lock. When working with this group, the key can be many different items. It can be as simple as a word or the name of a video game. The key can be derived by either observation, listening for repeated items or asking questions about their favorite game, toy or activity. The key can be the opening to the therapeutic process. It can also sustain the therapeutic relationship

and open the therapeutic relationship up to further necessary learning for life.

As these definitions may dictate, there is a lot of autistic spectrum disorder-level IIs. The ability for the caregivers/parents/average person to take the time and understand an individual with ASD-II is a monumental task, but it can be done. Individuals with this disorder are gifted to some extent. They have good memory ability, and some are very gifted and talented artists and designers as well as engineering types. To understand this disorder is to be able to give someone that has an exceptional talent an opportunity to blossom, grow, and have a very productive and satisfying life. There are going to be conflicts, however, and with understanding and reasoning, those conflicts can overcome and be used as a training/teaching experience that the individual may understand and benefit from. However, society has not had enough time even to try to gear them up to understand individuals who have this quality and therefore punish them as if they were the average individual with malicious intent and behaviors. For the most part, individuals with ASD-II, do not understand how the world works and all its twists and turns and incongruities and therefore suffer from this inability or lack of knowledge to deal with society the way they are expected to deal with it. It is only with patience and understanding can these individuals help those with ASD-II to comprehend and possibly adapt to those expectations and inconsistencies in the world that surrounds them. They have a lot to offer society if society is willing to work with them on helping them to allow their talent to come forward in their life and flourish.

To start with, the DSM 5 describes the ASD-II in the following way: level II: The severity level of requiring substantial support. Social communication, marked deficits in verbal and nonverbal social communication skills, social impairments apparent even with supports in place, a limited initiation of social interactions, and a reduced or abnormal response to social overtures from others. For example, a

person who speaks simple sentences has interactions limited to narrow special interests, and who was markedly odd nonverbal communication. Restrictive, repetitive behaviors, inflexibility of behavior, difficulty coping with change, or other restricted/repetitive behaviors appear frequently enough to be evident to the casual observer and interfere with functioning in a variety of context. They have distressed and/or difficulty changing focus or action. (DSM-5, 2012).

This inference from the DSM 5 is considered the most rigid of descriptions. However, there is some variability within the ASD-II level. It has been my distinct honor to be able to work with a lot of individuals who are at this level, and there is variability within this level to the point where, so far, I have been able to identify three levels within ASD level II with 6 sub levels. To some degree, intelligence, adaptability, and age dictate the ability of someone to be in a specific level. When I first started to be able to classify individuals, we were using as a guideline in part: the intelligence test referred to WISC-3 and grades from school and also progress or lack thereof within the social realms of school. The WISC-4 can also be used as a guideline along with school grades and other tests that the state may give such as the Keystone tests and even the PSSA exams. What has been observed in the school-age children is a differentiation between subjects that are either left brained or right brained in nature. In the preschool situation, some insight into autism comes from the observations of the teacher and behavior patterns that were noticed in the school as well as in the home setting. Nevertheless, these are not the only determinants of someone to be designated with ASD-2. These are some of the guidelines that I use along with descriptions of behaviors by the parents and activities that I used during the session. These individuals can be challenging and teaching them adaptive skills takes cooperation from the parents, teachers and other caregivers. Depending upon the individual's intelligence level and

willingness/ability to learn new behaviors, communication skills, and problem-solving, an individual can move up through the levels. Perhaps even achieve a level I. There have been some reports of someone who was able to do this, but this would take a lot of therapeutic interventions, support and someone willing to work with them on issues that may develop over the course of a lifetime.

ASD-II Low Level

ASD-2 lowest level has been determined in part by a borderline IQ test that may have (as determined by WISC-3) differentiation between the performance IQ and the verbal IQ. One of these divisions within the test may be in the intellectually disabled level any other one may be in the borderline to just above borderline functioning. The full-scale IQ (FS IQ) is the integration of the performance, and the verbal and these individuals may come out with borderline intellectual functioning or possibly just below or even mild intellectual functioning (F70). These individuals do have some skills, however, they have problems with verbalization or they can verbalizing but cannot perform. This would determine if they were right brain dominant or left-brain dominant. These individuals do have specific behavior patterns, and they are not necessarily adaptable to new behavior patterns or a change in their current behavior patterns. Depending on whether they are right brain dominant or left-brain dominant, the following definitions have been applied. A person, who is right brain dominant, may be able to understand but they have problems with verbalization. A person who is left-brain dominant may be able to verbalize, but they cannot perform. It is noted that they can learn some skills such as activities for daily living but not anything beyond some domestic skills and some self-care skills, may happen. There is a limit to their learning ability and to their performance ability. However, they do have some skills and those skills do need to be recognized. It is noted they may also have some of the more familiar issues such as the possibility of overstimulation coming in through one of the five senses. They may also have some

insightfulness, but they may not be able to understand or describe it. There can be emotional issues and the possibility of meltdowns, but if the caregiver keeps within the limitations of that individual's organized the world, most issues will be avoided. These individuals do have some skills, and they need to be recognized and encouraged. These individuals do like their routines, but some variation can be worked into the routine if the caregivers/parents/teacher takes the time to explain why there needs to be a change and to what benefit the individual may get from it. This may take some effort, but it is a lot easier to try and help the person understand why a change is necessary rather than to push the change and suffer the consequences of the possibility of a meltdown or something worse. This would then deny the person of any possible chance of any acquisition of adaptive skills because when the meltdown does occur, disciplinary policies will be invoked rather than the understanding of what actually happened. This seems to be quite the norm in dealing with any individual with autistic spectrum disorder is that schools/parents/caregivers are very quick to punish rather than try to understand. The behaviors that are displayed are usually stimulated by something that needs to be understood and rectified rather than disciplined. Any disciplinary action will not be understood and may cause the behavior to escalate or even exacerbate the situation. Individuals do not understand yelling and screaming, and they may respond to it by covering their ears. A parent may interpret this as some kind of defiance, but in all actuality, the individual is stating in a non-verbal that their ears are being hurt by the yelling and screaming. They do not understand why someone is hurting their ears for whatever reason they do not understand. It is also noted that a parent/caregiver/teacher should not ask a right-brained individual for an explanation. Individuals in this level have problems in explaining what they feel and usually act on them because they do not necessarily have the ability to explain. A left-brain dominant individual on this level may be able to explain things, but their behavior may still

be problematic. The ability to explain does not relate to the ability to perform the correct behavior. Their logic for the behavior is how they understand what they are doing but it still not be the expected or proper behavior. A word of advice here is that a parent/teacher/caregiver should never expect something more than the individual understands or can perform. Work with what is presented and do your best to understand the motivation behind the behavior and don't assume that it is defiance because it is probably not.

Individuals at this level are usually placed in a special education program that could be detrimental to their possible gaining of skills, and a very good IEP is needed to help them work on the skill that they do have rather than pushing skills that they cannot comprehend. Individuals at this level do require close supervision, and their adaptive skill achievement is limited. However, different skills should be tried to determine which ones are achievable and assimilated.

From the definitions that were explained at the beginning of this chapter, I will now do find them as the observance of the low-level ASD-2 individual.

Comfort zone: The comfort zone of an ASD-2 low-level individual is usually restricted to immediate family and maybe some extended family. For the most part, they will not go anywhere without a parent or first-degree relative. They may allow themselves, over time, to converse with a therapist as long as the first-degree relative is present. There are places they will not go due to the situation being too crowded or noisy. However, they will attempt to go to places as long as they are escorted by a first-degree relative or parent. That parent/relative should always be with the individual when any interaction with the outside world.

Familiar individuals: Parents and siblings are usually the most comfortable to be around. The individual will allow himself or herself

to be around other people as long as a parent or sibling or possibly a first-degree relative, such as a grandparent, aunt or uncle, is present. There are few if any friends that they will engage with and participation in group activities is highly unlikely without the encouragement of a parent or first-degree relative that is present and seen by the individual during the event.

Adaptive skill: the acquisition of any adaptive skills would be minimal. Personal hygiene would be considered one of the highest adaptive skills they can achieve. The possibility of operating simple household items such as a microwave or a toaster would probably be the most complex adaptive skill they can achieve. Individuals of this nature cannot drive or operate any other machine. Simple activities that require more than two or three steps are only possible using laminated lists and reminders.

Meltdown: This group does have meltdowns. They can be quite intense, as it seems at times that they are hard to understand what it is they are having the issue about. Depending on their age, younger individuals in this subgroup may have more severe meltdowns, which are more like temper tantrums, as older ones may become verbally disagreeable. However, meltdowns are not as frequent as will be discussed in the next group. Yet they do exist, and the parents/caregivers/teacher must know the individual and what those items may be that may be the trigger to this emotional outburst.

Social etiquette: Individuals at this level can be extremely shy and withdrawn depending on whether they are left brained or right brained. A left-brain dominant individual may talk but only with a parent/familiar caregiver or relative present. They do not freely converse, and they have problems with eye contact. A right-brained individual may make occasional eye contact, but they will not talk until they are familiar with the individual that is trying to engage with them in conversation. In therapy, this can take several sessions before the individual feels

comfortable enough to speak. They do not engage with strangers unless their parent or familiar guardian introduces them, and even then, it may take time for them to decide whether they feel comfortable in speaking. Their etiquette outside the home can be very appropriate unless of course, a situation happens that may trigger a meltdown and then it becomes evident that there is a problem. So for the most part, as minimal as it may be, they do go out into public, and they are relatively well behaved unless something triggers an emotional issue.

<u>Social awareness:</u> Individuals at this level tend to ignore, for the most part, the social environment. They may go out into the environment however they are very observant of their caregivers/parent that they are with and they have a tendency not to look around other than to keep their eyes on the individual that they are with. If they are asked about what they saw in their social environment, they may bizarrely look at you as if to say: "I was supposed to look." Some do observe some things in the environment especially if there are loud noises or something that distracts them for a moment. For the most part, these individuals do not like to go out of their comfort zone. They can be very well behaved in the social environment. However, there is a possibility that a meltdown may happen. This may occur anywhere especially in a store where they are told the word no. They do not care who observes their behavior at this time, and this outburst may be scary to the observers.

<u>Consequences:</u> Individuals at this level are aware there are some consequences, but they are very uneducated to the possible severity of their behavior. Individuals at this level are not known for being aggressive physically, but it could happen. A meltdown in public could lead to a possible physical altercation, but for the most part, it is not likely to happen, but still, it could happen. They seem to be more of a verbal nature or the kicking and screaming character rather than of throwing fists or physical altercation. However, it can occur and when

it does they are very much unaware of the possibilities of any legal, moral or ethical issues that exist in the world around them. Their understanding of good and bad is limited to what they have been taught and what they understand. They do not learn from the environment around them but only from direct instruction that has been introduced to them many times until it has become familiar with them. This issue will be further discussed in another chapter called "autism spectrum disorder-expectations." For the most part, these individuals do not learn from being in the environment. They are usually concerned with not losing the parent or caregiver that is with them and only show any attention towards items that can distract them such as loud noises, lights flickering, multiple colors and of course physical touch or pain. They only learn from direct intervention and instruction. Their understanding of consequences is entirely limited to their understanding of the word good and bad. They have no idea that there is something called a legal system and to what specific behaviors may lead to interaction with that system. Consequences for the most part other than not getting what they want or not being able to do something are about the extent of the word consequence.

<u>Right brain dominance:</u> Individuals with this level that have right brain dominance can perform some skills. However, if they are asked how or why they did it that very no explanation will follow other than a strange look that may infer: didn't you see me do it? They cannot explain how they did what they were able to do or why they did what they were able to do but to some extent, and they can perform specific tasks but, they cannot explain verbally what they did or how they did it. Individuals who work with right brain dominant individuals should not ask questions just look at the results and give compliments or show them how to do it better. Continually asking questions may lead to the possibility of some form of meltdown.

<u>Left-brain dominance:</u> A left-brain dominant individual can talk to some extent about what they think they can do, but they cannot necessarily

follow through on it. However, many individuals who are right brain dominant cannot explain what they did or how they did it, and there is also the possibility of a speech impediment or some form of speech problems, such as a lack of words or the use of minimal amount of words. The left brain dominant individual may have more words to use, if they don't have speech issues, and may be able to describe specific items when questioned but the individual may only be describing what they have seen and not what they have been able to accomplish. It can be said that individuals who are left-brain dominant can talk a good game but cannot always follow through on it. A caregiver who works with the left-brain dominant individual can expect some verbal ability, but they should not expect too much in the area of performance as they have problems following through and sequencing tasks. The possibility of a 1 to 2--step task is possible but may take encouragement and the person, even though they can talk about it, may not be able to follow through without instruction and encouragement.

Brain-behavior and thought process: **There is always a possibility of some type of brain insult or brain injury to individuals at this level. The possibility of a seizure disorder or epilepsy is also possible. In spite of those issues brain function seems to be somewhat or to some extent normal. Overall functioning is the question depending upon if the individual's right brained or left brained or what part of the brain is not functioning to its potential and what tasks or abilities cannot be gained through learning. Other bodily functions may be affected to some extent depending upon whether the brain has been injured or insulted in some way. This is a matter of continued research.**

Jaded by Life: **Individuals at this level have minimal interaction with other individuals and with the community outside their comfort zone. However, they may have some issues with specific people, places, and things but they are limited by their limits to where they have been taken and what experiences they have actually experienced. It may be**

that there is an individual that for some unknown reason they do not like, and they will stay away from even if they do have some familiarity with them. However experience-wise, they do not have a lot of experience, and this is a limitation to learning about life. If the individual is well taken care of by the parent/caregiver, they seem to be happy in their environment, and the parent/caregiver makes sure that the environment is safe for them and they are well cared for. For the most part, there is not a lot of life experience learn from. As their life experience is limited, so is their understanding of the world around them. They are usually well supervised, and there are minimal negative experiences encountered.

Vulnerability: individuals in this group are highly susceptible to the possibility of being taken advantage of and thereby the need for constant supervision. For the most part, they do not have any contact with strangers as they are always supervised. However, it is possible for someone that they have determined to be safe actually to take advantage of them in some way. Constant supervision is necessary even though individuals in this group may tend to shy away from anyone they do not know. They may not understand stranger danger, but they are still susceptible and vulnerable to individuals with unwritten agendas. This group should not be let out of the sight of whoever is supervising them or at maximum within line of sight. The line of sight, in this case, maybe within a very short distance, especially at an outside activity.

The key: in working with this group. The key can be obtained through either observation or asking simple questions. However, even though this group may be limited, they still have things that are very special to them. Talking about those particular items may open up dialogue and a sharing experience.

ASD-II Middle Level

The next group I would like to talk about is the middle level of ASD-2. This group is also divided into the right brain dominant in the left-brain dominant. Their IQ test scores and their behaviors differ from the ASD-2 low-level individuals significantly. The full-scale IQ for these individuals usually comes out in the average range (90 to 110). This differentiation in IQ accounts for a more dynamic individual complete with unique behavior patterns and gifted ability. The range of the IQ tests as determined by the WAIS-3 have a differentiation between the performance and the verbal scores of anywhere from one to two standard deviations. They will have one score somewhere between 75 to 85 and another score that will be somewhere around 100 to 110. This is not a standard by any means, but this is an observation as noted in my clinic. I will hope that others will go forward with this information and either further prove or disprove my observations. For the most part, however, these individuals intelligence, full-scale IQ, is in the normal range.

These individuals can be quite gifted with one, two, or even three abilities that they do very well. They seem to have some insight into the world around them, but they do have some vulnerability to individuals in the real world that may target them as an easy mark to take away their personal property or use them to some extent. These individuals may be more apt for verbal and possibly even physical altercations. They may be more emotionally charged as they do understand some emotions but they have the minimal understanding when it comes to long-term consequences. They are an interesting group to work with as they do have the ability to learn some adaptive skills. Nevertheless, other characteristics of autism do come into play with this group, and for the most part, they can describe them much better than the previous group.

Comfort zone: **In this level, there can be a lot of differentiation of what is considered the comfort zone. The comfort zone will include for the most part the nuclear family and a lot of first-degree relatives. However, it differentiates, as this group is more social and will develop some outside friendships. They may also participate in extracurricular activities to some degree. Yet they will be watched very carefully by anyone who is participating in the group as well as some adults. Their behavior may be somewhat odd at times, and their personalities and how they respond to the different external stimulus will be different. As long as no one takes offense to or talks to them in a derogatory manner, the comfort zone can exist outside the home. However if someone starts to say things to them of a derogatory nature or it is determined that those people around them are not friendly to them anymore, individuals at this level will begin to resist participating in those groups or organizations to the point they will be deleted from their comfort zone. Some of the organizations and individuals at this level will join as follows: Scouting, chorus, glee club, drama club and other organizations where they may be allowed to be themselves without criticism or any negative feedback. Therefore, therefore, the comfort zone has increased considerably in comparison to the previous level.**

Familiar individuals: **As was mentioned in the previous category, first-degree relatives continue to be familiar to this group. However, there may be a division between the mother and the father. For the most part, but not always, one of the parents is more understanding of the issue and is more willing to learn about what autism is all about especially at this level. However, the opposite parent takes a negative stance as they feel that this is some type of manipulation and should be corrected by punishment. This is where the possibility of a division between familial and familiar comfort starts to develop. Also, other first-degree relatives may or may not be understanding of the issue because it is more prevalent in certain circumstances and events. It**

seems that they will not take the time to understand what is going on but instead criticize it or avoided altogether. Individuals at this level have a lot of insight into the fact of specific emotions and behaviors, and facial expressions along with body language that goes on around them and they may make a conscious decision to stay away from certain people that they feel are negative towards them. Individuals become very familiar with individuals/people/caregiver/supervisors that take the time to try to understand them and work with them on helping to develop a very good relationship. Individuals at this level understand relationships and to some degree the importance of relationships. Other familiar relationships can be established with teachers, coaches and other individuals that they feel that they can have a positive relationship with. Individuals at this level have insight into who they can have a good relationship with to some extent. However, they sometimes try to develop relationships with people who are not suitable for them but actually try to take advantage of them. This does occur due to a trusting nature at this level, but they do have some insight into who should be good for them and who is not. This is another one of those variabilities within this level, but it also is an adaptive skill that they determine who they should be around and who is right for them and who is not good for them to be around. This is also a function of age and experience, which then, of course, can lead to adaptive skills and the ability to discriminate between someone who is actually their friend and someone who is just trying to use them. This is another adaptive skill that can be learned over time.

It is apparent that individuals at this level can develop, to some extent, symptoms of other mental illnesses. The president of symptoms, but do not fully meet the criteria for the specific disorders, is sometimes seen. These disorders are as follows: attention-deficit/hyperactivity disorder, obsessive-compulsive disorder, oppositional defiant disorder, intermittent explosive disorder, and what appear to be elements of conduct disorder. However, only

symptoms of these disorders appear but do not qualify for the diagnosis because it does not fit the total criterion. Some mental health disorders that do go along with this level are as follows: anxiety, reactive attachment disorder, posttraumatic stress disorder, and depression. These issues may meet the full criterion for that specific disorder, and it is usually in relation to the perception or actions of individuals who are supposed to be important in their lives. Other behaviors that may evolve, but are not limited to, frustration, anger and the possibility of anxiety type disorders and their related behaviors. These are usually a result of something they experienced in their environment and in trying to internalize it, behavior that comes out is often anger and frustration. This is usually brought home to the familiar environment rather than to be expelled in an extended familiar climate. Individuals at this level have a good insight for the most part that the best place to let out their frustration, anxiety, anger is in the home setting. However, if the anxiety, anger, frustration, and trauma are intense enough, they will tend to allow it to be expelled outside of their homes and into an extended familiar environment, which may lead to consequences of a legal nature. This is one of the major reasons why individuals at this level need to be diagnosed very accurately and the educational facility in which they are in needs to understand them and have specific interventions in their individual educational program. For the most part, but I'm sure there are some others, these instances happen in the school setting or possibly at an extracurricular activity, and it seems that if there is direct intervention immediately the situation will calm down. However, what has been reported on many occasions is that there is no direct intervention and the situation seems to be exacerbated by individuals who do not understand autistic spectrum disorder or the individual that is displaying the behaviors in that extended familiar environment. Under these circumstances, the individual may start to delete out that extended familiar environment and begin to look at it as a hostile environment whereby they will be on the defense the entire time

unless some intervention is already a protocol that will be in place in case of a situation of this nature. When an individual gets to this point, there is a possibility of some type of behavior, but that will be explained further in this chapter.

Adaptive skill: At this level, there is no delineation in age groups but when it comes to adaptive skills age plays a factor in learning and adapting and integrating adaptive skills. One of the first adaptive skills to be learned is to discriminate between someone who is actually their friend and someone who is actually trying to use them. However, in the earlier years or initial school years, it seems that individuals at this level want to make friends and their ability to discriminate between someone who is actually their friend and someone who is not. This skill needs to be learned. Another adaptive skill that needs to be learned are protocols such as fundamental living skills. These are as simple as cleaning up after oneself to a more elaborate version of the importance of doing homework and outside study. These items can be learned, but they may be met with resistance. If they are met with resistance, the worst thing a parent can do is start to yell at the individual. As I have noted in previous articles, a parent that is going to stand there toe to toe and yell at their individual with autism you lose. The child has won the battle, and they will not listen to you, but instead, this will lead to the meltdown. As individuals at this level age, their ability to discriminate becomes more precise, but their understanding for the need for simple things such as activities of daily living: showering, cleanliness, and prevention of acne does not seem to be as important as distractions such as smartphones, tablets and the computer and video games. It appears at this point that their discrimination between the "what's more important in their life" needs to be retrained. The adaptive skill of working with them on "understanding what the real world is about" will need interventions of an outside nature to work with them. Putting together a plan of action, which will be authored by the individual with autistic spectrum

disorder, and someone who knows how to put together a life plan of action is essential. The reason for this is that the individual is the author of this plan and therefore they will follow it. A pre-program, a pre-packaged plan will not be accepted and thus not adapted. A social skills training program should also be implemented which works with the individual's strengths and helps them with their social weaknesses. Some emotional control training should also be implemented at this time along with social communication skills. This group can learn, and they can learn adaptive skills well. However, this is no-touch and walk away routine. This is continued remediation until they have mastered the skill that is being taught to them. Some of them can assimilate this very quickly and others it takes several times and a lot of practice to assimilate an adaptive skill. However, they can learn adaptive skills, but some adaptive skills are limited because of the individual. These individuals can learn to drive, and it seems that they are good at operating machinery to some extent. Supervision and encouragement are always recommended when an individual is operating any machinery. The supervision and encouragement will also help them to assimilate the adaptive skill and to some degree perfected the skill, as any other person would be able to do.

Individuals at this level can be very adaptable but whoever is teaching them/working with them needs to find out what the key is to help them to assimilate the adaptive skill. The key can be very complicated or very simple. The key may be a specific person, place or thing that they are very familiar with and when the teacher/trainer/therapist mentions the key, they have the undivided attention of the individual. As was always the case in life once you find the key to the lock, the lock is open, and then the door can be opened, and anything can be possible within the extent of the ability of the individual. These individuals are limited to some extent in their adaptive skills, but they can be quite adept to a lot of everyday items in life, along with tasks and demands of the world and society around them. To some extent, they can live

alone with minimal supervision, and they can carry out activities of daily living on their own to the extent whereby they can ride public transit and go into restaurants and order their own meals. However, this is something that takes time and effort and someone who is willing to teach or train the individual at this level to adapt .

Meltdown: The subject of the meltdown seems to be in part related to the age of the individual at this level. Younger children will have total temper tantrums. These temper tantrums can be avoided, however when a parent wants something done, and they want their will to be carried out, they will stand toe to toe with the child. In the grand finale, the result is a total temper tantrum followed by some type of consequence. The task that the parent/caregiver/teacher wanted to be done does not get done. Nobody wins in this situation. Individuals are usually punished to some degree, but they do not quite understand why they are being punished and they may be resistant to the punishment. A simple intervention of talking with the child and "*why*" they are being punished could alleviate this entire problematic scenario. As the individuals get older, the temper tantrum ceases and leads to more acceptable behavior. A form of verbal resistance will take the place of throwing oneself to the ground and kick and scream. The verbal resistance is not necessarily talking back but usually revolves around the question of "why." Parents tend to interpret this as being resistive and disrespectful and immediately go into some type of tirade rather than to answer the question. This results in a verbal altercation whereby nobody wins, and the question is never answered. Therefore, as I caution parents, when the question "why" is asked, take a few minutes and answered to the best of your ability. The following answers do not work: "because I said so," "because I am the parent" or "or else." These statements will only be met with verbal resistance, and if they are pushed hard enough, some aggressive posturing may be the result. It is on a rare occasion that individuals at this level will strike out and actually cause a physical altercation, but

it is possible because the question has never been answered and they have become so frustrated with the person giving commands that the frustration becomes anger. Without an intervention such as, talking to the person in the situation or answering the question, it may result in what can be considered some type of aggressive posturing, which could end with a physical altercation. What the individual is looking for is to understand the "why" or "necessity" of the request/demand/command. They are not trying to get out of the situation or avoid what is being asked of them, but they are only looking for a logical explanation why it needs to be done the way it is being told to be done. In a good intervention on this point, a question should be asked back to the individual with autism such as "how would you do it?" Alternatively, "how do you think it should be done?" Instead, individuals who feel threatened by individuals with autistic spectrum disorder tend to be overbearing and do not use their head but instead allow their inferiority complex/feelings of inadequacy, issues of superior, come to the surface with this type of questioning. In the grand finale of all this issue minus any type of intervention or use of some thought and logic, the result is usually some type of problematic outcome. The problematic outcome will often result in hurt feelings, groundings or on the upper end of the scale legal action. Individuals who are adults at this level tend to become very loud when they recall specific issues from their past as it seems that they tend to have suffered from a lot of trauma and possibly abuse. They are quite verbal, and they do have many adaptive skills, but they still need some supervision and guidance at times to organize their life and help them reach the optimal activity level. Adults can be very independent minded and can be resistive to that the support/supervision, but with intervention, an explanation for the supervision/support will be welcomed.

<u>Social etiquette:</u> Individuals at this level may have some basic social etiquette skills, depending on what they have learned through initial

interaction with their nuclear family. However, there is a possibility of a total lack of any type of social etiquette due to a lack of family training and interaction. The most common social etiquette skill is a lack of eye contact. A lack of eye contact is a hallmark feature of autism, but this can be remedied through intervention/training. This specific group does have the ability to learn this skill and master it. Other social etiquette elements would also include a handshake, a smile, a greeting or some type of gesture of acknowledgment. Some of these come natural and others need to be taught during early intervention time in the early years. However, besides learning the skills, there may be some social interventions in the development of friendships that may or may not happen due to the understanding or lack of understanding of what social relationships become over time. Any of the traditional social etiquette skills need to be trained directly. Many individuals at this level will not pick this skill up by observation but only by direct instruction and practice. Verbalizations at this level can be from nonexistent to over-elaboration of some issue that may or may not have anything to do with them directly. This is a function of learning but also right or left-brain dominance. At times you will get nothing out of an individual at this level, and other times you will get explanations that go on and on and have actually nothing to do with the individual, but for some reason, they have made it part of their problem. This is where interventions in teaching social etiquette are essential because it helps the individual to discriminate between what is their problem and what is someone else's problem and to put in a boundary between the two issues. Boundary issues can be a problem at this level and need to be taught to discriminate and taught to the point of being mastered. A lack of a boundary issue could lead to other problematic outcomes and consequences, and therefore it is vital for them to understand social etiquette, to own what they own, and not own what someone else's problem is. It is essential to distinguish between their boundaries in their life versus someone else's problems. Individuals at this level do have some insight, but at times, they look

to try to fix things that they have no clue how to fix. They realize there is a problem and they have a desire to help but in some cases, helping this issue may lead to consequences for themselves that they did not deserve. It is imperative to teach people at this level social boundaries when it comes to social etiquette. This group can learn adaptive skills in relationship to social etiquette, and they can become quite adept at using them.

Social awareness: **In the previous level, the idea of any type of distinction when it comes to sex is somewhat concrete at best. It is understood what sex they are, but they do not necessarily understand the whole story of other issues that relate to sex. Therefore, they are aware but somewhat oblivious to what all social and sexual relationships are. However, at this level, they have become aware of social relationships, romantic ideation and to some degree sexual relationships. However, they do not always understand the emotional ramifications involved in social and sexual relationships. Individuals with autistic spectrum disorder have problems understanding emotions. They are very familiar with the emotions of frustration, anger, depression, anxiety, and disappointment but when it comes to other emotions that they may feel, such as love, caring, and concern, they may be somewhat restricted in their responses. When it comes to trying to understand the emotions of others they may understand the emotions to some extent but not to the depth in which that feeling, emotion, the issue may affect another person. This is another good case where interventions and therapeutic education come into play to help the individual at this level understand other emotions and how to respond to them as well as reading the emotions of others and responding appropriately to them. Individuals at this level can develop social relationships with the opposite sex but do not always understand or empathize with what the other person may be feeling. At times, they can have insight into their own feelings but not know what they are or have some insight into the feelings of others but not**

understand them to the point of what an appropriate response should be. Verbalizations can be quite crude, and the lack of a social filter is well noted. When an individual reaches puberty at this point, which may not be at the national normative level (11 to 15), parents/caregivers have to take the time and spend some time with their individual when they are entering this point of physical maturity. Interventions need to be in play to help individuals at this level understand what they may be feeling and the appropriate way to express themselves. They must also be schooled to some extent upon social implications of specific behaviors that may or may not take place and given the "why" or consequences to specific behaviors that may be of a sexual nature. For the most part, these individuals are not necessarily sexually aggressive. If they learn from others, they may become curious. However, if they learn from a parent/caregiver/qualified professional about what they are feeling and how they need to conduct themselves in society, they may not get the perverse ideas that can be shared among social contacts who they themselves do not know everything but have ideas. In this case, they may start to become sexually curious but not necessarily sexually aggressive. They may ask for specific favors from certain individuals of the opposite sex and then not understand why they were turned down. If this happens, instead of becoming sexually aggressive, they can become sexually withdrawn and withdraw from speaking to individuals in which they had asked for specific favors.

In some cases, individuals at this level have been abused, neglected or even sexually assaulted, but there has been no indication at this time, at least from the experiences of this counselor, that they become sexually aggressive, assaultive or even become sex offenders. It seems that from my experience, they seem to become withdrawn from those types of encounters that can become sexual in nature and take on a different perspective on what social and sexual relationships are about. It may be that they withdraw into themselves and become

depressed to some extent and express themselves in some type of bizarre or someone obnoxious external attire or they regress back to being more childlike behaviors. Those that do have some posttraumatic stress disorder at this level seem to be withdrawn from individuals around them and keep to themselves. Some individuals tend to spend time in the outreach centers and try to help others in some minor way. But, individuals at this level understand what it's like to have some posttraumatic stress disorder issues whether they are from being mistreated or sexually abused and seem to move forward without becoming sexual predators. This has only been my experience to this date. I am sure there's a possibility that this can happen to others but at this time I have not experienced it out of my clinic. There is always a possibility that someone who is at this level could become a sexual predator. However, at this point, I have not witnessed it or experienced it in my clinical observations or experiences over the past 25 years.

<u>Consequences:</u> In retrospect, to the previous level this level is aware of consequences but does not always understand why the consequences happen. They tend to believe that the behavior in which they presented themselves was not a problem but rather an expression. This expression, however, can be misinterpreted by individuals around them as possibly being hostile or threatening and therefore the consequence may be some form of legal outcome. The ability to understand consequences depends upon age and understanding how the behavior may affect others in the outside world. Individuals at this level do not always understand that their actions, behaviors, and verbalizations may be offensive and frightening to others. Therefore, since they do not understand or cannot sense the feelings of others around them, they do not understand why the consequence happened until someone takes the time to explain to them and about how their behavior affects others. Another hallmark issue of autism is that individuals with autistic spectrum disorder do

not always understand that people around them may be affected by their behaviors. They may not understand the social ramifications of the verbal tirade as it may relate or disturb others in the immediate area. This is a function that needs to be learned through adaptive skills training especially in a social etiquette environment. As the individual matures over time, they should learn some of the social boundaries and social etiquette issues that could affect them by not using a social filter or by not learning to give themselves a timeout and remove themselves from an area or location that seems to be of a problematic nature to them. These types of interventions need to be taught, and the individual can master them. Sometimes these displays of emotion in the wrong environment at the wrong time are due to their own feelings or could be the interpretation of someone else who is close to them and their issues. They will not understand that they will be suffering consequences for their own behavior even though it is not directly related to something that affects them. This is why interventions from a very early age for people at this level need to be employed along with understanding and good therapeutic interaction. Individuals at this level do understand to some extent, but they do not always understand that the outcomes/consequences can be more severe than what their logical thought process can understand. Teaching individual boundaries is very important, and the mastery of boundary setting is to help them to understand to avoid getting involved in something they cannot fix themselves. Is very important for them to understand if they intervene because it is someone that they have good familiarity with, they could share in the consequences that that person receives. This is very important to teach this concept to individuals at this level. Is very important to help them to understand this area of consequences, as they need to learn to mind their own business and put up boundaries. Their idea of helping out a situation may be interpreted as some type of interference from an outside observer or from the individual who is trying to fix the problem that seems to be an authority. Even after the consequences are invoked,

they still may not understand why they are being punished in this way. Further intervention is needed to explain the situation and then to help the individual understand that they need to put boundaries in place, so they do not get pulled into someone else's problem and therefore share in someone else's consequences. This is another important area that needs to be instructed and taught to the individual at this level masters it.

Right brain dominance: The right brain dominant individual at this level seems to be very good in mathematics and logic. They do have problems in trying to express themselves or explain what it is they did or how they did it. Instead, they point to what they have done, and you need to interpret as such. If they are pushed to give a verbal explanation, they may withdraw, shut down or possibly even get up and leave. They do have some mechanical ability and to some extent even some artistic ability when it comes to drawing and painting. They very much follow the quadrivium, as their strengths seem to be equated directly with those strengths. These individuals can be very orderly about specific things, but if it does not make sense, they will not be orderly with it. In other words, their logical construct, what they feel is essential, will be very organized but, areas that they do not deem to be very important will be chaotic. They do have a good memory, but it is directly related to the topic that they are interested in. Other topics that may be of a left brain nature may be problematic in learning, but it can be done through remediation and explanation of its necessity. They seem to be a little rigid in learning topics that they do not feel are important but with positive intervention and understanding and helping them to understand logically why they need to know the subject that they do not like may result in a positive outcome. They do have some flexibility in their learning ability when it comes to non-preferred topics.

Left-brain dominance: The left-brain dominant individual at this level is very talented with their verbalizations. However, at times they do not

have social filters and therefore may say things in a manner that is either not acceptable or is misunderstood entirely. These individuals' strengths seem to follow along with the trivium as they are gifted in their verbalization, they have a good reading ability, and they are or can be gifted musicians. They do have some problems in learning non-preferred tasks or tasks that are right brained in nature such as mathematics, sequencing and organizational properties specific to the right-brained individual. However, they are good at explaining what they did or what they want to do even though they may not be able to do it correctly. They will give very logical explanations on why they cannot master specific subjects and why particular subjects they just cannot understand. Due to their ability to verbalize some crossovers or bridges can be built between their left-brain dominance and help them function with some right-brained properties. They can be quite rigid when it comes to crossing over into right brain areas, but it can be done with the proper explanation and logical reasoning of why they may need these abilities that are not preferred and are right brain nature. They can learn through remediation and through good logical explanations.

Brain-behavior and thought process: Individuals at this level do have some crossover behaviors between the left and the right and the right and left, however, they still have a dominant side. This can be noted especially in the academic performance as well as older versions of specific intelligence testing. (WAIS-R is much better in delineation than the current version). The ability for individuals at this level to crossover between their dominant side and learning to improve the non-dominant side of the brain is a function of time, outside influences and of course qualified interventions. From previous chapters are written there are still specific things that you may say to an individual at this level that will make absolutely no sense to him and does not logically make sense, and therefore the expected result will not happen. Taking time out, explain things thoroughly and teaching and coaching the task will result in a much better outcome than getting into a verbal attack which will then result in a verbal altercation and possibly even some type of hostile outcome. This ability to build bridges between the dominant and non-dominant side of the brain gives them the possibility of advancing to the top level in this level, but there are some who will be resistive to any changes because taking on changes may result in a compromise of their comfort zone. Whereas others take on more adaptive skills and actually advance to a higher level because it enhances and even expands their comfort zone into areas they have a curiosity about and can master. Individuals at this level are likely to have some abnormal brain functions such as seizure disorders, or epilepsy. They may also have hypersensitivity as brought in through any of the five senses plus some very attuned insight into the world around them. They may not always understand what it is they are feeling or seeing, etc. but they are bothered, per se, by natural input from this world around them. So at times, they may look distracted whereas they are actually sensing something that the people around them cannot sense or cannot detect. So at times, they may look like they are distracted or off into another world. Individuals at this level also have a very good sense of electronics and tend to use them as a shield to hide behind when situations are tense or in the environment that they are uncomfortable with. In other words, they may be hiding behind their electronics in the situation that is outside of their comfort zone that they are trying to possibly either bring into their comfort zone or delete out of their comfort zone. This would also be considered some type of coping mechanism or coping strategy to try to regain some balance and establish some boundaries with the world around them.

The possibility that these individuals have had some traumatic experience, either due to them actually having a traumatic experience, or their interpretation of what a traumatic experience is, is very likely. They may tend to have some forms or symptoms of posttraumatic stress disorder either brought about by their actually

experiencing some type of trauma or they have witnessed some kind of trauma and feel that they also have been exposed to that trauma personally. They may become very loud when they are talking about specific issues that relate to some of their traumatic experiences. They may also tangent off into their traumatic experiences when some topic or subject that may be related to their trauma is discussed. I have found it is better to let them vent to a certain extent and after venting for a few minutes bring them back to the here and now. It seems to be very therapeutic for them to vent the frustrations from the past that seem to have built up over time that they have not been able to find some rational explanation. It looks as over time as they vent their frustrations and traumatic experiences. The intensity of the past trauma becomes less and the tendency is to focus on current goals rather than to bring up the past.

Jaded by Life: **Individuals at this level seem to have had some negative experience with life. As they age, these experiences may become more complicated for them to understand. They may also possibly have had some traumatic experiences, depending on their age and life experiences. As I alluded to in the previous section, Brain behavior and thought process, these traumatic experiences have resulted in some type of jading in their life. Those that have had major traumatic experiences seem to be very cautious about developing any sort of new relationships and seem to be happy at times, with what is going on in their life without any further acquisition of adaptive skills. However, there are some that are still learning and have not had any type of experience that has seriously jaded them from life. They continue to try to develop some adaptive skill or skills to help them to understand boundaries and their potential. The adaptive skill achieved to overcome being jaded in life is a function of therapeutic intervention. If a person who has had traumatic experiences or has experienced some traumatic experiences that led to some posttraumatic stress disorder symptoms, a good therapist with outstanding intervention skills can actually help them to gain adaptive behavior. The goal is to overcome this boundary that may have been adapted for the simple purpose of self-preservation. However, these boundaries are not always logical or practical and may result in some form of social isolation. This maladaptive boundary needs to be**

addressed logically, and reacquisition of a better adaptive skill needs to be put in place to keep the person from being so jaded by life that they refused to leave their home. Becoming a shut-in is one of the results of being jaded by life. This jading in life can be very real, but it also can be misinterpreted due to the inability of the individual to understand that there is a possibility that what they experienced was not something they need to be jaded. Rather, whatever that instance, circumstance, thing, whatever that has caused them to start to have this maladaptive skill of being either shut in, avoidance or hiding per se, needs to be examined and interpreted for what it really is rather than what it was possibly misinterpreted to be. Direct intervention needs to be used in this case to sort this out to make sense of it. The proper adaptive skill needs to be implemented to get the person to move forward and possibly away from that item that caused them to have those feelings and behaviors. This can be accomplished as they do have the intelligence and the ability to learn that there is a possibility that they misinterpreted something and then acted upon it incorrectly, which resulted in some consequence that in the grand finale resulted in the possibility of isolation or very limited interaction. Individuals may learn positive adaptation skills that result in proper coping mechanisms to whatever jaded them through life and may follow through, or they may retreat back to their comfort zone. Sometimes the skill that you try to teach somebody, and they may try it out, they may go back to what it is that is most comfortable for them. This is not a failure on the part of the therapist, but it is comfortable for the individual to possibly not move forward as they seem to be entirely happy where they are. As a cautionary to therapists, if your individual chooses not to adapt to an adaptive skill totally, it is their choice. So respect it.

Individuals at this level can be quite gifted. However, it takes someone who understands individuals with autistic spectrum disorder-middle level-level II to help them to develop and use their skill and even market them to the best of their ability. Individuals at this level can be misunderstood, but they have a gift, and they have something to offer society. Do not ever give up on this level because they can advance to the next level or even higher. Success for these individuals depends on their ability to acquire and assimilate adaptive skills and/or

identifying their talents and skills and encourage and promote them. If these talents are not recognized and encouraged, the person may shut down and settle for a lifestyle or job that is far below their talents and abilities. It is also possible that they may regress to a level that is minimally functional and they will need more supervision as they have become so jaded by the life they want to be shut-ins.

<u>Vulnerability:</u> Individuals in this group are not as vulnerable as in the lower group, but they still have a vulnerability. Individuals in this group do have or have achieved some social skills and the possibility of making some friends. It would seem that anyone who takes time to pay any attention to them may be considered a friend but may not really be a friend. Individuals in this group can be swayed by individuals they consider to be their friends to do things to continue to maintain this "friendship." They may question the motivation behind the activity, but to keep their friend, they may follow through on a maladaptive behavior. As an individual matures from this group, they may become less prone to becoming vulnerable. However, they still do have some vulnerability, as it seems that influence by individuals they consider their friends may result in being taken advantage of, and/or possible legal consequences. They may not be as easily persuaded as to the previous group but, put into consideration someone they think is their friend. They can be taken advantage of quite quickly. This group needs some supervision, but they also need intervention to understand and hold to the concepts of right and wrong, no matter what the consequence there is to the friendship. Individuals at this level may consider friendship to be significant and therefore they can be very vulnerable to someone who has an unwritten agenda.

<u>The key:</u> This group has many keys to work with. Sometimes with this group, a key may be an activity, an event, a television show or even an item of interest. In working with this group, the key can also be used to redirect an individual away from having some sort of emotional meltdown. Whatever the key may be, the individual may redirect themselves, through the use of this intervention, from a highly charged emotional state to a state of attentiveness and interest. In using the key, however, this group will then become over-focused on the key and until another key is employed, they will continue to repeat that item of

focus or interest until there is a resolution or an entirely logical explanation has been completed. This group is very workable when a key or sets of keys are developed and understood. It seems that using the key with this group is very successful in helping them to understand boundary issues, social issues and to develop some emotional control. Finding the key is essential in helping these individuals to learn and adapt to the expectations of the environment in which they reside. It is also important to teach parents/caregivers/teachers these keys to defuse possible situations in those environments and help the individual move forward.

ASD-II High Level

This group is at the top of the level II as determined by their behaviors, their IQ level and also their ability to learn and assimilate adaptive skills along with some other behaviors and abilities. However, they can be challenging to work with at times, because they know they can choose. They seem to be able to make decisions based on what they feel is important to them and what is not important to them. They do have some extreme derivation at times between their left and the right brain functioning. As individuals at this level get older,Level II-High level, they display behavioral traits that seem to have been acquired through experience, education, and contact with the outside world. They do have the ability to transcend the level II altogether if they choose to. However, at times, and depending upon age, they tend to not transcend to the next level (ASD-level I), but may in some cases revert to the middle level and possibly even show some traits from the low-level. However, they do have a lot of potentials to grow, to learn and to excel at whatever their strongest ability is.

<u>Comfort zone:</u> In regards to the previous levels that have been discussed in this chapter, the ASD-2 high level, has to some extent extended their comfort zone into the community and possibly even to a job site or even to some places that they should not be. The comfort zones at this time may be added to, or even parts of initial comfort zones may be deleted from the areas in which they will venture into. However, the individual will continue to expand their comfort zone

until they reach a place that is no longer comfortable and then they will wonder why it is not comfortable and try to find some way to make it comfortable. In retrospect, someone who may also be in that same position of finding a comfort zone that doesn't work for them may start a regression back to an initial comfort zone in which they felt safe. Either one can be listed as a personal comfort zone for this level. They can have variability in their comfort zones along with what people they are comfortable around. This group also looks for people that are more like them or have similar interests. It may be the interests that lead them into that comfort zone that may or may not be appropriate for them. For example, one familiarity may be that the individuals that they are trying to get to know also have similar interests, such as video games. As far as the person at this level, knows or believes, the person they are talking with may have something to offer them, but they do not have the wherewithal to understand that the person who has a similar interest of them may actually be trying to use them for something. This is why someone in this group tends to get into trouble because they do not quite understand why it is that people that they trust betrayed them. Therefore, a regression may occur back to another comfort zone, or there may be some rationalization for them to stay in that comfort zone that may be harmful to them, both financially and legally. So overall, a comfort zone with this level may expand; remain the same or even regress. It is essential for the therapist/parent/caregiver to understand this and help the individual understand why the specific comfort zones that they have thought were good for them, that turned out to be bad for them, will always be bad for them. This is not just an occasional item, but it is one of those warning signs that need to be understood and acted upon appropriately. It should also be mentioned that comfort zones may change with age and even with interests. As an individual gets older and acquires skills along with experiencing new things, the comfort zone may change, or it may stagnate for a time and then possibly expand rapidly. This can be dangerous to the individual. If their comfort zone expands too quickly and no boundaries have been established along the way, the individual can get into a lot of trouble very quickly by believing that their comfort zone is safe for them when it is actually a trap for them, set by an individual with an unwritten agenda.

<u>Familiar individuals:</u> In this level, the initial familial groups are the parents and extended family. This group seems to be very familiar to the individual, and they seem to have a very good relationship with their parents and siblings. However, if some type of event occurs that upsets this relationship, (divorce, death, major illness), the individual may seek some kind of solace by seeking out or expanding upon other people, they may meet. This does not lead to good judgment and at times an individual will put their trust and thoughts out in the open and anyone with an unwritten agenda can take advantage of them. For a time they will see that person as their friend or as a confidant. Nevertheless, eventually, that person either takes advantage of them or gets them into some serious trouble. This seems to be common with families who have had divorce, death or family conflicts or even in blended families and it appears that taking sides tends to occur. These individuals perceive problems within other family members but do not always seem to recognize that people outside the family may be more trouble than people in a family. They may develop friendships with people of the opposite sex and even engage in some sexual behavior, but it seems in their seeking comfort and familiarity with another person, they may be just setting themselves up for another disappointment. The perception of these individuals can become clouded by some thoughts of emotional comfort or emotional trust, and therefore they set themselves up for failure to some extent. They may be over trusting people that they do know only to be given some type of hope that never materializes. These individuals can be over trusting or, as time goes on, they can be very distrusting of anyone who actually is trying to help them. It has been noted that the people that they will let in their life are much like their addition and deletion that is similar to their comfort zone addition and deletion. At times with their non-discriminatory trust, they can get into legal problems because they just do not understand. For the ones that have had some life experience, they get into trouble because they won't deal with the system and therefore surrender and take whatever punishment is given to them even though they may not have actually done anything wrong. This will be discussed further in consequences. Their relationships with other people may change over the course of time and be depending on how their relationships with people go. They will

either add new people or delete people out of their life as they learn that not all people who want to be part of their lives are good for them. They also learn that people that they want in their life may not be good for them as well and therefore become discriminatory towards relationships and familiar people in their life.

Adaptive skill: **This group has the highest ability to accumulate/to assimilate and learn adaptive skills. However, they may be the most resistive towards learning new skills. If they are not given logical explanations why they need to learn the skill, as in previous levels, the explanation of "because I said so" and "you should know by now, "does not work. These individuals need bona fide reasons why they should learn new skills, but they need less training in adapting to them if they want to. This level also may accumulate and assimilate new skills and even master them, but they may also delete them later on because they feel they need them or those skills may take them out of the comfort zone, and they may regress back to a previous comfort zone. They can learn, but they also have the will to resist learning new skills. Parents/caregivers/therapists need to work on logical explanations that will help the individual to cooperate when they are learning new skills and in practicing with them the new skills. This can be very successful if the time is taken to explain before the demonstration and then to practice any new skills. It has also been reported that someone who has learned a new skill has decided that after a time it did not work for them, so they reverted back to a time and a different skill that worked for them in the past. This group may also develop new skills on their own. However, sometimes they will develop skills that are not good for them, such as smoking, alcohol and other possible, substance abuse. It is known that they will try these things if they are introduced to them by someone that they trust even though that familiarity is minimal. They may take up a bad habit or even possibly commit specific problematic behaviors that could get them into some type of trouble. However, these behaviors can be unlearned as well as more positive ones that can be learned to substitute for the bad ones. These individuals can take their individual qualities and skills that they already have and be very prominent in those fields if time is taken to understand what those skills are and how they can use them in the real world. If the skills that are**

developed and not encouraged, these individuals may settle for some employment that is far below their potential and make it part of their comfort zone. They may settle for menial labor jobs rather than to use their skills to their most significant potential.

Meltdown: **At this level, the meltdown will depend on the age of the individual. Some of the younger individuals that have been identified at this level tend to come home after school and have some sort of aggressive outburst. It has been recommended that families with these individuals have a punching bag or even a punching dummy available to allow these individuals to vent their frustration. The individual matures, and it seems that the meltdowns are more like minor adult temper tantrums. This include stomping of feet, verbal tirades and possibly cussing and swearing. This type of outburst is usually short in duration, but intense during its length. After the meltdown, it is advised that the parent/teacher/caregiver take a moment and ask the individual what happened that caused them to have the meltdown. In the younger group, you will either get a blank stare or possibly even the famous line of "I don't know." It is advised that the parent/teacher/caregiver then go through a series of questions to possibly identify what may have happened that caused the meltdown. If that does not work, then talk to them about the key topic which gets them to talk about anything. The key topic needs to be identified and to be frequently used when in situations such as this occur. In the older group, it is advisable to allow them to do their foot stomping, ranting, and raving for a period of time and then address them with the following statement, "Are you done." This should get them to refocus on the fact that you are paying attention to what is going on and then the dialogue can begin about what happened and why they feel the way they do. A therapist/parent/teacher may take this opportunity to try to understand what it is that the individual either misinterpreted, took personally or entirely overreacted emotionally too. Whatever the situation was that caused this emotional outburst it can be understood and learned from. These individuals are not usually violent, and by some time in their late teens to their early twenties, they are more verbal than physical. However, it is possible that they may take a swing at someone if they are interrupted before they are allowed to go through their foot stomping**

and tirade. It is best to allow them to vent this and then sit down and talk to them about what it was that caused this emotional outburst. It is then advisable to work with them on solutions other than going through a foot-stomping/verbal tirade. Therefore, depending upon the individuals' age will depend upon the type of meltdown that may be witnessed.

<u>Social etiquette:</u> Younger individuals at this level still are very shy and timid to some extent. There will be some eye contact, but initial verbalizations are rare until the individual becomes comfortable in their environment. Standard social greetings such as eye contact, handshake, and a greeting are unusual until a younger individual is comfortable or someone works with them on these gestures. They are not known to have any type of meltdown or verbal altercation in public. That seems to be saved for when they get into their comfort zone such as their home and then it appears that they tend to vent. In the older group, if they have learned any type of social etiquette, they will practice it. These individuals have learned that any kind of expression of emotions or anger in public could have consequences. They have a tendency to either remove themselves from the situation or give themselves a timeout or they will leave the situation and possibly isolate themselves at their residence. They may perhaps take a good deal of time to think their way through the situation. This group can learn many social adaptive skills if someone takes the time to work with them on adaptive social skills. They will not usually pick up the social skills or social etiquette by observation. The expectation that they should know certain things or they are at a certain age and should be aware of these skills is a profoundly erroneous thought. These individuals do learn on occasion from examples in the environment, but for the most part, need to be reassured that what they have learned is an acceptable skill. They may entirely ignore what is going on in their environment as they may have a tendency to hide behind their electronic device. However, if someone takes the time to work with them and encourage them to use specific social etiquette skills, they can adapt and assimilate those types of social skills into their everyday behaviors. Overall, anyone at this level can learn social etiquette and adaptive skills that have to do with social appropriateness.

<u>Social awareness:</u> The younger group has a tendency to be somewhat aware of their surroundings but at times has a tendency not to participate unless encouraged to do so. They will have a tendency to stand off when a new item is introduced into their social schema. However, they can learn new social thought process and well-being. By the time, these individuals reach early adulthood. They may have learned about boundaries and about social appropriateness. There may be times when they have issues that could lead to some type of meltdown, but for the most part, they seem to be able to adapt quite well to the social schema as described by normal society. As stated in the previous section, these individuals can learn but at times needs a logical explanation with good reasons why they need to become more socially aware. The younger group is less aware of the differentiation between boys and girls. However, the older group may have had some experience with the opposite sex. For the most part, from the experiences gained within my clinic, they are not sexually aggressive. It seems that they may be taught or experienced something from another person that may be sexually aggressive and therefore begin to adopt that social awareness as being somewhat normal. However, they will only seek those types of behaviors with that specific person who has taught them. They do not seem to go out and look for other sexual partners. It appears that their comfort zone is with the person who has taught them about their own sexuality to stay with that person. Individuals at this stage do not necessarily have multiple partners due to bonding with the individual who has shown them the affection that they have experienced. Over time, and as they age, these individuals may seek out a different partner, but this would be due to the fact that the partner which introduce them into their experiences has either hurt them severely or has moved on to someone else. It is not uncommon for an individual to be married to one person, divorce them, and then have them move back in with them due to the familiarity and the comfort, which was generated through that relationship. At times, they are very leery about taking on any other new relationships due to bad experiences from a previous relationship. They can be very suspicious of people especially after they have had several bad experiences. It seems that they have learned from those bad experiences and have moved on and become

somewhat isolated or they are actually actively seeking a new partner. This has been documented, and some individuals have suffered legal consequences by not understanding why the individual that they are so close to has decided that they no longer want them around in their life. When an individual at this level does make an attachment to another individual, it seems that that attachment is felt to be permanent. However, if an individual at this level has the unfortunate incident of having a relationship with an individual who is either using them or abusing them, they may find out that there are legal consequences, and they actually may be in legal trouble for not understanding that sometimes relationships do not work and people have to move on. It would be indicated that it seems that their learning when it comes to social awareness, is sometimes by trial and error without necessarily learning that the error needs to be walked away from. This is probably going to be a point of contention later on, but for the purposes of my putting this writing together, this is what I have observed and noted in my practice.

<u>Consequences:</u> This area is dependent upon age and experience. Whether an individual has advanced to this level or they start off at this level, the acceptance of consequences or the understanding of consequences is dependent upon both age and experience.
Younger individuals at this level have a tendency to push boundaries and need to be taught that there are consequences for bad behavior. Parents need to be working together on these consequences for the behaviors, and it needs to be a uniform code whereby both parents give the same consequences for the same behavior. These individuals are very intelligent. At a young age, they may end up playing the parents off each other and thereby getting away without consequences. This may lead to maladaptive behaviors later on and the possibility of other outside interventions, which could include children services as well as the legal system. However, over time as they age and gaining experience, they do realize the consequences are real and can develop their own boundaries.
Individuals in the teenage an older groups of this level have a tendency to have learned about consequences as they have been dealt with by outside interventions such as the legal system or another social service agency. However, they begin to develop a specific

logical response that if this happens then, this should also happen. They have a tendency not to dispute any type of claim against them but rather just accept the consequences. Although this seems to be somewhat self-defeating, this is part of their learning process and thought construct. For example: if an individual got into trouble for doing something and there were some legal ramifications, they believe that anything that involves legal consequences they will be punished. At times, this does not seem logical as it is an all or nothing thought process but, through learning, the individual believes that if there is any legal involvement, it is best just to take the consequences. They feel they are going to be wrong and prosecuted regardless of whether or not they were involved and just surrender to the consequences. In most cases, this makes absolutely no sense. Outside interventions to help them through the fact that just because the police are involved does not mean they are guilty are somewhat unsuccessful. However, through learning, and if they have ever had any contact with law enforcement, they will tend to surrender and accept the consequences even if they are not guilty. The reason for this seems to be that it is better just to accept the consequences and deal with the consequences rather than to try to prove oneself innocent or not guilty. It seems that they would instead just take the consequences then go through the hassle of whatever they believe will happen next and just serve the consequence rather than to fight it. This seems to be a part of the age and learning experience that has a logical thought process with an illogical conclusion, but this happens quite frequently in individuals with autistic spectrum disorder. If they cannot see the whole picture, then they just determined that the picture they have given is the only one they are going to see and therefore they will take consequences rather than go through a process to prove themselves not to be responsible for what had happened. In several cases, this starts off when an individual at this level begins to have a contact in the community, and people take advantage of them. Since their contact with the outside world is minimal, they do not understand why people treat them that way and start to develop the thought process that all people are going to treat me this way, and it's best to stay away from them. However, individuals at this level do tend to continue to try to have contact with people in the outside world. They do not always understand social functioning or the fact that individuals may

have an unwritten agenda that may cause the individual that has autism to look like they may be the source of the problem. However, since an individual with autistic spectrum disorder does not have the social wherewithal to understand that not all people are good and that each time there is any police involvement, they are not guilty. It seems that individuals with autistic spectrum disorder end up taking the blame due to a lack of understanding of the real world and how it works. That is why individuals at this level continue to need some forms of supervision and outside intervention to understand that the world around them can be very hostile towards them if they are not aware of it.

It is very often that individuals at this level have had some legal involvement over the course of their lifetime. It has been the experience of this counselor that individuals who have had some legal problems have a tendency to surrender rather than to fight. It seems that this surrender keeps them in a comfort zone rather than to enter into an arena where they have to talk about and defend themselves against what they are being accused of. Since individuals at this level sometimes have problems in talking and describing and being verbal about how to explain themselves, they have a tendency just to take the punishment rather than try and stand and fight for themselves. Individuals who do have fairly good verbal skills at this level have a tendency not quite to understand the meaning of certain words or certain terminology. The in-depth thinking they do and speaking in some specific phraseology, they might not fully comprehend, can get themselves into more trouble because of their lack of word understanding and usage. This is another reason why individuals at this level need some level of supervision and intervention especially when it comes to dealing with the legal system. There have been many times over the course of my practice that individuals with this level of autism end up being prosecuted for something that they have not done, but they have admitted to either directly or indirectly. Their own verbalizations that may or may not have been correct have caused them to be blamed for an offense they have been accused of. The legal system is based on initial accounts and verbalization. At times, these individuals' verbalizations may be good, and it may be accurate to them, but the interpretation of the verbalizations may not be exactly the way the individual understands them to be and therefore open to

interpretation by the legal system. Therefore, individuals at this level have a tendency to have legal troubles. It is not uncommon for an individual at this level to admit to something he did not do and face the consequences. They believe going to happen, only to find out later on that the consequences in which he believes will happen are not going to happen, and they may be more severe than what they have assumed. The assumption is based on their own learning experience and what they have experienced through their consequences. Any further consequences beyond what they have experienced are unknown to them. In this case, the need for outside intervention and clear explanations are needed for the individual to make sound judgments and decisions. It is not uncommon for an individual after they understand the whole scope of the legal problem. To then recant their story and explain it the best they can. At this point, from a legal standpoint, it may be felt that the individual is lying. However, the individual, finally seeing the whole picture, may not want the consequences that they do not understand to happen and therefore try to rectify the situation rather than just give themselves up. At this point, they may want to take a stand and clear themselves. This is why individuals at this level need supervision and also outside intervention to help with those things that may happen in their life that they do not understand or have not experienced or assume not to exist.

As this group continues to age, their life experience and learning experiences do have some bearing on their behavior. It seems that over time as they have had these experiences, both good and bad, they may choose to withdraw to some degree and only have minimal or marginal contact with the world outside of their comfort zone. This seems to be prevalent as the individual reaches into their thirty's and decides that they would like to stay in a comfort zone where they are out of danger and have minimal chance of developing any problems that they may not be able to handle. They may not want to deal with legal, emotional or social issues at this point in their life. It could be said that due to consequences an individual at this level will spend more time in their comfort zone because they believe it is safe and their contact with the outside world will be minimized due to a fear of further consequences and complications.

<u>Right brain dominance:</u> Individuals at this level with the right brain dominance show a high propensity towards mathematical skills. It also seems that they are very organized to some degree, but not completely. What appears to be important to them will be very organized what does not seem to be important will be very disorganized. The younger group, these individuals are very organized when it comes to important items such as their toys or their games. However, they are less organized when it comes to things like clothing, laundry, and cleanliness. You may see this as highly organized when it comes to items that are important to them. However, you may find them hiding their dirty close under their beds in their closets or even under their dressers. Intervention with these individuals can help them to be trained to do those other skills such as activities of daily living. The right brain individual can become hyper-focused on specific sports that require certain mechanical and mathematical precision to perform them to the best of their abilities. When the right brain individual finds what they are very good at, they need to be encouraged to continue on in pursuit of that path. The right brain individual is not as verbal and may become frustrated if they are asked for a verbal solution to a problem. They are very good with signs and numbers, but they do expect you to keep up with them. If you do not keep up with them, they will become frustrated with you and probably either grunt or walk away when trying to explain what it is that you want to know. Written work can be problematic, but it can be trained. A manual letter making especially with pens and pencils is possible through rote learning and encouragement. They are very adept at computers, computer skills, computer games and the mechanics of a computer. These individuals can also do computer programming as well as setting up systems. Individuals at this level are sometimes overlooked for their greater gift and are seen as problematic due to either their odd behavior, which is pretty benign or their inability to understand body language and verbal introductions. They have a tendency not to show eye contact and will only speak when they are asked to speak. This is a very intelligent group, and they have a lot of possibilities as well as potential. This is one of the important groups that need to be supervised and directed because they have a gift and without the proper supervision and guidance, that gift will be wasted, and they may end up in a menial labor job.

<u>Left-brain dominance:</u> **Individuals with left-brain dominance are very verbal. They have good logic construct and relatively good understanding of word usage. However, at times they tend to use words they may not quite understand and in the wrong context. This may lead to some major misunderstanding. They have issues with mathematics skills, but are very adept at understanding music in its presentation, but not necessarily in its written construct. Individuals that are left brained tend to be a little more social because they have confidence in the fact that they can verbalize and possibly converse with whomever they meet. It is also known that they may be able to talk a good game but mechanically speaking, and they cannot play it. Individuals like this are exceptional at making designs and can come up with ideas that are revolutionary but may not be practical. They may not understand the concept of the joke and will be looking for the meaning long after the joke has been told and explained. They are the excellent conversationalist, but if a topic comes up that, they do not understand they may say they understand because they may be taking the word apart to try to understand its fragments. However, in doing so, they may misinterpret what the entire conversation is about, and the other person may assume that they are following when in all reality they are not. When working with individuals that are left brained at this level, It is important to continually ask them questions of what they understand of what has been told to them. On occasion, they tend to agree when they have no clue, and therefore direct intervention in helping them to understand that they are allowed to ask questions and not assume that they understand is essential in the therapeutic encounters. These individuals have high potentials as writers and strategic planners to some degree. However, this gift must also be recognized and encouraged for them to take their gift and use it.**

<u>Brain-behavior and thought process:</u> **This level seems to have the ability to learn some crossovers between the right and left-brain. However, at first, they do look as though they may have the standard ability. However, with further examination, it is evident that there is a differentiation between the left-brain and the right brain processes. They can be taught left and right brain crossovers and also be**

instructed, worked with and can even master the non-dominant side of the brain functions. The deficits in differentiations need to be identified so they can be put into a specific program. In the younger group, an individual education program needs to reflect the fact that they need continued help/instruction/remediation on particular abilities. However, without this identification of these deficits, an individual may struggle through school and have differentiation in grades that would be considered acceptable, but this is not the individuals' best interest. For them to reach the highest degree of their potential, their deficits need to be identified and remediated. One specific tests that can determine the differentiation brain functioning is an IQ test called the WISC. The WISC-R, II, and III edition of this instrument to help you identify deficits in the brain functioning and can, therefore, be remediated through the use and employment of an individual educational program. As the individual progresses through school, this differentiation may become less evident if the individual educational program is successful. However, if the individual educational program is not as successful as possible, there will be long-standing deficits. These individuals may qualify for some type of vocational technical training, and they may become very masterful and whatever field they choose. Others who can close the gap between the left-brain and the right brain or vice versa can definitely go on to post-secondary education and be successful in whatever field of endeavor that they choose. The earlier the intervention, the better the outcomes and the more complete the person becomes. The later the intervention the outcomes may be questionable, and could even be catastrophic for the individual. Therefore, it is important to identify these issues as soon as possible and design a program that helps the individual maximize their potential. There is nothing worse than to waste someone's ability that has good talent that goes unnoticed because nothing is done to help them foster their gift.

<u>Jaded by Life:</u> Individuals at this level, especially starting in the teenage years and going forward, tend to ruminate on their negative experiences and begin to expect them to happen. It seems that what they learned from their negative experience seems to become absolute in their mind. Their thought process seems to take on the all or nothing, and if this happens then, this always follows. Intervention

during any of these times may help the individual not to become so concrete in their thinking. When it comes to their experiences in life, intervention, supervision and logical explanations go a long way to help them beyond this thinking construct.

Individuals at this level can be very trusting in their early years, and this can continue depending on their experiences. If they have not had a lot of negative experiences throughout their adult life, they may be very trusting till they reach a point where their experiences have taught them to not to be as trusting. It seems at times that they can be very idealistic in their outcomes in life only to have those experiences not materialize. However, with the ability to think their way through things, they may rationalize that it did not happen because something or someone intervened for a good reason. However, that good reason is rationalized even though it could probably be a bad reason. For example, someone using them for their own gain rather than sharing with them. Over time, however, these individuals can become quite wise to the ways of the world, but in this process, they tend to become more withdrawn and less social. Their learning curve in dealing with disappointment and especially with the inability to trust others seem to take a lot of experiences before they actually learn as compared to normative persons. They can be very optimistic and outcome positive. Even if the outcome has little to no chance of ever happening, they will rationalize it did not happen because it was for the best for someone else. As one can see from this line of thought, these individuals can get into legal trouble because they seem to be trying to feel and rationalize why the other person did them wrong but not looking at it is wrong against them but for the right for the other person. This is where the logic gets to be somewhat twisted as it is internalized logic and not logic on a global scale. Individuals at this level may take the blame for something they did not do to protect someone else who they may or may not have a good relationship with. It is not that they feel that they should be punished but in their experiences, whenever there is any type of legal involvement, it always leads to some kind of consequence. With this learning, they feel that any time there is any legal involvement; it will lead to that consequence, and therefore why to bother to fight it because it is going to happen anyhow. This is illogical on a global level, but within their logical thought process and through learning,

this makes perfect sense to them. Many individuals at this level are incarcerated for something they did not do because they rationalize the other person has more to lose then they do or that their learning experience has always led to this type of consequence and therefore it's going to happen. So why fight it. This is why intervention and continued supervision along the pathways and course of a lifetime are needed to be implemented due to these misunderstandings, illogical thought process, and negative experiences. This is one of the reasons why supervision is recommended to continue on through the course of a lifetime for individuals at this level. It seems that they have enough social skills and enough intelligence to get themselves into trouble without trying.

Vulnerability: Although this group is less vulnerable than the previous two groups, they are still quite susceptible to the underlying schemes of others. Individuals in this group have developed friendships over time through the learning process, but they can still be swayed to some extent by individuals they considered either friends or possibly even family members. Individuals from this group may also take the blame for something they did not do to protect a friend or a friendship. They are also vulnerable to issues when dealing with the legal system, as they may tend to avoid the issues by taking the easy way out. However, by taking the easy way out, they may be severely punished by the legal system. However, they do not understand, at times, the ramifications of the punishment that they have agreed to or the further consequences of the label that will be given them as a convicted individual. These individuals need continued therapeutic intervention, and they also need some supervision to learn that not all people that are your friends are good people. It would seem that they have or overlook the possibility that someone that has been their friend over time may have been setting them up for a long time to possibly take the blame for some unwritten agenda by the friend. This group seems to have blinders on as to the difference between right and wrong when the importance of friendship or family is involved or some important relationship. These individuals can learn that life has a lot of twists and turns in it and they may be caught up in the importance of a relationship rather than the importance of their own credibility. Even though there intelligent and adaptable they are still vulnerable to the

Ways and Means of individuals who could seriously take advantage of them.

<u>The key:</u> Individuals in this group have many keys that can be utilized to help them to understand, learn and adopt new skills. This group can also be taught to use these keys to practice some self-behavioral interventions. When working with this group, a therapist/parent/caregiver/teacher should be aware of many keys to working with any specific individual. It is essential to know more than one key when working with this group because they may not respond to a key that had been used in a previous intervention. It is essential to know more than one key order to use them to resolve the situation or to open up dialogue in working with this group. It is understood that they are very intelligent and they can be resistive to intervention. However, in working with them, and knowing several of their keys, intervention and therapeutic progress can be made by the utilization of this concept.

Other issues: ASD-level II

At this point, there is a need for an overall explanation of specific behaviors within each of the levels within level II regardless of which side of the brain is dominating. The ASD-level II-lower-level tends to spend a lot of time in their safe zone due to their vulnerability and their inability, due to a lack of social skills and social communication, to handle the real world. This is understandable as they make very easy targets for designing people. Therefore, therefore, they stay safe, and they stay out of harm's way. They will try to make some effort to go out into the real world, but overall their situation is simple by their minimal operations outside of their safe zone.

In contrast, ASD-level II-higher-level tends to continue to have a more open view of being out in society and in the real world. They do have an elaborate safe zone that they can very easily go to but they seem to be a little more adventurous, possibly due to their ability to learn adaptive skills and master them. They do maintain their safe zone to some extent, however; they are more willing to engage in the real world outside of their safe zone. As they continue to adapt and learn

new adaptive skills and master them, they may have a tendency to change their safe zone or add other safe zones beyond their initial safe zone and therefore can and will spend more time in the real world. This is a great adaptive skill that this group can master and utilize.

The ASD-II-middle level is the most interesting of this group. It seems that there are two distinct groups within this group. It has been noted through my experiences that this group can go in different directions. One direction, the most beneficial to the individual, comes into contact with the outside world, some good supervision, and encouragement from parents, teachers, supervisors and their therapist. This group is referred to as the "PROGRESSIVE." It seems through exposure to the outside world in a minimally supervised environment they seem to want to embrace the real world especially when it comes to the incentive of money. Given the situation, and they can, learn a trade and have a marketable skill. They will spend more time in the real world developing zones outside of their comfort zone whereby they accomplish the task of earning money and self-expression through their job. It seems that they learn many of the adaptive skills needed to function in the real world with only minimal supervision over a period of time. They seem to embrace working and getting paid and being able to have some independence with minimal supervision. It seems that there is a good success with these individuals, as they seem to learn adaptive skills, master their adaptive skills and take responsibility for working a job and their own needs. They still have a comfort zone, usually a bedroom or their apartment, that they can find comfort in if needed. It seems that they like to get out into the real world and at least experience or observe the world around them. They know they still have their comfort zone they can go back to if they become overloaded or there are too many activities going on. They have the wherewithal to go back to their comfort zone and refocus if they become overstimulated or anxious. They also have a tendency to ask questions about situations in which they have observed in order for them to come up with a solution set to handle the situations if they are ever involved in them. Therefore, through the skills they have acquired they have learned to adapt to society and have no problems in going out into the real world. In stark contrast, there are individuals at this level who spend way too much

time in their comfort zone and are enabled to stay in that comfort zone because of a lack of motivation and/or encouragement by their parents. They are referred to as the "REGRESSIVE." It seems there is also a lack of any type of outside interventions that is community-based. These individuals seem to be totally focused on their comfort zone and start to spend less and less time outside of their comfort zone. It was noted that they begin to overindulge in thought processes that may be related to the entertainment in which they continue to entertain themselves with to the point where they are starting to have a problem with distinguishing between reality and fantasy. There was a time when this would be called "schizophrenia"; however, these individuals can be brought out of their comfort zone and this fantasy world if they are given the right incentive, encouragement, and supervision to do so. However, until that time, they become somewhat dangerous to other individuals because of indulging in the fantasy world, which is usually a factor of overplaying video games, over watching specific television and the lack of planning for the future. These individuals can become very reactive to situations in which they may feel threatened or challenged, and they will react with what they have learned through the video games, television and possibly other factors in their safe zone. They may become very verbal about what they are thinking, and their verbalizations may sound dangerous and threatening. However, their verbalizations are the venting of trying to rationalize and emotionally deal with, some situation that they have no reference for dealing with. The verbalizations can become very disturbing to anyone listening, but for the most part, they are verbalizations with no real behavioral outcomes. In other words, a lot of negative thoughts with no actions but possible consequences if there is no intervention by someone that knows them. If someone does not know the individual and they vent these thoughts, they may be considered a threat, and legal action may be taken. This is one of the many reasons why this group, Level II, needs closer supervision. The solution to this problem, which I highly recommend, is therapeutic interventions with the individual and the family. Bringing this individual back to reality starts with challenging the thought process that has been brought about by too much time creating a fantasy world where they are in control and bring them back to the reality that they are really part of. This is going to take some time and a lot of effort, as it

seems that in the enabling process, allowed too much time in their room playing video games, watching television and being on the computer, needs to be divested in a manner by which the individual will not become angered. This is a slow process and all individuals: therapist, parents and other concerned members, need to all work together off of a solid plan. Without the coordination, this will not work, and that individual will become hostile because they are going to defend their thoughts about who they think they are rather than whom they really are. With all the concerned individuals, working together there is a chance of a good outcome goal for this individual who has autistic spectrum disorder-level II-middle level. There must be incentive involved in this program, encouragement, and patients in order to make it work. This is going to take time to accomplish because this individual has spent way too much time developing their fantasy in their safe zone and they believe they can take it out into reality but they can't. Therefore, it is going to take time and effort on all parties to help this individual to become a productive member of society. This can happen but it takes the patience, and the cooperation of all the people involved to help the autistic individual become an adaptive member of society that has abilities they can contribute to the real world.

Conclusion: Throughout this chapter on autistic spectrum disorder-level II the reader should be reminded that this is the experiences and observations of this counselor. These observations and recommendations are what this counselor has experienced in his office over the course of the last seven years in private practice and his experiences working for specific institutions and outpatient practices. I have been in mental health for over 25 years in total. Since the redefinition of autism in the DSM 5, it seems that people have a problem with understanding what autism is today. Hopefully, with an open mind, anyone reading this will have a better understanding that there can be several levels within a level and that there are many abilities within each individual in each level that need to be discovered, encouraged, fostered and of course help the person to discover the highest level of their potential. Not all people have the ability to reach the highest level of their possible potential, but they do have a gift, and that gift needs to be discovered and encouraged. The

individual needs encouragement and some supervision and interventions to continue on a course to develop their talent. It seems on many occasions that these individuals have been warehoused, neglected by society and have ended up either in the criminal justice system or are just living their lives on day by day basis, without any real direction. It is my goal, as it is in these writings, to inform the public that these individuals can live amongst us and need to be given every opportunity for a full and fulfilling life.

CHAPTER 6

Autistic Spectrum Disorder

Level III

Autistic Spectrum Disorder-Level III

Of all levels of autistic spectrum disorder, this level has been documented over the years as what a true individual with autistic spectrum disorder looks like. This has become the mindset of many people, and it is very incorrect. Individuals with autistic spectrum disorder-level III may have the most severe issues, but not all individuals with autism are at this level. This level has been overgeneralized and plagiarized as the typical autistic spectrum disorder. That is not the case, but I hope that the information contained herein will help people to understand that this level, although it is severe, individuals still have qualities and individuality that needs to be discovered and then through good training programs can be mastered.

When somebody says the word autism, the general population deems that individuals with autism fall into this category of level III. However, this is not the case. Individuals that are at the level III have severe deficits but can be taught to do specific tasks if the proper programs are put together for them based on individual needs and abilities. Although this group, the level threes, has been the most recognized throughout the history of this diagnosis, they are not the majority of individuals that fall under the autistic spectrum disorder. They are the ones most in need of qualified individuals to help them to determine their limitations and their abilities. Therefore, a highly skilled/trained/patient individual would be the only one who can help individuals with autistic spectrum disorder-level III achieves some skill sets and goals. Although they have been categorized and generalized these individuals, still have abilities that need to be discovered and then mastered.

According to the DSM 5, the autistic spectrum disorder-level III is defined as the following: "requiring very substantial support."

Social communication: "severe deficits in verbal and nonverbal social communication skills cause severe impairment in functioning, very limited initiation of social interactions, and minimal response to social overtures from others. For example, a person with few words of intelligible speech who rarely initiates interaction and, when he or she does, makes unusual approaches to meet needs only and responds to only very direct social approaches.

Restricted, repetitive behaviors: "inflexibility of behavior, extreme difficulty coping with change, or other restricted/repetitive behaviors markedly interferes with functioning in all spheres. Great distress/difficulty changing focus or action. (DSM-5). It was also noted in several notations from the DSM-2, DSM-3, DSM-3R, that there was a possibility of some intellectual disability, childhood schizophrenia and possibly even some neurological deficits due to many etiologies. Individuals with autistic spectrum disorder-level III have a lot of issues and need constant support and supervision.

Over the course of my career, I had encountered individuals with autistic spectrum disorder-level III that were institutionalized and younger individuals that were still being supervised by their parents. It is tough to get any intellectual quotient (IQ) from these individuals, but it is possible. Due to their restrictive behaviors, minimal speech content, it can be tough to relate to these individuals, but it can be done. Specific training programs have been designed to work with them and what strengths they do have. As it was quoted from the DSM 5, some individuals are verbal to a minimal extent while others are not verbal but may understand specific signs and body language. These are two major factors when it comes to individuals who work with level III individuals. In my current practice, I do not work with individuals that are at level III. These individuals are best served in specialized facilities and possibly even long-term care environments where they can get the specialized treatment programs that are available at those two major institutions.

Throughout this chapter, I will be using the markers that I've used for the level I's and level II's and I hope this sheds some light on what these individuals possibly have a potential for and how difficult they are to work with. Although my interaction with individuals that were diagnosed with autistic spectrum disorder level III is somewhat limited, (mostly with Level I and II), the following areas of interest are somewhat generalized however they are applicable. I hope that someone will take from this article and possibly even expand upon it. It is also my hope that people learn from this article that individuals with autistic spectrum disorder level III are human beings and need to be treated as such even if they do become combative and assaultive.

<u>Comfort zone:</u>

Individuals with autistic spectrum disorder level III have specific places where they are most comfortable and are less likely to have behavioral issues. They may still have behavioral issues in their comfort zone however not as likely as if they are taken out of their comfort zone. This comfort zone can be their home of residence or a specific area in a specific room. Their comfort zone may be tied to a specific seating location, chair, or part of a couch. It seems when they are in this comfort zone they are most calm. It is also in the comfort zone where individuals who work with them can approach them to some degree. It has been my experience in the inpatient setting that I can sit next to an individual with autistic spectrum disorder level III, and they will touch your hand. Depending on the person sitting next to the individual with autistic spectrum disorder level III, they may be calm and enjoy the minimal contact, or they may have a possible meltdown due to the individual. This will be discussed further in this article. However, individuals with autistic spectrum disorder level III have specific comfort zones, and they also have specific people with which they will interact to the best of their abilities which may be no more than a hand touch or that occasional glance.

In the outpatient setting, the individual may have a comfort zone in their home of residence and in the specific facility in which they are going through their daily activity. This may be a function of age as well as the severity of the level III individual. It has been experienced that younger level III individuals that live at home with their parents seem to be restrictive when brought into a new environment. However, it was observed that after a few minutes they were able to engage in individual play behavior with toys. This may be a function of the fact that they were younger and did respond somewhat to their mother's voice. However, it seemed that they were quite relaxed in that environment and played with whatever toy they got their hands on.

In the clinical environment, in my own experience, the individual seems to be slightly resistive but, both parents were present, and the individual remained calm. The individual did not have any eye contact with me during this evaluation. There were no behavioral issues or incidents during this encounter. The individual did respond to a specific song that was being played on a laptop along with the visual stimulus of the colors as they flashed across the screen. The individual looked up and was watching the different colors and the different color patterns on the laptop screen as a song played. There were no incidents of any behavioral issues and the time seemed to be somewhat productive as the individual found a comfort zone in an office that he'd never been in before, with music playing and some colored lights flashing. It seemed that for the most part, this was a temporary comfort zone, but it was a comfort zone.

The comfort zone should be noted with these individuals for the simple reason that their best behavior will be found in these comfort zones for the most part. Specific things in the comfort zone should also be noted for the individual such as the seat they are sitting in, the texture of the seat they are sitting in, any items nearby they may be especially attached to, and any individual they may have a relationship with. Removing any of these things from the individual is very likely to

cause a behavioral outburst or some bizarre behavior. Maintenance of the comfort zone is paramount to the individual, and this contributes to the relaxed and behavior-free area.

Familiar individuals:

As a comfort zone is an essential part of an individual's life, specific individuals are also an integral part of their life. Caretakers may develop a specific relationship with a specific individual. It should be taken into account that a caretaker's approach towards the individual with autistic spectrum disorder. It may be something very specific such as the sound of their voice or even their approach to the individual. Ultimately, individuals with autistic spectrum disorder level III can be very specific towards their behavior with specific individuals. It has been observed that if you removed caretakers that they are familiar with there is a good possibility of some behavioral outburst.

To some degree, the most familiar individuals that have the best relationship with individuals with autistic spectrum disorder level III is one or even both parents. Over time, it may become necessary to have the individual in day programming or even possibly institutionalized to some degree. Autistic spectrum disorder level III individuals will pick and/or choose the individual in which they want to be addressed by. This may be a preference that they have that may not be entirely understood, but through observation, it seems that individuals who talk to them gently and do not try to over stimulate them may be the most familiar individuals to them. It has been observed that individuals that are very familiar to the autistic individual can be the most significant in the autistic person's life. Individuals who become very familiar with the autistic spectrum disorder level III individual can be utilized as a key to helping the individual in dealing with his day-to-day life as well as performing activities of daily living or even assisting the individual in getting those activities of daily living done. The familiar

individual is as important to individuals with autistic spectrum disorder level III has the comfort zone.

<u>Adaptive skill:</u>

Individuals with autistic spectrum disorder level III do have some ability to learn some adaptive skills, but it has to be repetitive and simple one-step procedures. These procedures may be very fundamental, and patience is needed in teaching and re-teaching them. It has been observed that some fundamental skills can be taught and learned, but they are just what they are fundamental skills and abilities. Simply: activities of daily living such as eating, toilet training, and dressing abilities are a few to mention. These still must be supervised and guided to some degree.

These are not great works like the other levels can learn, but they are still some skills that have some possible independent outcomes such as when they dress or if they brush their teeth with minimal supervision. These things can be taught to some degree, but patience and persistence on the part of the caregiver are needed. Individuals may not be able to complete the task, and gentle encouragement and direction may be needed or even required. They may not remember or follow through on parts of a task.

<u>Meltdown:</u>

Level III individual is quite prone to meltdowns. Due to their inability to communicate effectively, their frustration level seems to lead directly to a meltdown. Since they cannot state what they are feeling or what is going on verbally, for the most part, they act out. I witnessed on many occasion meltdowns by individuals with level III autistic spectrum disorder. It seems that if you do not know the person and have not worked with them before the meltdown can seem to be very spontaneous. However, individuals who have worked with that person have some insight into their behaviors before a possible meltdown and

therefore can try to prevent it to some degree. The familiarity with the level III individual is essential in trying to deter possible meltdowns. Meltdowns seem to occur spontaneously at times without any precursors or any behaviors that may have been observed that lead to a meltdown. Meltdowns themselves can be very simple as a person may sit in place rock rapidly and wave their hands in the air to, on the more severe, assaulting other individuals within arm's reach. I have witnessed both types of these meltdowns and variations in between.

In order to prevent the meltdown, individuals with familiarity who are included in the person's comfort zone are the only ones who can intervene efficiently to deter the meltdown possibly or to minimize it to some extent. A person that intervenes that is not part of this group of familiar individuals, or part of the comfort zone may end up putting himself at risk for possible bodily injury if they intervene without knowledge of the autistic individual's behavior.

It would be to the benefit of the individuals who are part of the familiar and/or are part of the comfort zone to come up with protocols to help the autistic individual, knowing what the precursors are, before the possible meltdown event and preventing them from happening. Knowing what could lead to the possibility of bodily harm and possibly restraints and possibly even emergency medication is to the best possible care of the autistic individual. With the caregiver, knowledge of the individual's behaviors, not only prevent them from having a behavioral outburst but also assist them in having a better experience in their life. Although these individuals may not be verbal, they still understand kindness to some degree, and any kindness or positive gesture may also help prevent any meltdown. Remember these are human beings, they should be treated with dignity and respect, and to help them to avoid a meltdown is therapeutic. The results of a meltdown are not therapeutic and can lead to possible future adverse outcomes. This is an area that needs further study and investigation. I hope someone takes it from here and works on it. For the most part,

this has been my experience with meltdowns with autistic spectrum disorder level threes. I was a familiar with one of these individuals, and he did not have any meltdowns when I was in his comfort zone, and he knew that I was there. I was able to escort him out of his comfort zone for a time, but eventually, there was a meltdown. Therefore, there is a possibility that even if you are a familiar a meltdown may still happen.

Overstimulation can also lead to a possible meltdown. As with other levels of autism (level I and II), individuals with autism may become over stimulated by events or other issues in their environment. Since the individual with level III autism is minimally verbal, they cannot tell you what may be overstimulating them. This stimulus may come in from the five senses (Seeing, hearing, touch, taste or smell) and may start to cause some behavioral issue. The familiar caregiver should be aware of any abnormal or erratic body movement and seek to find out what the over stimulus is and try to calm the individual down before things get to the problem point where a meltdown is probable. The familiar caretaker may be the only one who will notice this behavior and therefore will be the only one to prevent the meltdown. The caretaker or any substitute caretaker should have a written protocol of interventions to help the individual calm themselves and no have the meltdown. More work is needed on the extent and to what stimulus or stimuli may trigger behavioral issues in the level III person.

Social etiquette:

Due to erratic behavior and nonverbal ability, level threes have minimal social etiquette. For the most part, they only communicate with those people who are part of their familiar individual group that has been welcomed into their comfort zone. If an individual is taken out of their comfort zone, there is a possibility of some behavioral issue that will occur rather quickly. Some individuals can sit at a table and eat with others in some proximity, but this has only been observed

when they are in their comfort zone. It is noted if there are taken out of their comfort zone and some activity is expected of them, refusal to even a possible behavioral meltdown will occur.

Anybody who works with individuals with level III may be able to teach them a few social gestures such as waving and maybe handshaking, but this is going to take a lot of work and a lot of repetition. Therefore, they can learn some very basic social skills, but overall the social etiquette cannot be taught to any significant degree as it is in the other levels. This is also an area that needs further study, and also I hope that someone else carries this on.

<u>Social awareness:</u>

Level III individuals do have some sense of social awareness. It has been observed that they will notice or glance around the room from time to time but for the most part, they engage in an activity unto themselves. This activity can be as simple as sitting still and staring at the floor to playing with one toy or a couple of toys, which they prefer. Social awareness has always been a key feature of individuals with autism from the beginning of the study of autism. It was noted that individuals with autism sit by themselves for the most part, and sit and rock in place and make noises. This was one of the early hallmarks of autistic spectrum disorder. From my own observations this seems to be consistent but, at times, a familiar individual that is allowed in the comfort zone can take an individual with autistic spectrum disorder level III for a short walk or even walk with them to another comfort zone area.

In my observations from the clinical standpoint in the private setting, level III individuals, upon seeing something they like, move towards that item and grasp it in their hands and either hold it, play with it or rub it between their hands. An experiment that was conducted in the private setting was with an individual that was diagnosed with level III autistic spectrum disorder. The individual was of grade school age, did

not speak, and the only familiar people in their environment was the parents. He would only listen when they spoke, and he would only listen to them. It was unknown what education the young man was receiving, but he was in for an evaluation. As an experiment, I turned my laptop to him and turned on the music. The laptop responded with different color schemes going across the screen. I believe it was the music that got his attention, but it was the color patterns going across the screen that sustained his attention. It seemed that I had been able to reach out to him to some degree and get him to observe color schemes going across my computer screen, but also it was the music that got his attention. The parents were encouraged to play music for him to see if he starts to pick up any behaviors, good or bad when he listens to music. Unfortunately, I never saw the family again, and it is unknown what the outcome was. At that moment in history and time, an individual with autistic spectrum disorder level III crossed over a bridge, listened to some music and watched the color schemes go across the screen.

Since I do not work with autistic spectrum disorder level III individuals, I would challenge anybody to start working with them and having them listen to music coupled with the possibility of some color schemes and patterns. This may have been a fluke; however, I would challenge anybody to take up from this experiment and see what kind of progress could be made. These individuals are human beings, and for the most part, they can hear, and they can see, but they cannot or do not verbalize. This type of experimental session seemed to have had some impact, at least for the moment, on this individual with level III autism.

Consequences:

For the most part individuals with level III autism do not understand what consequences are. It seems they do not necessarily learn from the imposition of consequences on them for their behavior because

the behavior seems to continue even though some consequence was imposed. From my own experiences, I do not see that they understand or even fathom the consequences of right and wrong. What I did observe and have observed is that consistency in their environment with the familiar individuals, and the consistent comfort zone or zones may avoid any problematic behavior that could lead to consequences. They do not learn from consequences. Any severe consequence such as restraint or being removed from their comfort zone will lead to further problematic behavior and possibly injury. Returning a person to their comfort zone or possibly emergency medication will calm the person. Punishment for removing the person from their comfort zone or removing a familiar individual is punishment, and a behavioral issue will probably follow. I do challenge anybody to continue this work for the sake of the individuals with level III autism.

Right brain dominance:

The right brain dominance can be observed if it does exist in the individual. The behaviors that may lead one to conclude that the individual has right brain dominance may be some behavior that shows some organizational skill or some building exercise. These types of observations may be possible if the individual is presented with Legos for some building items. Depending on the individual, they may not respond at all and observation should be done at a distance. It should be noted that an exercise like this must be monitored closely because individuals with autistic spectrum disorder may try to eat the Legos or any other type of puzzle presentation. Due to their limited skill levels trying to determine whether one has right brain dominance can be difficult to impossible, but it's always probable that somebody will come up with some test in the future to work with individuals with level III that could determine the possibility of right brain dominance.

Left brain dominance:

Much like the right brain dominance; it is difficult to determine if an individual with autistic spectrum disorder level III has left brain dominance. However, observations in response to music may indicate the person has some left-brain activity. This may not mean that they are left-brain dominant, but at least there is a clue to the fact the left brain is working to some degree as the person may respond quite favorably to music or have a meltdown. This may be evidence of the left-brain function and possible dominance. On the other hand, the possibility of leaving out crayons and a coloring book or sketchpad and giving them space to see what may happen could be a useful screening tool or at least see if there is a left-brain function. There needs to be supervision on this issue because individuals at this level do tend to stick things in her mouth and ingest nonedible items (pica). Caution should be used during this type of observation but pay close attention to see if the person does try to do something with crayons or sketchbook. Hopefully, other institutions will pick up on this and even try it once in a while with individuals with level III autism.

Brain-behavior and thought process:

It is tough to determine what brain behavior and thought process are going on with level III autistic spectrum disorder. It is possible through a PET scan or an MRI to possibly determine brain behavior; however, the thought process might be documented and observed through standard observations. We know to some degree these individuals do think, and they do process events in their environment, but it is unknown the consistency of the response to these stimuli in the environment. Someone who works with individuals with level III autism and behavioral staff should pay close attention to specific stimulation in the environment, which leads to specific behavioral outcomes. I do not know if there is any consistency to this, but it is possible. My experience with this is limited, and I hope that someone else will

continue working with individuals with level III autism to try to help improve their lives through positive stimulation in their environment, which could lead to less behavioral outbursts and more serenity. Therefore, it is a challenge, and I challenge anyone to continue with this work.

Jaded by Life:

Individuals with autistic spectrum disorder level III do have experiences in life. They do to some extent understand who has been kind to them and who have been not as nice as they would expect. It seems to some degree they have been jaded by life as not all caregivers or other individuals they may encounter in life are kind to them. It seems they do have some ability to discriminate. It is unknown exactly how they may discriminate between someone who is kind to them and someone who is not; however, they do have that ability. Any caregiver that has ever been mean to an individual at this level beware that the impulsive behavior may occur and that will be a clue to back away quickly. For the most part, their behaviors are reasonably good with individuals who are part of their familiar group: specific caregivers, parents and even siblings. If you are not part of that familiar group and you want to be, take your time in allowing them to get to know you with kind words and a calm and relaxed tone of voice.

Although this type of jaded by life is different from the other levels, it does exist because at some point in the individual's life someone has been either unkind to them or has been rough on them. There is a high probability that they may become erratic in their behavior around someone who has mistreated them in the past. For some unknown reason, they remember specifics about individuals who have mistreated them as well as specifics about people who have been kind to them. It is hoped that further work will be conducted and to possibly answer this question but at this point, it seems that it's

partially due to memory or memory of something that they picked up from the person who mistreated them. It is also the same for people who are kind to them, and they remember them very well.

Vulnerability:

Individuals with autistic spectrum disorder level III are very vulnerable to the real world. It seems, and it is recommended that they are supervised 24/7. They can be taken advantage of by individuals with an unwritten agenda or what we call designing individuals that may try to use them for something. Supervision, specifically close supervision, is recommended.

It is noted in the previous section that they do have some discrimination skills. However, they may not discriminate from strangers who have done them absolutely no wrong up to this point but may have the agenda of either physically or emotionally harming the autistic individual. This is one reason why constant supervision is recommended and consistent contact with individuals who are in the familiar group.

The key:

The key to working with individuals with autistic spectrum disorder level III in my experience and opinion is consistency. These individuals need constant supervision by individuals that they are comfortable with. A good rapport between the caregiver and the individual is paramount in preventing possible behavioral outbursts. There are probably other keys to working with this group but, in my limited experience in working with them, this is all that I can give you at this time.

The key lies in familiarity with the individual with autistic spectrum disorder level III. Caregivers who work with them have to pay very close attention to their body language and possibly even noise that they may make. Any abrupt body language or possible erratic behavior

should be attended to immediately and with protocols that are set up to defuse the situation and not make it worse. The caregiver that is part of the familiar group that the individual has welcomed into their comfort zone is someone that needs to use a calm voice, say kind and nurturing things but also be aware that this individual could explode at any time. So, exercising caution and a predetermined pattern in which to get out of the situation is a good idea for the caregiver to have on hand at all times. One technique that I used to use was to approach the individual from either side. Do not approach the individual straight on because this leaves you vulnerable to being kicked or them jumping at you. This technique seemed to work in those cases in which I was dealing with individuals with autistic spectrum disorder level III that was in an institution. In the outpatient setting, I have only worked with individuals who were of school age that were level III. It seems that some types of pleasant noise, such as music, or some entertaining colors, seemed to keep them calm and cooperative to some degree. Building rapport with an individual with autistic spectrum disorder level III and maintaining that rapport is the best key that can be given to anyone who works with individuals with autistic spectrum disorder level III. Always treat them with respect, dignity, and a calm voice saying simple positive things such as saying their name or talking to them about something they like.

Summation:

Individuals with autistic spectrum disorder level III are very challenging to work with. Their behavior can become very erratic at times and even combative to the point of being assaultive and injuring those people working with them. It is unknown what may cause them to explode at any given moment, however, if you are a caregiver that is part of their familiar group the possibility is much less but it can still happen.

Individuals with autistic spectrum disorder level III, their inability to verbally communicate, for the most part, are usually medicated to some degree. The medication is due to the behavioral outbursts and possibility of injury to themselves and others. However, if someone works with them at a young age, the potential is unknown at this time. In looking back at the experiment, that I did with a school-age young man who was a level III and his response to music and colors broke through, and he responded to them. I wonder, and I challenge others to pick up on this possibility that individuals with level III that are young can have possible potential. It is going to take someone who wants to work with them, patience, diligence and the ability to notice subtle changes to make a difference in the world of the person with ASD-level III. For the most part, I have not worked with individuals with level III in many years. My forte is level I and level II. I hope that throughout this chapter, I have sparked interest in the possibilities that one could learn if they were close enough to individuals with level III autism. I hope that someone continues and tries to work with them to teach them something but their potential has to be found, and that takes time. There are limits to what they can learn and what they can do, and therefore patience and persistence have to be used in working with them. Therefore, I challenge others to take note from this chapter and move forward on the possibility of trying to find whatever potential individuals with level III have even if it is very small it is still their potential and it needs to be discovered.

CHAPTER 7

Autistic Spectrum Disorder

Noted Issues

Autistic Spectrum Disorder-Noted Issues

Throughout the previous chapters, we have talked about the development and diagnoses of autistic spectrum disorder. Although the disorder can be very prevalent to the point of the need of constant supervision (level III), to the possibility of an individual mastering many adaptive skills and needing almost no supervision whatsoever (level I), however, other associated issues may be present in the ASD individual. I will do my best to outline the most prevalent ones, but I am sure there may be others that have not come to my attention at this time. This list of associated issues is to the best of my knowledge and experience to this date. Please be aware and mindful of the fact that these other issues may be very prominent or may be very minimal at times, but they do exist and reasonable understanding should be used in working with these associated issues. If you are a parent, this can serve as a guideline to help you with your child. If you are a caregiver, teacher or someone in a one-to-one contact or group contact with individuals with autistic spectrum disorder, consider this before you react. Being proactive is a key to helping individuals with autistic spectrum disorder achieve the highest level of their potential. This awareness will help any caregiver to support the individual with ASD and to feel good about helping the individual with ASD reached the possibility that they have.

Before moving forward in this chapter, there has to be some old psychological jargon explained at this time. There is a model out there, at least it used to be, that when according to this following sequence:

Syndrome-symptoms-etiology-treatment

This was abbreviated by S-S E T

Syndrome-

A group of signs and symptoms that occur together and characterize a particular abnormality or condition

A set of concurrent things (such as emotions or actions) that usually form an identifiable pattern (Merriam-Webster dictionary)

Symptom- It is a deviation from what it is considered normal, and it indicates the mental or physical disorder to the person. They should be in a recognized pattern to decide if a person has symptoms of a specific condition. (Psychological dictionary)

Etiology-
plural -etiologies

CAUSE, ORIGIN; specifically: the cause of a disease or abnormal condition

A branch of knowledge concerned with causes; specifically: a branch of medical science concerned with the causes and origins of diseases (Merriam-Webster dictionary)

Treatment-

The act or manner or an instance of treating someone or something: HANDLING, usage the *star requires careful treatment*

The techniques or actions customarily applied in a specified situation

Substance or technique used in treating

An experimental condition (Merriam-Webster dictionary)

An understanding of this model would help any professional to understand that the total of all symptoms equals the syndrome. However, it seems that many professionals are hung up on single details and look specifically at individual details rather than the

total of the details equaling what the correct diagnosis is. It seems that this model is being ignored at this time in history and it needs to be relearned and to be used. The total use of this model gives proper diagnoses, therefore the appropriate syndrome, and the correct treatment. It seems that the focus on symptoms leads to ignoring the syndrome and leads directly to possible improper treatment. This article is based upon in part of the lack of use of this model and therefore leading to improper diagnostic syndromes and inappropriate treatment. Without the careful consideration of all the symptoms, the proper syndrome will not be arrived at. Treatment may not be the most effective and the person will suffer.

When it comes to the autistic spectrum disorder, it seems that many professionals see the symptoms but do not see how all the symptoms lead to the correct diagnostic syndrome. Instead, they look at the symptoms and try to treat the symptoms, not the syndrome. Further, they do not look for the cause/etiology of the problem but rather ignore that and go right into specific treatments. If an improper diagnosis is made then how can the treatment ever be therapeutic? If the wrong therapy is applied the outcome goals will never be accomplished, and the individual will not benefit from any of the treatment programs. This is why the learning and use of this model are essential when it comes to diagnosing individuals with autistic spectrum disorder. As this disorder continues to evolve, there may be more symptoms of this syndrome. The etiology should be determined, and then proper treatment modalities can be implemented that may help individuals with autistic spectrum disorder become more successful.

Other issues associated with or observed in conjunction with the autistic spectrum disorder.

ADHD Symptoms

The interesting thing about individuals with ASD, they have been confused with individuals with ADHD. When determining that the individual has ASD with some ADHD symptoms versus a person with ADHD with all needed symptoms for ADHD, this can be an issue. In chapter 17 in this book, using the physics model (Autistic Spectrum Disorder-A Physics Model) specifically using an oscilloscope to illustrate the differences between behavior patterns of the individual with ASD versus the individual with ADHD. There are some similarities to the behavior pattern such as: easily distracted, cannot sit still, moving from one activity to another and at times having problems paying attention. Where this differs is in the following areas: individuals with ASD may seem not to pay attention. However, they are picking up items from their environment, but they are not paying this type of "close attention" as some people may want them to. It is noted that individuals with ASD may prefer specific tasks over others but will try, with encouragement, to continue working on those tasks that are not as preferred. At times, it seems that they are not paying attention, but they are. An individual with ADHD does not seem to retain anything in their environment when they are in one of their behavior patterns where they cannot sit still and cannot pay attention. When it comes to moving from one task to another, the individual with ASD may look like they have ADHD. However, the individual with ASD will get several things done when it comes to the final product. Someone with ADHD may never get anything done without outside intervention and specific directions from an external source.

These specific similarities have caused many individuals with ASD to be categorized under the ADHD heading. Although some of these behaviors are similar, the specific behaviors related to ASD individuals differ due to the achievement of outcome goals or tasks and the ability of an ASD individual to organize what it is they want to do and how they want to do it. An individual with ADHD does not have

organizational skills and will only do the task at hand if and only if it is the preferred task. This diagnosis of ADHD has been given too many individuals with ASD in the past. It shows that someone is just looking at specific symptomology rather than the overall behavior patterns. If all the behavior patterns are looked at and put together, the clinician will evaluate the individual to have ASD rather than ADHD. However, sometimes, the clinician in determining the diagnosis should spend some quality time observing the individual rather than jumping to conclusions due to some of the observations made by parents and outside sources. It seems that everybody who works with any individual whether it is children, adolescents, adults and has no clue about all the parameters of autistic spectrum disorder should become educated as quickly as possible so an accurate diagnosis for individuals with autistic spectrum disorder can be made. There have been many occasions when I have had to look at the documentation sent to me by an outside source only to question its validity and how it is worded only to find out that they were overgeneralizing and using the fewest words possible without making useful observations. Always look beyond the similarities and see the bigger picture.

Emotional Outbursts

Individuals with autistic spectrum disorder have a specific pattern that they follow behaviorally. That pattern in a simple format is the following: F-A-MD. This roughly translates into the following: frustration, anger, and meltdown. Individuals with autistic spectrum disorder tend to be very verbal, or they give lengthy explanations on particular topics in particular situations. If they feel you are not listening to them, they will start to become frustrated. Their body language will become slightly stiff, and they start to look like they are staring at you very intently and looking for you to acknowledge what they are saying. If you do not acknowledge what they are saying, they began to get angry and probably loud. If they feel you are still not acknowledging what is going on with them, the meltdown will occur.

Emotional outbursts are easier to spot and recognize and therefore avoidable in the more verbal individuals. This group would include all level I and the level II -high and middle levels. The level II-low level may not be as apparent because they are less verbal than the upper levels in the level II designation. Level III can be highly unpredictable, but they do show some body language before their meltdown.

Level II-middle group is well known for its emotional outbursts. It seems at times that they lose control and will start yelling and screaming when they have their meltdowns. The level II middle-middle group may pace or even be silent and stare before they have a meltdown. In other words, there may be a delay before the outburst, or there may be a minor outburst.

Level I-both static and dynamic have emotional outbursts. They seem to be short in duration, and after they have them, they tend to ask for forgiveness for their bad behavior immediately. This is due to their adaptive skills, and they realize they did something wrong, and now they want to make up for it. This leads to the next topic.

Verbal aggression and violence

For the most part, anyone with autistic spectrum disorder can become verbally aggressive and even violent. Level III have the spontaneity issue whereby they do not often give off signs unless of course you work with them for some time and were able to recognize their body language or possibly even some of their verbalizations. They have a tendency when they have their meltdown to become physically aggressive. When working with this specific group, be very careful, and make observations on the individuals in which you are working with so you know when there is a possibility of a meltdown followed by physical violence.

Level II tends to become loud, verbally aggressive, possibly even violent, and physically aggressive. It has been through my

observations and studies of the individuals, in this group, in which I have worked with over the course of the last several years that for the most part, a level II will not become violent unless backed into a corner. This is what I have found through working with my individuals. If someone else has another observation, please feel free to share it with me in the future. But for the most part, when you talk to the individuals who are at the scene of the incident, the individual with autistic spectrum disorder was either physically touched by someone, hands were placed on him by someone else in an aggressive manner, such as in trying to restrain them or they were backed into a corner. The issue of physical restraint is something that many individuals in specific institutions have not learned that you do not single out an individual because of their mental health status such as being autistic. I have come across many instances over the past years whereby, there is an individual with autism that happens to be in the environment, and there may or may not be a real conflict that they are involved in. However, the first person to have hands laid on them or to be verbally confronted is the individual with autism. In this type of situation, there may not be a meltdown right away. However, verbal aggression will happen along with a lot of cussing and swearing. In many cases, this situation has been handled most inappropriately, and the individual with autism was either pushed to the point of a meltdown followed by physical aggression. They were inappropriately treated by whoever was in the situation and felt that the autistic individual is causing the problem, which led to further issues and possibly even charges. In this situation, individuals should not be focusing on an individual with autistic spectrum disorder but should instead solve the problem. Perhaps, even just tell the individual with autism to leave the area. However, it seemed, time and time again, when someone sees an individual with autism that has a little bit of a reputation for being loud, they will focus on them and do something really unnecessary which, will then lead to a meltdown and possible physical aggression. It seems individuals who are in the situation do

not want to seem to learn that the fact the matter is if an individual with autism is in an environment where something is going on; the best thing to do is to talk to the individual with autism and instruct them to go someplace else. This eliminates a lot of problems in the long run.

Level I individuals seem to tend to try and explain things to people that they are experiencing, seeing or feeling and the result is the individual either does not want to hear the explanation or the explanation is too complicated for them to understand. Because the listener does not want to listen, the individual becomes frustrated and may become loud. Level I individuals are known to be very long-winded and can get verbally aggressive; however, they tend to stay away from any physical aggression. Their frustration level is not easily achieved as they have learned some level of patience. Their verbal explanations may be too technical, over detailed or possibly a little loud due to their excitement and they seem to quote the following: "why can't they understand what I'm trying to tell them." It seems that they are trying to understand why the other person does not understand what they are trying to help them understand. This can lead to some verbal aggression but for the most part, the frustration seems to just linger along with the unresolved question is "why don't they listen to me"?

Trauma and Posttraumatic Stress Disorder

This is a very prominent issue when it comes to individuals who have the autistic spectrum disorder. It seems that all levels have some traumatic issues that have occurred throughout their lifetime. Individuals with autism have been abused, teased, bullied and made fun of throughout their entire life because they are unique. It seems that in the family home the parents are the first ones that do not recognize this issue and start this issue off with negativism, criticism and overall making fun of them. The worst thing that happens is that the parent does not recognize what is going on and tries to treat their

child as if they understand what the child is doing. Parents take advice from another person, who has no clue what is going on in the home and may have different interventions that are unacceptable to anyone who has autism. Trauma starts in the home. It may also include siblings as well as extended family members who want that person to act a certain way but they cannot. In trying to mold them into something they are not, the abuse happens followed by long-term traumatic injury. It has been documented that siblings are some of the worst offenders on this issue. It seems that they will make fun of their sibling because they are different. Siblings pick up on the verbal abuse being used by the parents and may use the same verbal negativity towards their sibling. This makes the home environment very toxic and causes trauma to the individual with ASD. This lack of positive emotion in the home contributes to ASD individual to be loners and not understand emotion.

After the family has had their time with causing trauma, the school is the next one to create further trauma. Issues on the school bus have been going on since the invention and use of the school bus. When it comes to having autism, riding the bus is a very traumatic experience. Autistic individuals who have sensory overload have a myriad of issues when riding the bus due to noise, visual stimulations, and possibly the other stimulations of the other senses to the point where they are overstimulated. It is hard sometimes for an individual with autism to ride the bus. At times, it is impossible for an individual with autism to ride the bus especially if they have audio sensory issues. That is only the beginning, and the individual gets off the bus and goes to school. Now the individual has problems or issues with the teacher and other students. The classroom has many possible sensory overload items starting with: noise, lights, colors, and smells. It seems it is kind of hard to learn when your senses are on overload and it is hard to pay attention. This is where the individual with autism may tend to have problems sitting still during the school day due to all the sensations

and the overloads. However, they may be disciplined as just another student and therefore not understand why they are being punished because all the overloads in their environment are causing them to feel a certain way and behave a certain way. The teacher may have no clue why the student is behaving the way they are. The teacher will then take standard measures to try to discipline the student into trying to sit still and learn. This does not work, and the student may fall farther behind along with having all these traumatic experiences in the classroom such as: being yelled at by the teacher due to the teacher not knowing what is going on with the student. This is one reason why autistic spectrum disorder issues need to be in-service to every teacher in every school district throughout the entire planet. The lack of understanding of autism produces traumatic experience and therefore possibly even long-term posttraumatic events. A proper IEP will help in this situation if the school district accepts the fact that they have students with Autistic Spectrum Disorder. School districts are very well known for being in denial of having students with ASD. This denial causes trauma to the student and can be long term.

After school, any community activities may also cause the individual with autistic spectrum disorder to develop some type of trauma. Being around other individuals and not understanding why they act the way they do, the autistic individual, will act the way they normally do and therefore be either chastised, ridiculed or possibly physically assaulted by other individuals. This leads to further trauma and long-term traumatic memories.

Some individuals with autistic spectrum disorder have been incarcerated and/or committed to some institution for a period of time. It seems that from their experiences in these institutions they have developed further trauma beyond what they would normally experience in the home, school, and community. It seems to be indicated that the individuals who work at these institutions have no clue about what autism is about and try to use the usual methods to

try and "help" the individual to follow through on what is expected of them. What ends up happening is these people are not trained and act more like bouncers that are going to make the individual do what they want them to do no matter what it takes. This further adds to traumatic incidents and long-term trauma.

As far as trauma goes, the autistic individuals (namely level I and level II) do not seek revenge for what has been done to them. It seems they are looking for an understanding of what has happened to them and are trying to rationalize and even find a way to forgive what has been done to them. As a footnote, for the most part, people with autistic spectrum disorder level I and level II are not physically aggressive. I will repeat that they are not usually physically aggressive. It seems they will try to do whatever they can to avoid any and all physical confrontations. However, they can get loud, and they may posture, and they may even push people out of the way, but they are not looking for any type of physical confrontation. However, autistic spectrum disorder level III individuals are highly erratic and can explode at any time. It seems that the level I and level II individuals can learn to deal with their traumatic history and can avoid the triggers that could cause possible verbal aggression. However, it seems that working with autistic spectrum disorder level III, it is unknown what they feel or what they will do which is probably due to the majority of them being nonverbal. They still have issues with trauma, but they cannot tell you about them. Instead, they may act out at any given time when any possible traumatic thought crosses their mind.

Trauma and traumatic experiences and posttraumatic stress disorder are some of the significant experiences that individuals with autism have experienced throughout their life. If a therapist/teachers/caregiver/parent wants to work through these items with the individual, they can help the individual come to some level of peace in their life whereby they can start to let it go. This takes a lot of time, a lot of patients and an excellent understanding of the

individual and the experiences that have been inflicted upon them. However, it can be done, and in many cases, it needs to be done.

Trauma can last a lifetime and is never forgotten. In some cases, it becomes an overgeneralization and is used as a precautionary measure by which they may limit activities in their life and not try new things. This is well illustrated in previous chapters on the different autistic levels and is described as jaded by life. One of the main reasons why trauma is not let go of because trauma, traumatic events and their occurrences by people around them, have no logical reason. Some of the individuals with autistic spectrum disorder level I and level II cannot let it go because it made no sense that it happened. Until they figure it out and find a way to let it go, they will continue to have some issues with their past that may dictate their future.

Other possible associated mental health issues

Anxiety

Anxiety seems to be experienced by many individuals with autistic spectrum disorder. The life of an individual with autistic spectrum disorder can be wrought with anxiety issues. It seems that after suffering trauma from family, friends, school and the environment, autistic individuals seem to have anxiety about trying to experience something new in their lives. It appears that the learning experience, although it was mostly negative, may cause them to have any anxiety about trying new things in their life. However, there are some that do not allow anxiety to keep them from experiencing new things in their lives. It seems that this group was shielded or sheltered from a lot of the traumatic experiences that seem to be common with other individuals with the autistic spectrum disorder. Some individuals with autism do not have anxiety due to being sheltered from some of the traumatic issues. They do not verbalize their anxiety, as other people would do. They go into a shutdown mode, or they become verbally aggressive to some degree. This is a good indication that they are

having anxiety. In dealing with this issue, therapist, teachers, parents and other caregivers should pay close attention to the shutdown or the loud verbal tirade that may come along with the anxiety. In working with individuals who start to experience anxiety, a lot of support is needed by those individuals who are in the autistic individual's comfort zone. Individuals within the comfort zone can help the autistic individual through their anxiety issue and help them to gain some new skill; skills set or experience something that they would not usually do. Being an individual in that comfort zone will be highly beneficial to the individual that is having the anxiety attack as it will help them defocused from the anxiety and refocus on the individual's comfort zone and then focus on the task at hand. This is one of the major components to helping individuals with autistic spectrum disorder get through their anxiety and experience new items they are not typically engaged in.

Depression

Depression is another issue that comes forth from the negative environment. There is a good possibility that the individual has been around other people that have teased or taunted them or even bullied them on a bus and they come up with the thought process of "why cannot I be normal." This is not uncommon in school-age children, as they seem to be the targets of most of the bullies in school and on the buses. It appears that depression comes forth from not being able to solve this issue of being unduly picked on by individuals on the school bus. However, this can also be a function of negative issues in the home brought about by family, extended family, and friends of the family. The individual can get to the point where they feel unloved. They may feel that everybody around them is making fun of them. Individuals who experience this type of depression may feel that people around them are talking about them. They do have a high degree of perception and insight when it comes to the environment and how hostile it can be towards them.

Their reaction to the negativism from the environment which includes: family, extended family, friends, school environment and of course the community, can be seen in the form of the individual isolating themselves, crying and possibly even getting very loud. To some degree, they may use some vulgarities. Helping an individual handle their depression is unique. It takes someone from their comfort zone to help them believe in themselves because the world seems to have caused them to retreat or shut down. The autistic individual needs to be told positive things about themselves, their uniqueness and what they can do that no one else can. This will help build up some self-esteem, self-worth and an appreciation for their gifts. However, this must be done by someone who is in the comfort zone of the autistic individual. Other people outside of that comfort zone may not be acknowledged or may be ignored. Someone that is in the comfort zone and has been accepted by the autistic individual is someone they want in their comfort zone and has an excellent chance of helping them to learn to deal with depression and learn those skill sets not to allow depression to become part of their life.

Obsessive Compulsive Disorder

An obsessive-compulsive disorder is one of the hallmarks of individuals with autistic spectrum disorder and almost every woman I have ever met in my life. Although most women have a specific order to their obsessive-compulsive disorder that seems to follow a logical path, individuals with autistic spectrum disorder have their own unique order in which they do things and in which they organize things.

Some observations, in individuals with the autistic spectrum disorder, are that they feel that things need to progress in a particular order. This is part of a behavior pattern in which they may show a precise sequencing to whatever they are doing. It may be as simple as lining up their toys in a particular way to a specific color-coding or numerical pattern in which they find it to be very specific to the task at hand or

how they organize their world. Although they do come up with their own patterns, they can be altered to some degree with an explanation that must make logical sense. If a parent tells them, they cannot do it that way. The following reaction will happen frustration to anger to melt down. Nothing is solved, and things will continue the way they were before the demand for the change. However, behavior patterns can be altered away from the obsessive-compulsive issue of things having to be done a specific way. However, this does take some work, some patience, and some very good explanations to the individual with autism for them to adopt the change, more so adapt to change into their normal routine. If they are taught a proper sequence of how to perform, behave or organize their environment, they will stay with that until something else changes.

For anyone working with an individual with autistic spectrum disorder, change can only come through patience, logical explanations, and practice. The autistic individual has to be part of this program from start to finish to adopt the change. If they are not part of this program, the program will not be adopted and probably will have a toe-to-toe fight on your hands. Nothing will be accomplished. I cannot stress enough that if your child has obsessive-compulsive disorders they can be altered and even changed to some degree but it has to be done through negotiations, and the individual has to be part of the program. This has been done successfully on more than one occasion, and it was only accomplished through cooperation, patience, and practice. But it was accomplished.

Reactive Attachment Disorder

Reactive attachment disorder is also known, as RAD may also exist in individuals with autistic spectrum disorder. Reactive attachment disorder is an issue that comes about when an individual wants a relationship with, usually a parent, that they are not given. There are expectations on the part of the autistic individual and often the parent

that causes unresolved conflict as the individual has expectations about the relationship between themselves and the parent. This has to do with the expectation that the individual with autism will be accepted and that the relationship should evolve between themselves and the parent. However, it seems that the parent tends to reject the individual with autistic spectrum disorder because they are not what the parent expected them to be. This is also entirely true and individuals without autistic spectrum disorder but, individuals with autistic spectrum disorder may end up in a situation, with the parent that will not give them the relationship that they want. This could turn into some type of conflictual situation. This can happen with other family members especially if the autistic individual is being raised by other family members or is in some foster care situation. This conflict may start off very simply with the individual with autism questioning the parent about the relationship or something related to the relationship or an event that they feel that the parent should've handled better. The parent, on the other hand, takes this is a challenge, and instead of asking a question back, they usually instigate the situation further by some very snide or snappy remark. This causes the autistic individual to reach the level of frustration whereby they may start to posture, pace or even get loud with further questioning or statements. If the parent at this point is not explaining themselves or trying to amend this relationship the next level may occur which is the anger level. The autistic individual may even begin to cry or also get louder, and possibly even stomp their feet or start flapping. If this situation is not rectified immediately, the autistic individual will go to the next level, which is the meltdown. Autistic individuals are not known for becoming physically violent or taking the first swing, but it could happen, in this situation, but at this point, if the parent continues to be obstinate in standing their ground and not trying to rectify the situation, a meltdown may occur. A very ignorant parent may try to grab the individual, and this could set off a chain reaction with the possibility of someone getting hurt and authorities

being called. Chances are the autistic individual will be arrested for possible assault charges.

The result of conflicts like this become part of the trauma which the autistic individual will remember the rest of their lives. They cannot always explain what they are feeling in terminology that would be familiar to anyone who is not well versed in dealing with individuals with autistic spectrum disorder especially those who have a component of reactive attachment disorder. It seems that this issue will continue to come out throughout the individual's life and even though they may feel anger toward the parent who will not give them the relationship they want, they will express certain feelings towards that individual that can be very positive.

Reactive attachment disorders should not exist if the parents are willing to accept their child and love them in spite of their differences. However, it always seems that one or possibly even both parents tend to reject their individual with an autistic spectrum disorder. These parents do not have any skill set to work with their autistic individual and should seek out services that will help them in dealing with behavior issues in regards to their individual with autism. It is pretty sad to think about the fact that a parent or both parents reject their child just because they do not measure up to their expectations. If there is an understanding between the parents and the autistic individual, then reactive attachment disorder may be minimal if at all. However, over the course of the observations, it seems that one parent will not put forth the effort to try to understand their child. In some unfortunate cases, it appears that both parents will not accept their autistic individual and try to treat them and disciplined them with the way they were brought up. It is very apparent the disciplinary policies of the last century do not work in this century and even more, so they do not work with individuals with autism. No matter how much a parent wants their child to be something else, they are what they

are, and they need to be loved, listened to, appropriately worked with and cared for.

Reactive attachment disorder in individuals with autistic spectrum disorder seems to be very prevalent and can be resolved if the parent that the individual wants to have a relationship with will take the time and try to understand and give them the type of relationship they want and desire. Conflict in regards to this associated issue is very preventable and avoidable if the parent will take the time to learn, practice and master those skills needed to work with their individual. Help them understand what they are trying to work with them on. However, sad but true, most parents will not take the time and will not bother to work with their autistic individual the way they need to. It is regrettable when parents do not love their child because they are different but more so, it is criminal if they do not love their child because they have autism. This issue seems to continue into adulthood, and it is treatable with the right therapeutic interventions and of course, with the right therapist who is aware of these relationship issues. In the grand scheme of things, it is the parent that needs to accept their individual as an adult. It seems that the conflict resolves itself to some extent, but there continues to be the trauma of the way they were treated in childhood through early adulthood. But this also becomes part of their trauma issues.

Intermittent Explosive Disorder

Intermittent explosive disorder in regards to individuals with autistic spectrum disorder is part of the symptoms of autism but does not fully qualify the diagnosis of an intermittent explosive disorder. When an individual with autistic spectrum disorder reaches the third level of the typical autistic behavior pattern (frustration followed by anger followed by the meltdown), the meltdown behavior resembles intermittent explosive disorder. However, it is the third level of behavior that happens when the individual with autistic spectrum

disorder becomes frustrated followed by his anger followed by the meltdown, and the meltdown is what looks like intermittent explosive disorder. However, the meltdown is the final result of people not interpreting what the autistic individual is trying to say, not listening or not trying to diffuse the situation. This can be one element in the autistic spectrum disorder. However, that is not entirely covered in the diagnostics of the DSM-5. This behavior may be interpreted as part of the symptomology, but in fact, it is only one aspect of a very large possible symptomology that the autistic individual may display. It has been experienced that members in the mental health field have misinterpreted this behavior as being the syndrome but in fact, it is just another symptom of a broader syndrome of autistic spectrum disorder. Do not be surprised if your autistic individual has one of these behavioral outbursts. It is the final expression of their emotional outburst due to either: not being heard or not being understood. At any time during the emotional triad (frustration followed by anger followed by emotional meltdown) this can be prevented by interventions such as: asking a question, refocusing, giving full attention to the individual and telling them you are giving them your full attention. Interpreting what they are saying not as what they are saying but what they are trying to say. At any time during this time, this emotional outburst/meltdown can be avoided and rectified.

These emotional outbursts are more prevalent in individuals that are level II and III autistic spectrum disorders. Level IIs can be very emotional because they start to understand emotion and they are trying to interpret it. In doing so they may have these emotional meltdowns that resemble intermittent explosive disorder but, upon an interpretation of the environment and situation it may be nothing more than their over emotionality of the situation without quite understanding what's going on but they are displaying what they are feeling. This is more prevalent in the level II-M (refer back to the chapter 5 on ASD-level II) as they are starting to grasp something

about emotion but do not have the necessary skill set to display the emotion in such a way that it is acceptable in the environment they are presenting. Therefore their emotional display may be misinterpreted by the individuals around them as being something dangerous, and consequently they may be disciplined rather than understood, and that could lead further to even a more massive negative behavior/meltdown. There is a possibility that they may not have the sizeable emotional outburst but instead want to retreat somewhere where it is quiet and take the time to refocus themselves on something else. Other issues may also be that they might become very quiet, cry and even want the isolation to regroup.

Individuals categorized under level II-H (chapter 5 ASD level II) have a little better emotional control however they still are learning, and therefore situations that they may not have mastered may evoke a total emotional meltdown. However, they are more open to intervention and can be redirected and refocused. They may also just become quiet, or they may cry, or they may want to isolate themselves rather than deal with the emotional issues that they are feeling that they do not quite understand and have problems displaying.

Individuals categorized under level II-L (Chapter 5 ASD-level II) may have an emotional meltdown, but it may not be as severe as the other levels in the level category. However, they may have a very subtle meltdown such as becoming quiet, crying and want to be alone. Depending upon the ability of the individual, interventions have to be very subtle and nurturing to some degree.

Individuals with level I autistic spectrum disorder may show a myriad of emotional outbursts, but it seems they will just become quiet and isolate themselves. There could be of course an emotional meltdown with some verbal outbursts, verbal aggression, and even posturing but for the most part, this group has learned a lot of the skills and may not allow themselves to go that far. However, it could still happen, but it is

usually due to their inability to handle a specific situation in which they feel they should be able to handle but have issues in doing so. They are very good at redirection, refocusing and taking time to regroup and move forward.

Individuals with level III-autistic spectrum disorder need to be carefully supervised at all times. Their caregivers need to understand their body language because, for the most part, they are nonverbal. Without understanding their body language, their occasional eye contact, and their behavior patterns, they will have outbursts and meltdowns that resemble intermittent explosive disorder. However, their outbursts and emotional meltdowns are due to the misinterpretation of what they feel, and this seems to be the only way that they can get people's attention. However, if the people who work with them closely understand them, take note of their behavior patterns, their posturing, and their occasional eye contact, interventions can be applied before any type of emotional outburst, or behavioral meltdown occurs. However, those people have to pay close attention, and they have to educate each other about what is actually going on with this individual. Behavioral meltdowns are not uncommon for individuals with level III autism. However, if the caregivers pay close attention, the meltdown, explosion, however, the event can be over to some degree. However, they can be very emotionally and behaviorally erratic and therefore a behavioral meltdown or explosive behavior can and may occur at any given time. This behavior is usually categorized into some form of physical altercation. However, it is possible that they may start to cry or they may want to be left alone and push people away. This group is very hard to understand, very hard to work with but with the right dedication, there can be some good intervention and some prevention.

When someone sees the intermittent explosive disorder diagnostic, it would be to the benefit of the individual who has been given this diagnoses and the betterment of the:

parent/teacher/therapist/caregiver to look further into the situation as it may be autism rather than an intermittent explosive disorder. Using some of these techniques as explained above may help an individual with autism to learn new skills in handling emotional situations. However, if some of the conventional methods are used on the autistic individual, the outcome will be catastrophic. There is no question in this case that when an individual with autism is at the third level of the emotional behavior state (emotional triad) that only a proper intervention will prevent this from becoming the worst case scenario. Further explanation of this will follow in the section on emotionality.

Emotionality

Emotionality can be explained as simply the emotions being displayed that may or may not be appropriate for the situation in which the autistic individual finds himself or herself. Due to one of the hallmark issues, not understanding emotion, individuals with autism may be in situations where they do not display any emotion, display the wrong emotion, or become over emotional. This is due to their level of understanding emotion, their ability to show emotion and learning how to control their emotions.

The individuals with level I autistic spectrum disorder tend to have skill sets in dealing with their emotions and the emotions in their environment. They still are learning specifics about emotions and how to convey emotions. If they are in a situation where they cannot quite understand what to display, they will become quiet. They may become what some people believe is argumentative however what they are doing is stating their point of view from a logical standpoint which has no emotion at all attached to it. They will become frustrated when someone does not listen to their logical side of the argument because they can become quite over-elaborated in their explanation. On occasion, their emotionality can become a little inappropriate but not to the point where there is an emotional meltdown. Instead, they state

their position and if no one listens they will retreat from the environment and go to someplace they feel is less stressful (safety zone/bubble) and distract themselves by doing something else. They do tend to hang onto emotion especially when they feel there could have been another way to handle the situation. This is where their learning ability comes into play, and they want to learn about how they could have dealt with the situation better. It seems that they do understand that maybe they did not handle the situation correctly and will seek out new skills to handle similar situations in the future. Other activities they may get into to deal with the emotionality that they cannot quite diffuse are as follows: outdoor activities, art, video games and chatting on the computer or phone. They seem to have an excellent fundamental ability to handle any type of emotionality they encounter but they are still learning, and there is the possibility that an inappropriate emotional display may happen during situations in which they are not comfortable or do not feel they have the right skill set to handle. They are still learning, and when this is brought into therapy there is usually good productivity, and the individual feels better about himself or herself, but they do not typically show the emotion expected. The therapist may get no emotion to the possibility of a smile. A proper intervention at this time is to ask the individual how they feel about what they have accomplished and instruct them to give themselves credit for what they have accomplished. This usually results in the proper emotional display of a smile to even the look of accomplishment.

Emotionality seems to be very prevalent in the level II autistic spectrum disorder. It varies throughout the three levels within the level II autism categorization (level II-high, medium, low: refer to the previous chapter on autistic spectrum disorder-level II)

Level II-high category seems to learn different ways to display their emotions and emotionality as they have learned different skill sets over the course of their lifetime. However, the ability to understand

and present emotionality is dependent upon what they have learned in their skill sets and their age. The older the individual is in this category, the more time they have had to learn skill sets on emotionality, how to display it, how to understand it and how to interpret it. Younger individuals (school age through middle teens) do not necessarily have that many skills, but they do display them in the following ways: isolation, video games, becoming quiet immediately and withdrawing to some degree and some type of work that requires skills such as art, carpentry, and model building.

Older individuals in this category seem to have learned a lot of different skill sets over time and try and match the possible emotion with the emotions expected in the situation. However, they still make mistakes, they still become angry, although they may not go all the way to having a behavioral or emotional meltdown. However, it still could happen. They are still learning how to handle their emotionality and understand the emotions and the environment as well as interpreting the environment and its emotions. They are still learning, and proper intervention will help them to continue to learn and sort through emotions and skill sets on how to handle their emotions.

Individuals in the autistic spectrum disorder-level II-middle, have a hallmark of having emotionality problems. They seem to feed off the emotion in the environment and to some degree allow themselves to display the emotion that they feel without thinking. In many situations, this is a charged environment, and they immediately go on the defensive and show some verbal aggression followed by some aggressive posturing, but they do not usually do anything beyond that. As it is, they are interpreted as being dangerous or trying to get into the situation in which they are not connected to directly, but feel a connection to, and find themselves that they have become part of the problem rather than the solution to the situation in which they find themselves in and around. Individuals at this level can be taught several skill sets and several scenarios in which they learn to control

their behavior and either: avoid the situation or go to a safe zone where they will not be involved in the situation. This group tends to interpret environmental emotion very quickly, but they tend to respond rather than to think about the possibility of responding the way they do and the possible consequences afterward. However, they can be taught to avoid certain situations or if they find themselves in those situations to avoid their over emotionality as the interpretation of the environmental emotions or other emotions of individuals so they do not display the type of emotions that could cause them to be interpreted as part of the problem. The most significant intervention they can be taught uses cognitive/behavioral therapy as in getting them to think about what is going on, behave appropriately, and have escape routes and plans to get away from the situation.

Level II-M individual will stand and argue. They argue about their emotional feelings and standpoint rather than use any logical type of thought process because they are highly emotionally charged individuals. If working with one of these individuals and they start to argue with you, the worst thing you can do is argue back. If a parent stands and argues, they have now leveled the playing field, and they will lose. One of the techniques I teach with individuals is to try to stop and think. However, if they are emotionally charged and this interaction is between a parent and child, I instruct the parents to back down. Either talk about something that they know their child likes and get away from the emotionally charged topic. Otherwise, this situation will go from bad to worse, and there may be outside interventions such as some type of legal intervention. Shouting will solve nothing if you are a parent towards an individual that is a level II that is having an emotional outburst. If you are lucky, all they will do is: stomp their feet and maybe punch a hole through a door or a wall. If you persist there may be some physical altercation that may result in a lot of bad feelings, no resolution to the problem and somebody will probably get arrested. A trip to the psychiatric ward is possible.

A useful intervention if you are going to work or have to work with individuals at this level (heads up parents) is don't stand toe to toe and argue. Nothing good will come of it. Asking questions, redirection to something else and a positive intervention will result in more understanding of the individual's emotionality.

Individuals who are at level II-low level have different understandings of emotionality and at times may show absolutely no emotion or display no emotional behaviors or improper emotion for the situation. However, they do feel and they can at times explain things, except in one word are two words or short sentences, but they do have ways to communicate their emotional feelings. They may not be able to put it in words, but they may put it into behaviors. Some behaviors may include silence, staring, crying or possibly talking with no coherence or stuttering and stammering to get the words out. However, they do try very hard to express what they are feeling, but they do not have the necessary skill set to do so. They can become frustrated and go into an emotional shutdown. Nurturing action will help the situation, but it must be done by someone that they trust and is part of the group that is inside their comfort zone.

The individuals with autistic spectrum disorder level III do have some skill set to express their emotionality. However, it takes someone who has worked with these individuals along with working with each individual to understand what their skill set may be to express their emotionality. Their emotionality may come in the form of guttural sounds to some screeching, screaming or some unintelligible noises, or even in the kind of some types of animal noises. They may also become very agitated by pacing, rocking in place and even flailing their arms or swinging at people or other objects in the room or even walls. It is imperative at this time that intervention is done to keep the person from injuring themselves or others. More work needs to be done with this group of individuals, and more observations have to be made to help this group of individuals further. I hope that someone

takes this further because the understanding of Level III's is difficult and challenging.

<u>Oppositional Defiant Disorder</u>

When it comes to individuals with an autistic spectrum disorder, they sometimes have been given the diagnosis of Oppositional Defiant Disorder. This diagnosis, once again, being tagged to the autistic individual is very precarious at best. It seems that this diagnosis comes from the fact that individuals with autistic spectrum disorder tend to debate situations. It is unfortunate that parents with individuals with autism do not take the time to understand that their child is either asking a question, debating the motivation for following through on what was requested or cannot see the logic in doing what was requested. At this point the parents become angry. Guess what? You just lost. Parents who do not take the time to understand and listen to what their individual is telling them are going to lose the argument one way or another. They might think they have won by getting their individual diagnosed with the oppositional defiant disorder but the bottom line is, it is not the oppositional defiant disorder. It is more likely that the parent feels that they have been disrespected by the individual either asking a question or staring at them because they don't believe what they just heard from their parent or that the parents' "ego" is being challenged and they feel they have to challenge back. As I had explained earlier when the parent levels the playing field with their autistic individual, the parent has beaten themselves, and the best thing is to retreat. Standing toe to toe in debating with your autistic individual over the need or purpose of whatever was requested or was demanded of them is not as important as taking one's time and trying to figure out what it is they're asking you about the request that you gave them. Each group has a different way of handling the situations, as it seems to some degree this is a universal behavior amongst all three levels, but each level has specific ways in which they handle the situation.

Autistic level I individuals that display this type of behavior are basically trying to see the logic in the request. They will also question people's motivation and behavior to some degree about why things are being done a specific way when there is probably a more practical way of doing it. This can be misinterpreted as being disrespectful or oppositional in the individual in which they are talking with, addressing or have received instructions from may take offense to this, and the ensuing questioning back, demand, or commands are going to lead to further debate and possibly even some verbal outbursts. In order to avoid this situation the individual making the request should make the request in a very logical manner stating the following: what the request is, why this task or objective needs to be done and the final desired outcome. In doing this, level I individuals will formulate a plan on how to complete the task as quickly and efficiently and accurately as possible. Being given a demand without these parameters being involved will lead to further questioning and possibly even interpersonal problems. It may also result in the individual walking away and not following through on the task, which was demanded of them. Individuals at this level are very intelligent. Treating them anything less than an individual with intelligence is causing them to question your intelligence. Basically, be prepared with those three parts when asking a request. If you feel that the individual is doing something not quite to the specifications of which you asked for, observe what they are doing and ask them if it's the most efficient way to complete the task. If an individual is working on a task and someone asks a question of a fascinating nature, like for instance "what are you doing?" The individual will probably state in their mind "he told me to do this and why you ask me what I might be doing if you already gave me the task to do, can't you see him doing it?" This will also lead to silence and possibly frustration as the autistic individual is given the task. If you do not know what task it was that you gave them you better figure it out quickly, their frustration level is growing because you just interrupted them from

following through on completing a task. The best thing in this situation is to apologize for disturbing them and tell them to continue. Otherwise, they may stop what they are doing or even just walk away.

Here is a specific illustration of this problem. The individual was a level I, and he was doing his homework. His mother interrupted him by asking him what he was doing. He growled at her. In addition, she verbally went off on him. The outcome was that he was punished by being stood in the corner and the homework was not completed for at least another day. This is an illustration of what I refer to as parents who tend to engage their mouth before they engage their brain and therefore interrupting the individual from completing the task that is their responsibility to get done. Observation of what is going on and then thinking before speaking is an excellent rule to follow. The task will get done, and the situation will not exacerbate to the point of arguing and then some form of consequence. In this case, the parent should be punished and not the individual.

If a parent does interrupt an individual level while they are doing a task, they may not transition into the next task that you want them to do because they feel they need to complete the last one first. In doing so there may be a debate, and therefore the parent may interpret this as being defiant, and usually, there is punishment, and thus the relationship is strained. Words of advice here, if a parent wants their individual to transition to another task, have them complete the first one. If there is a need to transition to another task, do not just stand there and start demanding. What is needed at this point is an explanation of why they need to stop the task that they are doing and the necessity for them to go to another task. Explain about completing the task of transition first and then going back to the initial task in which they were transitioned from or an explanation of what else is needed after they complete either task. Any transition is not easy, but there is no reason to make it impossible. Taking the time

with explanations will help the transition, and the follow through goes much smoother.

Level II individual-high level has several ways in which they supposedly showed defiance. One way specifically is they will totally shut down. They will not say a single word, and they will stare at you. It seems in this case that they are no longer willing to say anything because they feel that by shutting down it is better than having a meltdown. This group will debate to a certain extent and ask questions, similar to level ones but probably not as detailed, but are still detailed. Parents report that they find this to be annoying and usually become angry and start to get very short with their individual. However, these types of parents are not answering the questions correctly and find themselves in a debate where the playing field is level, and they have now lost. Corrective action is usually done at this time such as sending the individual to their room or threatening punishment of some nature. If the parent takes time to listen to what the individual is telling them maybe this would not ever be looked at as oppositional defiant disorder but rather an inquisitive mind trying to find out all the details of the task in which they were asked and why it was important for them to do it. Some answers are needed here and practicing this will save a lot of screaming, yelling and even prevent possible emotional meltdowns. This group is not known for major emotional meltdowns, behavioral meltdowns, but it is possible they may have one when their frustration to anger to meltdown occurs due to the parent not answering their question or their interpretation of the fact the parent is not listening.

The autistic spectrum disorder level II-middle level may tend to miss details in the request in which they were given. This group is known for their high emotionality and, in dealing with them, it is better to state the task in very specific words and then ask the individual to repeat backs to them what they were asked to do. Giving them a time frame and possibly even some type of privilege after the task is

completed will help the task to go to full completion. If a parent wants to play boss with this group you can expect some quick emotional responses at times and possibly even some holes in walls or doors. This group has a low frustration tolerance for being talked down to or commanded. Some of the responses parents may see are as follows: posturing, questioning, and possibly even some raising of the volume of the discussion. A parent who is very attuned to this will use an old method known as "grandma's rule." The request is respectfully given along with the reward at the end. Alternatively, they may explain the task by stating: "the task is needed for this reason," "you are the only one who can accomplish this task," and "when you are done this is the outcome and this will be your reward."

Although this group is not known for its violent behavior, there is always the possibility that a parent pushes them through the behavioral triad and there may possibly be some type of altercation. However, the best way to avoid the altercation is to practice the advice given in the previous paragraph. If you are looking for an altercation and possibly have your individual arrested or sent to the psychiatric ward, then continue with your behavior. However, remember there will be an investigation, and you may be held accountable for your behavior.

Individuals at this level may also ask questions because they may not be able to follow the sequencing precisely the way it was stated. It is best to give a simple to medium tasks for this group to follow through. Nevertheless, always provide them with the option after they finished the first task to come back and get instructions on the next task. Complex, long and detailed instructions will only frustrate the individual. Always give them an option to finish a task or a step of the task and come back for further instruction. The job will get done to the best ability of the individual but not as fast as what you expect. However, the job will get done to perfection.

Level II-low level individuals have problems understanding sequencing. It may not be that they are refusing to do the task; it may be that they do not understand the task. Working with this group, give simple tasks with simple instructions and possibly give only one-step at a time. It is possible over time that they will learn to sequence to a better degree, however; if too many instructions are given, you will see an emotional shutdown or possibly even emotional or behavioral meltdown, which may include crying, screaming and probably even some isolation. If any of these are observed the best thing a parent can do is be nurturing and understanding and talk to them in a calm, positive emotional voice and that will help them to regroup and then possibly you can start over again with simp,le instructions. Encouragement from the individual giving the task is always a huge plus in helping this level of individual to complete tasks.

Misinterpretation of these behavioral demonstrations can be very detrimental to the individual's feelings, behaviors and possibly even future outcomes. For the most part, oppositional defiant disorder gets put in with individuals with autistic spectrum disorder, but it is incorrectly interpreted and is not valid. If the parents/teacher/caregiver or anyone involved with individuals with the autistic spectrum disorder observe, pay attention and be patient, they will see that the individual does not have the oppositional defiant disorder. What they have is either questions about what is being asked to do a task, a lack of understanding of what is being asked or too many instructions are given at one time. The incorrect handling of these situations could lead to a traumatic event, which then leads to long-term traumatic memory. Following these simple steps will avoid conflict meltdowns, behavioral outbursts and of course traumatic memories. If you are a parent/teacher/caregiver or anyone else involved in the life of individuals with autism, take note of these techniques for they will work. Your relationship with the individual and the individual's success in life may be much better than the

consequential outcomes of treating them in a very demanding, demoralizing and illogic manner.

Possible Long-Term Brain Functions Issues Due to Being Overmedicated Due to the Lack of the Proper Diagnoses

Autism has been around a long time, and it has undergone different labels over the years, and due to a lack of insight into the problem, people with autism were given incorrect diagnoses. In the past, it was easy to spot and understand someone with what is now called autistic spectrum disorder level III. However, the other two levels (level I and level II) seem to have been overlooked and instead of given the proper diagnosis of autistic spectrum disorder, mental health care professionals were looking at the symptoms rather than the total diagnosis that encompassed all those symptoms. As I indicated earlier, an individual with autistic spectrum disorder either level I or level II may present with symptomology that may fall under other diagnoses. However, when taken in sum total, all the symptoms, the diagnosis of autistic spectrum disorder is overlooked. It seems for the most part that mental health care professionals only want to deal with some of the symptoms that the individual is displaying. A level I or level II individual may exhibit behaviors that look like attention deficit hyperactivity disorder, but then they finish what they start without outside intervention. They may display anxiety, depression and of course posttraumatic stress disorder. Other symptoms may fall under other categories that look like a mood disorder or intermittent explosive disorder but, when all of these symptoms are put together, the diagnosis of autistic spectrum disorder encompasses all the symptomology. However, because each mental health care professional is looking at the symptoms rather than the whole syndrome, the autistic individual is usually treated for one of the related symptoms but not the entire syndrome. Due to this issue, the possibility of overmedication or medicated with the wrong medication has happened in the past.

In some cases, individuals with over-emotionality, lack of emotional control, were tried on many of the antidepressants as well as some of the anticonvulsants. There is always the possibility of some adverse long-term reaction to medication, and it seems that this group was overmedicated because of their emotional outbursts. It was also noted that some were treated with the general class called mood stabilizers and may have developed long-term side effects from the medication. It seems that without the total syndrome being identified the symptoms being treated may have caused long-term damage to the individual. Also, some anti-psychotic medication may have been used, and other neurological problems may have precipitated in the individual.

When there is a prevalence of some of the attention deficit hyperactivity disorder behaviors, the use of stimulants may go on for years. However, it seems that the behaviors seem to speed up into their own pattern and even though the person is focused at times in the environment in which they are in, several thoughts are going through their head at any given time. Therefore, they have trouble focusing on just the one task at hand, or they may focus on the one task, but they may seem to drift off at times. Therefore, the stimulants do not work, and usually, the dosage is increased. Depending upon when the stimulants that were first used, there were studies about long-term side effects of the stimulants and growth and physical development. However, it seems to be a case-by-case study.

So in the past before the release of the DSM 5, and still today because it seems that individual mental health professionals have not even opened the DSM 5 and studied it to the extent it should be, the possibility of a misdiagnosis and the improper medication could very well happen. Therefore, a word to the parents would be, make a list of all the behaviors that you see and that you hear about and present them to the mental health professional before starting some medication regiment that may end up in some possible problematic

outcome. Or for the most part, seek out a mental health professional that deals and are quite versed in autistic spectrum disorders.

Other Issues That Need to Be Noted That Have Been Long Associated with Autistic Spectrum Disorder but for Some Reason Have Been Overlooked.

Some of the traditional issues related to autism seem to be overlooked at this time in history. Those issues at one time were key features in determining the extent of the autistic disorder. Those issues are as follows:

Tactile: To the degree of anything touching the body of the autistic individual such as clothing, personal hygiene items and of courses their hair. In addition, to include textures that they may experience while eating. Specific textures of food may cause the autistic individual to go into an overload due to the over stimulus. The tags on clothes, the texture of the fabric can cause over stimulation.

Smells: an individual with autistic spectrum disorder can become overloaded by the smell in a specific environment or by a specific smell in general. Olfactory overload is possible especially if it is an unfamiliar odor.

Hearing: individuals with autistic spectrum disorder may hear things that may or may not be audible to the average individual. For example, some autistic individuals can hear the sound of overhead tube lights. They may also have problems if they are in a closed environment where there is a lot of noise going on.

Sight: individuals with autistic spectrum disorder see things in detail as well as how all the details fit together to make the whole object they are looking at. They may describe something in detail that they see, rather than give a general description of what it is they are looking at. They may also become overloaded with too much color in the environment, details that do not seem to have a significance and

even people and the environment that they do not see a need for them to be there.

Taste: individuals with autistic spectrum disorder have a specific taste that they have had bad experiences with and will not swallow something that does not taste the way it should to them. Except for medication, at times, an individual with autistic spectrum disorder who put something in their mouth and they do not like the taste will spit it out.

As one can gather from the previous paragraphs, we are talking about the five senses. Individuals with autistic spectrum disorder can have a specific issue with a specific sense or a combination of the senses. This should be taken note of because they are not doing this because they are trying to manipulate their environment, but more so, they are responding to their environment in ways that others may not understand.

For example, an individual with autistic spectrum disorder can be sensitive to input from one or more of the five senses and therefore the behavior may become somewhat erratic. If you are familiar with the fact that the individual may have sensitivity, by all means, an intervention is needed. Because the following may happen: if an individual becomes overloaded by sounds, they may have a meltdown, and all you have to do is get them out of the environment. Easy solution but others may misinterpret this as some sort of manipulative behavior. It is not manipulative because they are responding to the environment and they have no control over this.

Therefore, the overloading of the five senses seems to have been one of the key factors in autism throughout history that appears to be overlooked at this time, but it is still prevalent. My question is why don't people look at these parts to decide on how to design interventions for individuals with autistic spectrum disorder? It seems that these basic components of autistic spectrum disorder have been

overlooked, as it appears that the behavior (symptoms) is being looked at rather than the actual problem (etiology) and therefore the diagnosis may be incorrect, and the person may end up suffering. Yes, suffering. This suffering is due to the wrong diagnosis, wrong medication, and the wrong interventions. All can lead to long-term side effects and behavioral issues.

Another feature that seems to be overlooked at this time is the socialization or association with other individuals. Autistic individuals have a safety zone or a bubble in which they live in per se, and only familiar people that they allow into the safety zone or bubble are the ones that they will associate with. Individuals with autism recognize other individuals with autism to some degree. Those individuals that they do recognize with autism, they may pull into their bubble because they see them as being like themselves. This does happen but again it may not happen, but it could happen.

It was indicated throughout other manuscripts and of course, other DSMs that individuals with autism don't understand emotion. This may be true until they learn what emotions are. They may not understand the emotions of others, but when it comes to individuals within their safety zone or bubble they seem to have good insight into that person's emotions, but they do not always know how to describe it or what to do about it. It appears that they can be quite comforting to individuals that are within that safety zone or bubble when they interpret their emotional states. When it comes to people outside that bubble or safety zone, the autistic individual may not understand the emotions of another person, and it may not make sense to them that they feel that way especially if they do not understand the situation in which the person is displaying emotions. It has been seen that individuals with autism can learn emotion and to some degree understand emotion but this must be taught outside of their safety zone or bubble. Therefore, the lack of emotions and a lack of emotional understanding still exist in the autistic individual but over

the course of time and excellent intervention skills being taught, they learn about emotion and how to display the proper emotion.

Another observation is that autistic children tend to play by themselves or someone that they have welcome into their safety zone or bubble. If anybody that has not been welcomed into that safety zone or bubble gets too close to them, they push them away by either growling or becoming slightly physical. However, when they get older and, if they do learn some social skills, they have a tendency to let others into their safety zone or bubble. This mainly happens if there is some commonality or common factor or if the other person has autism. What I mean by commonality or common factor is that they are interested in the same activity, item or concept. Such as an activity, video games, Legos or computer video programs (YouTube). They may develop some relationships.

Safety Issues

As an individual with autistic spectrum disorder continues to grow and become more independent and ventures into the community, they may have experiences where they have times and tendencies to be non-discreet, nondiscriminatory and have a tendency to be taken advantage of by designing people. This may happen when an individual learns a lot of adaptive skills along with social skills and may have some practice with all of them but does not learn cautionary principles of being in public. It would seem that they may be picked out of a crowd by designing person(s) and possibly be taken advantage of. This is one of the essential adaptive skills for an individual with autism to master because it will save them from a lot of problems down the road. Designing individuals may come off as someone that wants to be their friend, but they have some agenda to take advantage of the autistic individual.

Autistic individuals (level I and level II) may not have a fully developed sense of right or wrong. There may be the possibility of seeking people

to bring into their bubble or safety zone. They may not be discriminatory towards the individuals that may be offering to be their friends. These people may be designing individuals, but they may also be individuals who are problematic and are looking for another individual to be with them. Because they are trying to be just friends and it seems that they may not be designing, the autistic individual may have a brush with the law because they are with these individuals. This is another adaptive skill that needs to be taught if the environment in which the individual is being introduced to seems to be acceptable and not problematic. However, the individual's ability to discriminate between acceptable and problematic is something that must be learned. It is a well-known fact that individuals with autism end up in trouble with the law quite frequently and this adaptive skill/social skill must be taught and mastered to keep them from becoming a victim of being a friend with someone who has issues with the legal system. Autistic individuals are usually guilty by association, or they have done something that they do not understand is wrong. The problematic issues were part of the friendship or behaviors in the friendship, and therefore they are found guilty by association or by acts of volition without the thought of the act being incorrect outside of the group. This is another intervention that must be done with individuals with autism. They can adapt to the community as they seem to need to understand the difference between people who really want to be their friends and people who are trying to be their friends. Both need them or want them for something that may or may not be suitable for them.

Therefore, the safety issues must be taught, practiced and mastered or the autistic individual may find himself in a correctional institution where they may be further taken advantage of.

Other physical issues

Tic disorder has been noted in individuals with autistic spectrum disorder. The Tic disorder can be physical tics or even vocal tics, but it has been said that individuals with autism may display some type of Tic disorder or involuntary muscle movement at times. Deformity of the limbs may also be present along with some type of muscular or muscular skeletal or back issues have also been noted.

There may also be some vision issues in regards to the eye muscles. The possible deterioration of the eye muscles and the ability to see without the employment of glasses may also lead to confusion in the individual's life.

These are only a few of the noted issues in which I have come across in my private practice. Many autistic individuals are very healthy and have excellent coordination skills. However, some individuals with autism have problems with coordination; have some evidence of limited growth potential and some manifestation of a deformity. More research and observation need to be done on these issues, and I hope someone picks it up from here.

Level II individuals-low level

These individuals are unique. Depending on whether they are right brained or left brained determines whether or not they have the ability to communicate either verbally or in writing efficiently. In uncertain terms: either their transmitter (verbal ability) is working very well, but their ability to comprehend (receiver) may not be working at the best comprehension level. The opposite is also true in this group that their verbal ability may be compromised to some degree but their ability to understand functions quite well. This can be determined either by an intelligence quotient test or by several hours of one-on-one intervention through a well-trained therapist in autistic spectrum disorders.

Level III issues-intellectual disability-the receiver may be working, but the transmitter is broken.

Level III autistic spectrum disorder individual has been associated at times with intellectual disability. For the most part, they are nonverbal and therefore there is a limited set of tests to be given to the individual. However, any testing to be done would have to be by someone they have allowed into their comfort zone/safety zone/bubble. Individuals in their comfort zone are limited, and any testing may have to be done by one of the parents that are in that zone. It is possible that after time they may let somebody else in their zone, and therefore they could do the testing, but this is going to take time, patience, and a lot of effort. However, it is evident to anyone who has worked with any level III's that something is going on there. The problem is how you find a way to help them to help you understand what is going on there. Only time will tell, and hopefully, with more research, there could be an answer to this or maybe not. I guess it depends on how willing professionals are to work on this subject matter.

Typical issues-as mentioned previously-overload of the sensory receptors-taste, touch, smell, hearing, vision-five senses

As discussed previously in this chapter these basic autistic issues need to be understood and to be watched for and the proper interventions need to be put together to help the autistic individual learn different ways and adaptive skills in dealing with the overload of their senses. This is extremely important, and as the individual learns the adaptive skills needed for them to deal with their sensory overload, they will be able to live a better life and have an understanding of what is causing them to have their overload and how they can either handle it or avoid it.

Misdiagnoses

The DSM 5 has been out for six years now and should have been read by all mental health professionals along with anybody associated with dealing with individuals with autistic spectrum disorder. There have been training programs out there already to help the caregivers with individuals with autistic spectrum disorder. However, it seems that no one or a limited number of people has looked into the DSM 5 to understand how autistic spectrum disorder is now in three levels and the characteristics of each of those three levels. It has been noted, and I have heard this on several occasions the reference to something called Asperger's disorder or even a reference to someone having high Asperger's disorder. Neither one of these classifications exists anymore. In addition, they have been out of vogue in the classification of individuals with autism. Therefore, the misdiagnoses are entirely possible if people are not up to date on the current diagnoses and diagnostic criteria.

When the word autism was used at one time, it seems that everybody had a panic attack or a total freak out. The type of autism which appears to be still used in generality and thought process is that of the characteristics of which is now the autistic spectrum disorder-level III. It seems when an individual is given the diagnoses of autism it is automatically thought of as the characteristics of autistic spectrum disorder level III. That is entirely erroneous and shows a lack of insight and any type of thought process. It seems that when an individual may be diagnosed with autistic spectrum disorder, the parents may go into total denial. This is brought about by the fact of their lack of either understanding or information on the fact that there are now three levels of autism.

Addiction and Addictive Behaviors

Individuals with autistic spectrum disorder are not immune to addictions. The groups that are most supervised (level III and some of the level II's) are least likely to develop any form of addiction due to the supervision level. However, there can still be some type of addiction possible. There is the possibility of caffeine, nicotine, alcohol or even some medication addiction. It depends on the supervisor and the level of supervision. However, it can happen, and there is someone responsible for it.

Addiction in the level II's, not supervised, may develop an addiction to caffeine, nicotine, alcohol and other street drugs. They may get involved with drugs as a lack of supervision is prevalent. They may try certain street drugs to "fit in" with their so-called "friends." In fitting in thee is the possibility of addiction. They may also try drugs to self-medicate. They suffer from depression, anxiety and posttraumatic stress disorder and possibly other mental health problems and may self-medicate and therefore become addicted. Drugs they may try to become addicted to alcohol, marijuana, and possibly opiates. Lack of supervision and a need to "fit in" with their "friends" can lead to the use, abuse and addiction to substances. This can also lead to the possibility of incarceration or a rehabilitation facility.

Level I addiction can happen to a significant degree. This group has social and communication skills and knows how to obtain addictive substances. It seems that even though they have the skills to achieve them, they do have the skills to avoid them. It seems that level I individuals choose to become involved in the harder drugs and find some type of logical reasoning to continue use to a point. It seems that sooner or later, after they become addicted, that they want to become rehabilitated. This is a positive step, but rehabilitation can confusing and sometimes contraindicative (depending on the program), and the individual can become confused by the

rehabilitation program. They may decide to continue to be addicted rather than go through all the steps to become rehabilitated. The programs seem to be confusing due to a lack of continuity. Too many thoughts that may have logical and illogical parts may case a level I to give up and stay addicted. However, if a rehabilitation plan is designed with their specific thinking and learning process in mind, they may be able to rehabilitate. That program would be tailor-made to the individual, and there would be more significant hope for success. In this case, the therapist must get to know the individual to design a program for the maximum positive outcome. A program based on the individuals thinking and learning style will utilize the strength of the individual to help him to help himself to recover.

Summation

To summarize this chapter to anyone who reads it is straightforward. It seems that the mental health community at this time is not up to speed with what autism is or the associated features or possible associated features that may occur with autism. It would be noted that the mental health community has not studied the DSM 5 when it comes to the levels of autistic spectrum disorders. It would also be noted that many in the mental health community only look at the symptoms and not the sum total of all the symptoms, which is known as the syndrome. It seems the treatment at times has been for the symptoms and not the syndrome and therefore the treatment was in error and may have caused possible long-term issues. My advice to anyone who believes or suspects that their child or even they may have some form of autism is to go to someone who is well versed in the autistic spectrum disorders. Going to anyone else may bring about a multitude of other issues and the actual syndrome may never be treated with the best possible interventions. However, this is a choice between the parents and the individual. However, if some progress or some learning of adaptive skills and positive behaviors is what is being sought after, find a professional who can help you to get the

most out of therapy. Autistic individuals can suffer from addictive disorders. There are positive outcomes if the rehabilitation program is designed for the individual and his abilities. Autism can have issues associated with it that may look like something else, but when looked at in total, autism is the diagnosis that should be given.

CHAPTER 8

Autistic Spectrum Disorders

Behavioral Patterns

Autistic Spectrum Disorders-Behavioral Patterns

"The key to understanding behavior is by observation. Taking note of the behaviors and using the observation defines a key to dealing with the behaviors and directing them for a positive outcome goal."

Throughout this book, I have alluded to different behaviors, behavior patterns and about different keys to understanding autistic spectrum disorder behavior. In this chapter, I will talk about two very specific behavior patterns that have been alluded to but not defined. At this point, I will explain them and give recommendations for the possibility of how to work with them. I will talk about the different levels of autism and possibly how to spot these behavior patterns as they emerge. Although there may be other types of behavior patterns in autism, these are the most prevalent that I have seen and therefore can write about them with certainty. Please take note of interventions, because in working with anyone with autism intervention is the key to helping them to achieve the highest level of their ability and good quality of life.

Behavior Triad

The behavioral triad consists of the following behaviors: frustration, anger, then followed by a behavioral meltdown.

Frustration can be observed in different ways depending upon which level the autistic individual is on. At the level I-autistic spectrum disorder, frustration may appear in the form of arguing to as mild as just the individual being quiet and staring at you. If the individual is quiet and staring at you, your best intervention is to ask them a question. If you do not take notice of the frustration and continue whatever you are saying to the individual, they may just walk away, or

they will continue to argue with you. In the level I, at this point, they may just walk away or continue to argue with you, but your best intervention is to stop what you are saying to them and ask them a question. The question does not have to be about what the issue is at that moment but rather a redirection or direction in another direction that would help to stop the situation at this point. The frustration that a level I feels has to do with the fact that they are not being listened to or they are not being understood. They may also just stop talking to you altogether and/or walk away.

The level II autistic spectrum disorder, high-level individual, may behave very similar to level I. They may even show some emotional outbursts such as crying, silence, staring, and possibly even just walk away. The level II-medium level may display the same behavior at this point. If the level II individual has high emotional issues, they may not back down at all but rather start to posture and gesture and even intimidate the other person. These individuals can be unpredictable to a degree, but for the most part, they seem to follow the pattern of frustration to a point where they may become physically violent. Level II-low level, depending on their physical abilities, may become argumentative, probably become very quiet, but there is a possibility, that they may become verbally aggressive and have emotional issues that may lead to some inappropriate behavior. When it comes to describing the level to individuals, the ones that fall into the middle of the level II diagnosis are the ones that can be the most unstable. It seems individuals at this level are either learning new adaptive skills on how to handle their emotional issues or, they continue to stay inside their comfort zone and make that comfort zone the only reality they know. Therefore, level II-middle level autistic spectrum disorder individuals can be aggressive, and it seems that sometimes they have reality problems because of too much time in their comfort zone and not enough time in learning adaptive skills. It can also be explained that they have reached the limit of their learning of adaptive skills and

have made their comfort zone the only reality in their life. This can be quite detrimental to the individual as it seems that they may have issues in dealing with the real world as their comfort zone has become somewhat of a fantasyland. Great care should be taken in dealing with individuals with level II-middle level diagnoses.

Level III individuals tend to be very subtle in this first part of the behavior Triad. In working with them in the past, it has been very subtle such as: immediately stopping what they are doing and looking up, a glance, a grunt and of course sometimes it is direct eye contact at the person that is nearby them. This is usually a good indication to either intervene or back away as level III individuals can be extremely impulsive and unpredictable.

The next part of the triad is anger. Anger may take the form of just raising one's voice, to aggressive behavior, to absolute silence, depending upon what level you are dealing with.

In the level I individual anger can be as simple as raising their voices during an argument to having somewhat of a stomping of their feet and walking away. It seems the level I individual has learned some adaptive skills that basically they will utilize to avoid any further confrontation at this time. Their argument may become lengthier and possibly even louder. It seems they will vent their anger at a later date depending on what type of support system that they have. It is also possible that they may internalize their anger and think about it for several days before finally giving up on it and therefore showing signs of a change in their mood. Sometimes level I will become depressed if they cannot resolve their anger issues. Over time, they seem to dismiss these issues to some degree. However, they remember what the anger issue was about and continue to seek out ways in which to resolve it. At times, they may even seem to be moody after they have dealt with their anger for a period of time and have not resolved the issue. However, they continue to think about how they can resolve the

issue, and hopefully, they come up with several solution sets to finally fix the problem. For the most part, their anger is internalized or to some degree externalize, but they are not necessarily known to become physically aggressive. I am sure there are some cases where these individuals may become violent, but for the most part, I have never experienced it firsthand.

The level II-high-level individual may have developed adaptive skills or solution sets for becoming angry. It is noted that when they become angry, they may become whiny, or they may cry, or they may even raise their voice to some degree, but it seems that they may continue to argue the point to some extent. They may use some argument skill, or they may become a little intimidating such as posturing or even yelling, but for the most part, they have not been known to become physically aggressive. It is possible, of course, that those individuals at this level will become physically aggressive. However, at this point, I have not experienced this, and there has been no report to me that this has happened. However, it is always possible.

The level II-middle level individual may have issues with anger. This level seems to have either mastered specific skills, by which they will argue, posture, and they will even try to intimidate another person, but for the most part, they will not become physically aggressive. It is also possible within this middle-level group that individuals have not mastered specific social skills or have been influenced by violence (video games, first-hand experience, and television) and they do tend to act out what they have experienced through this media. I have had experiences with both types within this level, and it seems that as individuals reach a peak, or at a point to what they will learn, or what they could learn, at the time, they may tend to have a problem with the real world. However, there has been good progress on the part of the level II-middle level to achieve particular social skills along with work skills, and they may tend to be more goals directed then emotionally overwhelmed. As I mentioned earlier, individuals at a level II-middle

level may manage to have reached a certain level of their learning. If they have not found anything more to master at this time in their life, and they have a tendency to spend too much time in their safe zone or bubble and depending upon what is in that bubble, becomes their reality. If in this bubble is violent video games, first-hand violent experiences and also violent television, the individual may tend to act out these influences because anything else of significance is not influencing them. Their individual world becomes what they are doing: video games, watching television, and they are not being prepared for the real world. In allowing them to indulge themselves in their safe zone for too many hours a day, and indulging in this influence, they may have a whole incorrect thought process when it comes to what they can do in the real world. Therefore, with all this negative influence on them, as they progress from frustration to anger. At this point, they may become physically aggressive. Therefore, it is essential to know in dealing with an individual who is a level II-middle level, who has emotional issues due to spending too much time in their safe zone and having too much influence from negative and unreal media, and what is going to happen next. The intervention would be to back down and possibly even leave the environment and allow that individual to go back to their safe zone and go back to what they were doing.

Level II-low level individual may become angry, but their expression of anger could be anything from crying, screaming, yelling and even silence and staring. A useful intervention at this time would be to give them something to eat or allow them to exit the environment and go and calm down.

Level III individuals are very subtle at this point. You may witness the following behaviors: hyperventilation, noises, balling of fists and tensing of muscles and a stare that could scare anybody. Intervention at this point should be done with someone who is extremely familiar with the individual who has been allowed into that individual's safe

zone or bubble. Anybody else trying to intervene at this time will probably suffer the result of the next level, which will be the meltdown. It is essential for the level III individual to be around individuals they are familiar with that they have accepted. This is the consistency part of dealing with level threes that should be observed to the T. Any variation of this at this point will lead to the next issue, which would be the behavioral meltdown.

The Behavioral Melt Down

What is meant by a behavioral meltdown? The behavioral meltdown can be something as simple as the individual becoming very silent, to as severe as the individual becoming violent and trying to harm other people by swinging at them, kicking at them and even biting them. Behavioral meltdowns can be extremely scary and can cause parents/teachers/caregivers to have issues after the behavioral outburst is over. The behavioral meltdown may then cause the Parents/caregivers/teachers to become jaded by the autistic individual, and they may even expect that person to have a behavioral meltdown. A behavioral meltdown occurs when people fail to intervene at either the frustration or the anger level. Behavioral meltdown is the final result of the total frustration and anger not being calmed. This is a failure of the people who are observing the behavior and their lack of intervention. Simple interventions may prevent this from happening to level I and level II individuals. However level III individuals being quite unpredictable, intervention may or may not be applied in time to prevent the individual from having their behavioral meltdown.

Level I individuals who have a behavioral meltdown may retreat from the environment rather than to go any further with the issue. They may go into their safe zone and not come out for a time. They may become depressed or even a little anxious. It seems that level I individuals have learned several adaptive skills, social skills, and communication skills and when they feel they are at a point where they are about to

have a behavioral meltdown, they may isolate themselves in their safe zone. However, other things could happen such as crying, whining, continuing arguing and even some cussing and swearing. A Level I individual is not known for aggressive or assaultive behavior but it is possible, and it could happen. For the most part, they will either leave the environment or display some emotional outburst and then retreat. Individuals at the level I that do have a behavioral meltdown may think about their behavioral meltdown for several days afterward. With some direct intervention and counseling, they will let go of it and move on. It seems that the level I tend to feel guilty about feeling the way they do after they have had their behavioral meltdown. With interventions afterword and some role-playing, the issue that led to the behavioral meltdown may be resolved.

Level II individuals can be variable to a significant degree. The level II-high-level individual will continue to argue and even stomp their feet and possibly even cuss and swear. They may also just extend the argument and have the behavioral meltdown: crying, whining, silence and even retreat to their safe zone. For the most part, they are not known for aggressive behavior, but it could happen in the behavioral meltdown.

Level II-middle level individuals can have a wide variety of behavioral meltdowns: depending upon their emotional level and their level of understanding of reality. They may start to posture, they may begin to argue vehemently, they may stomp their feet, they may wave their arms and possibly become verbally aggressive. Those individuals who are continuing to learn adaptive skills may stomp their feet and walk away along with several negative verbal comments. However, those individuals, as mentioned earlier, that have a problem with dealing with reality may go into a full-blown aggressive outburst, which could include a fistfight, use of weapons, kicking, and the need for outside intervention such as the police. These individuals are very unstable as they are not dealing with reality, but they are dealing a lot more with

handling their problems in a fantasy thought process. As mentioned earlier, this is because they spend too much time in the fantasy world and not enough time in learning about the reality around them. Possible interventions for this level, especially if they become physically violent or assaultive with weapons or some other implementing to use as a weapon, is to try restraining them, call 911 and get the police. They will not stop until they are restrained. This type of outburst happens, although it seems rare at times, and depends upon the individual's thought process and whether or not they are dealing with reality. This problem is brought about by not having enough contact with reality and working on adaptive skills, and possibly even some long-term life goals. Being allowed to spend too much time in the fantasy world, especially when the person could excel in the real world, may lead to this type of behavioral meltdown.

Level II-low-level individual may show different behaviors during the meltdown. They may show simple emotions such as crying, whining, screaming and even pounding on the table, flapping arms and even some posturing that seems to be more aggressive. They can be unpredictable as to what the total behavior meltdown may consist of, so intervene as quickly as possible before it gets to this point with this group. Quick intervention with this group will be very therapeutic for the individual as well as the person working with them.

The Level III individual going into total behavioral meltdown can be extremely dangerous. If the meltdown is happening, intervention can be as severe as medication and isolation, to as minimal as just a short restraint. It seems at this point that the individual has become so overstimulated with their emotions, such as anger or anything else that happened in their environment to cause them to become angered, that the behavioral outcome will result in the meltdown. The mechanism of what happens in this situation is not entirely understood. Further study would be beneficial for the continuation of understanding how level III individuals function as well as how they

lead up to their behavioral meltdown. In working with these individuals, it is tough to gauge what the final behavioral meltdown will be as it is sometimes tough to understand their frustration and their anger, and therefore the meltdown is not entirely understood. Caretakers who work exclusively with this group should take notice of any type of behavior change whatsoever, as you will be the key to helping this individual by helping them to prevent themselves from going into a behavioral meltdown. However, the behavioral meltdown will probably still happen. It is an excellent idea for caretakers who work with level III individuals to pay very close attention to their behaviors and their patterns. It would be recommended that behavior patterns are profiled, and there should be protocols involved for the caretaker if they see specific behavior patterns. In putting this all together in the form of written documentation, caretakers and others who work with level III individuals may become more familiar with how to prevent behavioral meltdowns from their individual. In putting this all together in some easily understood format, the level III individual will be better-taken care of if people educate themselves on how they behave. Without this, the misinterpretation of the level III's behavior may always be somewhat extreme and not to the benefit of the level III individual. In this case, observation, education, and intervention as quickly as possible can help a level III individual to avoid the possibility of extra medication and isolation.

The behavior pattern of frustration to anger to behavioral meltdown can be like a chain reaction. In addition, a chain reaction can be stopped at any one of those parts. As a firefighter once told me, it is best to put out the smoldering little flicker rather than to try to fight the burning inferno with a fire extinguisher. Such as in this behavior pattern, it is easier to stop it at the beginning rather than to try to put out or deal with a total behavioral meltdown.

Some of the behaviors that you may see in the first stage (frustration) are as follows: pacing, standing in place, moving one's feet, stomping, lack of eye contact, and of course, the flexing of specific muscle groups, especially noted in the hands. You will hear an argument, possibly even foul language and of course the repetition of the same statement over and over again. At this point, pay attention to the statement and try to use the simple tactic of what we call using the behavioral key. The behavioral key is a substitution of a much more preferred item or activity to refocus the autistic individual away from what they are currently thinking or feeling and put them in a more stable mood and behavior. This may also be referred to as redirecting or refocusing the individual from one specific thing they seem to be fixated on towards a more preferred task or privilege. This tactic works very well for level I individuals and level II-High-level and level-II-Middle-level. The level II-Low level, the key may be the suggestion of some food item or giving them a bowl of ice cream. Either way, the situation will de-escalate rather quickly and you the parent/caregiver/teacher, can then work with the individual on what it is they really want/need and help them move in that direction. This may or may not work for level III individuals. Quick intervention on the part of the familiar individual and following through on the possibility of directing them out of the situation or something that may calm them down such as singing to them, talking to them, or reading to them, may prevent this situation from going into a full-blown behavioral meltdown.

For the most part, this tactic of using the behavioral key or redirection works in keeping the behavioral triad from going from frustration to full behavioral meltdown. Another tactic which can be utilized mainly in level I, level II-High level and level II-Middle level, is to ask them a question then have them stop and think. By getting them to stop and think, the situation can calm down rather quickly. The level II-Low-level can be distracted with a food item, but they can also be redirected with a hug or something very simple. This would depend

upon the observations and understanding of the caretaker of a level II-Low level individual.

In dealing with the level II-Middle level, there is a subgroup within this level that may not be easily redirected. This group has spent way too much time in building a safe zone that consists of some type of fantasy idealism. In certain cases, this has to do with the individual being allowed to watch television and play video games rather than the caregiver/parent talking to them and redirecting them towards what they could be doing in the real world. If the focus of conversation with this individual continually circles back to some unrealistic possibility, that subject matter may be what can be used as the behavioral key. These individuals need to be redirected back to reality and not be enabled to continue to play in fantasyland. My experience with this subgroup is that they are very verbal and trainable and have skills. They have decent abilities in both the right brain (performance) and the left-brain (verbal). They are spending way too much time in fantasyland and therefore start to reject what they could be doing in the real world. They constantly talk about something that they may never attain and about one specific subject that may be in the real world, but nothing more than entertainment. It seems they have become over-focused on something not attainable or possible. They need to let go of that fantasy and move forward into the real world. They have the ability, but they need to be encouraged to perform in the real world. Money seems to be a factor in getting them to let go of the fantasy world. Earning money and working a job seems to help them let go of the fantasy and adopt the real world. At times, they will want to talk about a new game or a game that they are currently engaging in. Take an interest in what they are talking about and ask questions. Find an opening and re-direct. The video world may also be in their safe zone, and they may use this as a way to relax after a day at work. In this was the fantasyland becomes a therapy to reduce stress from the real world. This subgroup (level II-Middle level-

emotional/over-focused on a fantasy world, having good verbal skills and some performance skills), may become violent to the point of physical aggression without thinking about it because it has been programmed into them by all the influence of this fantasy which they want to become real. This group may have to be restrained because it is unknown during this emotional upheaval what they are going to do. Talking them down is a start, but there is a possibility that they may continue on in whatever thought process or pattern they think is going to work. This group, as I have described before, is having over-emotionality. In other words, their emotions seem to take over, and any and all rational thought is overcome by emotional and a behavioral pattern that is usually unknown to others in the environment. There is a key to this, as they seem to talk a lot about things that are negative and to some degree violent. This is a key to the caregivers that this individual needs to be dealt with rather quickly. Refocusing them on what they can be doing in the real world may be the key to getting them out of this fantasy world in which they believe they can make happen in the real world. Further work and study need to be done with this subgroup as they also seem to have a component of posttraumatic stress disorder and it may be at this emotional moment that they are reliving a possible abusive event in their life and they are reacting to it in total self-defense. In this case, the parent/caregiver may have to restrain the individual, and they have to talk to them and redirect them while in restraint. They have to redirect this individual away from whatever behavior pattern is going on in their head especially if there is a history of posttraumatic stress disorder. The possibility of legal intervention such as the police and possibly even a short stay in a psychiatric ward with medication and future medication may be necessary.

In summation of this behavioral triad, the quicker the intervention, the easier it is to redirect the individual back to being calm, thereby preventing the behavioral meltdown. The key to each individual is only

known by those who spend the most time with them such as parents, caregivers, and teachers. They need to use what has been learned from observing and listening to the individual. This knowledge of the individual will help the individual become more stable over time and even help them to learn adaptive skills to de-escalate themselves. This is much the case in level I and level II for the most part. The level III individual will be well known by their specific caretakers in whom they have let into their safety zone. Caretakers, in this case, should put together a protocol and plan of action on how to deal with the individual if they start the behavioral triad. Planning with level III individuals is the key to helping them to avoid behavioral meltdowns and not experience trauma. Prevention is the key along with being pro-active and not being reactive. Reactivity will lead to the chain reaction and the behavioral meltdown.

<u>The 4P's</u>

The following description is very prevalent at the level I and level II-High and Middle levels of autistic spectrum disorder. It is less prevalent but could be present at the level II-Low level. It is unknown whether or not level III individuals follow this type of system. The system is known as the 4P's.

The 4P's are as follows: Protocol-Program-Process-Product

Although this seems a little complex and complicated, individuals as mentioned above (level I, level II-High and Middle) tend to live their life through this organizational pattern. The following program can be translated into the following:

<u>Protocol: An</u> event or activity that will be engaged in, engaged with or an endeavor that needs to be completed or a situation that happens.

Program: The technique and utilization of the means to accomplish the task as designated by the protocol. This leads to the further steps in the procedure.

Procedure: The steps involved as outlined in the Program to achieve the final product. There may be several procedural methods involved. There are side steps in the procedure such as "if A does not work then go to B"..and so on.

Product: The outcome goal. The achievement of the goal through the use of a protocol that has several programs but one is chosen, and through the procedure, the goal is attained, and the Protocol is successful.

This process has been reviewed over the course of time and changes may be made by the individual. In some cases, following the protocol may lead to changes in the program through the use of adding or deleting steps in the process to achieve the goal in a shorter or more proficient amount of time. On the other hand, some individuals set up their protocol, program, process, and product and never change any part of this because if it works for them, why change?

When this thought was presented to level I individuals, they found a model in which they could explain why they do things a specific way to others. The level II group found this model helpful in designing total protocols and following through in the completion of tasks. Specifically, in Level-II-High and Middle levels, it seems that these groups were still learning and were able to adopt new behaviors and form them into a protocol. It appears that the Level-II utilizes this model to learn and master adaptive skills and more positive behaviors.

CHAPTER 9

Autistic Spectrum Disorders

Communication Issues

Autism Spectrum Disorders-Communication Issues

The simple art of oral communication seems to have started a very long time ago with the caveman and over time has progressed and even to some degree became complicated when more and more words were developed. Oral communication as it is his complicated as it has several components. It seems that not all components of oral speech are attended to at any given time, which leads to a miscommunication, misunderstanding and other neurotic processes. Communication between the average individual is at times complicated and misunderstood which leads to hurt feelings, misunderstanding and afterthought processes. The goal of this article is to start to bring an awareness of the problems that people with autism have oral communication. Their ability to understand, comprehend and interpret oral language differs, as does that between the average individual, however, the results may be more tragic to less responsive than the average individuals may. The components of the communication may not be interpreted as would be expected and therefore the outcome may result in anything from a meltdown to no response. Thus, the following chapter will try to inform the reader as to how people with autism understand communication and of course, respond back with oral communication.

The components of oral communication are this: the words being used, the tone of voice, and body language. The words that are used in communication to an individual with autism must be specific and to the point. If there are any margins for interpretation, the individual is autism may choose one of those margins rather than interpret what is being said to them by the specific individual. The outcome may not be the desired on without the specific content of the words. For example, an individual told his child who has autism to go and wash the car. The autistic individual went and got a bucket, soap, and the sponge along

with the hose and proceeded to wash the car. What the parent really wanted to be done was that the individual is autism take the hose and spray out just the underside of the car. As one can see the words that were used were open to interpretation, and therefore the autistic individual proceeded to do what they thought was supposed to be done. The result was not what the parent expected or wanted and consequently chastised the individual, which then led to a meltdown. A word of advice when it comes to this is being particular as to what you want from the individual who has autism. Do not use large words or words that can be misinterpreted as something else be, very specific. The more specific the words that are used in the interaction, the better the outcome goal of what you desire from the autistic individual.

In contrast, when an individual with autism tries to communicate the best way they can to whomever they are trying to speak to, the individual being spoken to may become intimidated by the use of wording by the individual with autism. In other words, the person with autistic spectrum disorder may start off with a complex word or a word out of context, that the individual who is being spoken to does not understand and that person, of course, quits listening, and the person with autism continues to speak. The individual listening may start to get bored and look away, but the individual with autism does not necessarily read the body language and therefore continues to speak. After it is all said and done, they may ask the question, and the other person was not listening after the first couple of words and therefore has no answer to the question from the autistic person. The autistic person will then become frustrated, and either has a meltdown or walk away.

Tone and inflection are sometimes just as important as the words being used in communication. The tone in which someone speaks at times can be misinterpreted as possibly negative or in a positive sense. An autistic individual will clue in on the tone and inflection of

the communication being directed at them. If the tone and inflection are loud and negative, they may not hear it because the loudness of the tone is already hurting their ears. They are dealing with the pain in which the tone and inflection have caused, or they feel the individual is angrily speaking to them. If they feel they have done nothing wrong they are already watching for some secondary sign of the possibility of some type of punishment. Now there are hurt, and they are scared. It has been noted that on several occasions when parents yell at a child with autism, the child seems not to hear them. It has been pointed out that the parent continues to yell and possibly even takes it up several octaves to the point where their communication is loud enough for the next-door neighbor to hear. However, they claim that the child did not hear them. It should be noted for the most part that the child did hear them, however, when either the yelling started, they felt anxiety, pain or felt that it was not directed at them because they did nothing wrong and they continued with what they were doing. This seems to happen on a regular basis with parents who do not take the time to calm themselves down and then, calmly talk to their autistic individual. Instead, they treat their autistic individual in such a way that they feel that their yelling and screaming will garner them the desired effect in which they are trying to invoke. However, the autistic individual is not listening because they feel that the communication is not directed at them or it has already hurt their ears and they will ignore the parent who is yelling at them. If the parent becomes violent, then the child will have a meltdown as of course, the parent has a meltdown. This is not rocket science, if you decide to yell at your child who has autism they may not respond or they may meltdown because you hurt their ears and scared them.

Body language is what we refer to as a nonverbal form of communication. For the most part, individuals with autism do not understand body language. It seems that they have a minimal

response if any to the parent who is frustrated with them who puts their hands on their hips in that commanding fashion that they feel will make a big impression on their autistic individual. However, since individuals with autism do not pick up on body language, this component of communication has little to no effect on them, as they do not understand what it is the individual communicating with them is trying to communicate to them. Therefore, this component of communication is not understood nor interpreted for the most part by people with autistic spectrum disorder. Accordingly, if the parent tries to do the commanding posture or any of the other postures in which I have seen many parents do, their child with autistic spectrum disorder does not respond. If the parent becomes violent and displays angry and aggressive body language, the autistic individual may do any of the following: ignore them, walk away from them or in the worst case will stand up to them and mimic the posture. This may lead to a physical altercation, which will solve absolutely nothing but will lead to some type of sensitization on the part of the individual with autism.

In general, communicating with anyone with autistic spectrum disorder will also depend on the fact whether they are right brained dominant or left brained dominant, a child, an adolescent or an adult. Communication differs when it comes to which side of the brain is more dominant. I will cite specific examples throughout the rest of this chapter, as I will now divide into those three sections.

Before I get into the significant part, I would like to talk about individuals with autistic spectrum disorder keeping in mind particular things that may be going on when you attempt to communicate with them. It has been noted that at any given time an individual with autistic spectrum disorder is thinking about several things at one time and maybe over-focused on two or three of them. Interrupting this focus may lead to situations that will be described throughout the rest of this article. It should be noted that when interrupting an individual with autistic spectrum disorder when they are focused on the task,

video game or drawing, would not lead to the expected result that the parent/caretaker/teacher may desire but will instead end up in something they do not expect. It should also be noted that people with autistic spectrum disorder have specific issues that also need to be taken into account. These issues are the possibility of sensitivity to light, sensitivity to sounds, texture issues especially when it comes to food and of course cloth and clothing textures when it comes to being in direct contact with them physically. At any time if they are abruptly interrupted from their over focused task or if they are working on a non-preferred task and they are interrupted, they may display behavior similar to attention deficit hyperactivity disorder whereby they will go from one task to the next till they find the preferred task again. In communicating with individuals with autistic spectrum disorder people who are involved with them need to be very patient, perceptive of the child's likes, dislikes, preferences, non-preferences, and ways in which they may try to communicate back. It is noted that the meltdown/temper tantrum that has been observed by parents/caregivers/teachers due to the interruption is misinterpreted as bad behavior, but instead, it is a function of their frustration in not being understood by those individuals trying to communicate with them. I definitely hope that this thumbnail sketch of the following parts of communication with autistic spectrum disorder individuals at various ages will help shed some light. Help parents to be better parents when it comes to dealing with helping and encouraging individuals with autistic spectrum disorder. Further, to work towards the highest level of their proficiency and not be condemned for those things that they do not master quite as well.

Child

A famous quote did I'd like to share with you at this time comes from a very old manuscript which implies that you reap what you sow. Raising children and trying to communicate with them is a complicated task with an average child. The parent tends to get angry very quickly and

the infamous word "NO" is used several thousand times a day. Parents wonder why when their child starts to become very verbal that the first word out of their mouth is always NO. This is somewhat one of the few generalities that may carry over to some extent to a child with autistic spectrum disorder. It is also noted that the parent has to play a huge role in developing intervention strategies when they are working with a child with autistic spectrum disorder. This is one of those occasions where the quicker it is identified, the better and the earlier the interventions could lead to the possibility of the better outcomes in the long-term. However, it has been my experience that most that parents do not understand why the child behaves the way they do and has a tendency to yell and scream at them at the top of their lungs hoping for some change in the behavior. A child with autistic spectrum disorder may be very good at interpreting the word no; however, do they really know what it means? In other words, even though the parent knows what the word no means, does the child understand what the word no means? In all my experience, I have seen thousands of times this major mistake that parents have played throughout the ages with their children. Back in the day when a child did not respond to the word no, they were usually disciplined in a very painful manner. However in this day and age where that type of behavior is supposed to be eliminated, yeah right, striking a child with autistic spectrum disorder is not teaching them anything. Their interpretation of the word no may be very generic and other words the word no may mean something else to them other than no. As incredible as this sounds when the parent is using the word no in a generic sense the child then has to interpret what the parent actually wants from them. A child with autistic spectrum disorder will associate the word no, with whatever they are doing the present time and that will be the interpretation of the word. Imagine a child with autistic spectrum disorder being told no in regards to many different behaviors. There is a good possibility he will interpret the behaviors with the word no and start to call the behavior no. Of course, the

parent will interpret this is being belligerent or be obstinate or oppositional and then becomes angry with the child who has absolutely no clue why the parent is now becoming angry with them because they are repeating the word back to them that they have heard several thousand times. Most normal children are confused by this for a period of time, but for some reason, they tend to figure it out over the next couple of years. However, a child with autistic spectrum disorder may start to associate the word no with just about anything in their environment. In other words, he may start to call their toys no or a game no and this is where the parent misinterprets the word no as a name the child has interpreted from the parent to give to whatever the parent was yelling no at him about for. Parents who do not understand, or in some cases refuse to understand, autistic spectrum disorder will become very enraged with the child and cuss and swear at them trying to get some result. Usually what happens next is the nonverbal posturing along with the yelling and screaming. A child with autistic spectrum disorder interprets this as not in the language sense in the sense that mommy or daddy is yelling at them and they are hurting their years. Many times the parents start to scream at a child with autistic spectrum disorder, and the first thing they will do is cover their ears. The average parent misinterprets this as an oppositional gesture meaning, "I don't want to hear that," but what it actually means is your hurting my ears. This is where parents tend to become frustrated because they do not understand that their child does not understand that yelling and screaming is a form of an attention-getting behavior, probably invoked on them by their parents, and will not work as attention-getting behavior on the child with autistic spectrum disorder. If anything the child will start by covering their ears because you have just hurt their ears and they may have a meltdown due to the pain that they have just experienced by the yelling and screaming. Some parents have interpreted this as a temper tantrum rather than the reaction to having his ears hurt, and you are trying to tell your parents you hurt my ears by your yelling and screaming and to please

stop. At this point, this is where parents who do this to their child need to pay close attention. If you are doing this to your child, you are abusing the child, and if a mandated reporter hears about this, CYS will be visiting you. Therefore, wise up, all the cussing, swearing, and screaming and yelling will not get an autistic child to perform the task you want. This is abuse so be warned.

This is one of the significant misinterpretations in communication between parents and children with autistic spectrum disorder, language. If intervention is brought in at this time, the possibility of a better outcome and reduction of the parent's anger issues will be successful along with the ability to interpret what the child is actually trying to communicate back to you. In children, the right brain and the left-brain are still in developmental stages, and it seems quite difficult to interpret which side of the brain a child with autistic spectrum disorder is dominant. However, by the beginning of preschool to kindergarten or even in 1st grade the dominant side of the brain should be showing some qualities more advanced than the submissive side of the brain. It is also during this time that some behaviors are very closely related to attention-deficit/hyperactivity disorder. However, they are usually in response to the child boredom, and there is no incentive for them to do other things or the work is too, and they cannot seem to handle the situation in a more appropriate manner. This is usually where the infamous attention deficit hyperactivity disorder diagnosis is put into play although only one maybe two of the criteria for the diagnosis are seen. In general, it is diagnosed as ADHD, and the child is then diagnosed with ADHD. However, the child has autistic spectrum disorder with some of the symptoms of ADHD. If someone takes the time to sit and talk with this child, they will find out what the child is thinking and why they are behaving the way, they are. However, for the most part, the child is yelled at and told to sit down or told to pick their head up or told some other command by a teacher or a teacher's aide in a loud voice. This then only triggers the

response that angers either the teacher or the teacher's aide such as hands over the years, head down or just not paying attention. What these people in charge need to do is to take the child off to the side, sit down with them calmly and talk to them about what their problem is. The problem is, however, the teachers and teachers' aides are not very well trained and how to handle and/or deal with school-age children that have autistic spectrum disorder. It seems it is much easier to call them attention deficit hyperactivity disorder and give the medication, so they sit there and seemed to be doing something. However, a child with autistic spectrum disorder given some type of medication for attention deficit hyperactivity disorder may be able to pay attention a little better, but this is only putting a Band-Aid on the problem rather than trying to solve the problem. In talking with a school-age child with autistic spectrum disorder, the individual talking to them must understand that the child may or may not interpret what they are saying. Therefore, they must be very specific, simple and to the point and then ask the child to interpret what they say and speak back to them in their own words. This is where that virtue of patience will come into play, and the more patient the person, the better the outcome and the better the child will benefit both inspirationally and educationally. If a child with autistic spectrum disorder tries to explain what they are feeling or what is going on with them and the adult/teachers are not listening and would rather is trying to push their own agenda the child will become frustrated. If this issue was pushed without intervention, the chance is that the child will be either given a timeout or sent to the principal office. The process of communicating with children with autistic spectrum disorder revolves around the adults' ability and willingness to restrain themselves and to be open to the possibility that what they say is not always interpreted as what is understood. This is where I talk about the fact that say what you mean and mean what you say and then have the child repeat back to you what they understand. This will be much more successful than yelling, screaming, and seeing a total meltdown, which then leads to some negative outcome, which results in some form of sensitization and possibly even a lack of building a bridge with the child with autistic spectrum disorder. So if I were to sum this up briefly, I would say that in working with children with autistic spectrum disorder, take time, invest time, be patient, listen closely and ask the question why to the child don't assume they understand what you're saying. Always be prepared for some different response and what you expect because after all, the child may not understand or interpret what you are saying the way you want them to understand and interpret it.

The other issue that everyone should be aware of is the response that the child with autistic spectrum disorder may give you. If the question is too complex, you may hear the answer "I don't know" or nothing at all. One of the worst things that an adult can do with a child with autistic spectrum disorder is pressing them for the answer that you want to hear. What has been discovered over the time that I have been working with children with autistic spectrum disorder is that they have the answer but do you have the right question? This becomes more apparent with the adolescent and the adult, but children tend to be looking for the right question to give you the answer they already have. In one specific case and it should be noted at this time, that children with autistic spectrum disorder have many thought processes going at any given time and in interrupting the process by a surprise response from behind them or a stupid question may invoke an answer that the parent does not like or they may be ignored. My advice to parents with children with autistic spectrum disorder is very simple: do not sneak up on your child and do not ask stupid questions. Instead, observe what they are doing make some noises such as tapping or whistling or heavy footsteps approaching them from behind especially, if they are playing a video game or are busy coloring or possibly doing some form of artwork. This approach gives the individual with autistic spectrum disorder a heads up that an individual may be engaging them while they have many thought processes going.

On many unsuccessful occasions, I have heard about parents walking into a room where their child with autistic spectrum disorder may be playing a video game or busy coloring or playing with their preferred toys. The parent walks into the room postures himself in such a way of an authoritarian manner and utters a question in a loud voice such as "what are you doing" or something the effect of "didn't I tell you "with some previous request. The individual with autistic spectrum disorder, if they heard them, is already disturbed by this approach and several responses may ensue such as ignore the interruption, a brief period of silence followed by the response of WHAT or even guttural sounds such as a growl, a snarl or a one-syllable utterance. This, of course, causes the previously explained chain reaction of anything from a minor meltdown to a major meltdown to possibly no response at all. What I have been able to ascertain from working with individuals in this age group with autistic spectrum disorder is the following: they claim to be highly focused on what they are doing plus other thoughts are going on in their head at that time, and the adult is disturbing them and therefore ensures the meltdown. If the individual knows that the parent is present and they ask a stupid question, the individual will look at them in the infamous look of, "you talking to me." Alternatively, if the correct question is asked or the parent/caregiver sits down with the individual or sits next to the individual and actually asks them how they are doing rather than to stand over them in the posturing stand, barks out some order, communication can be established, and cooperation can be obtained. However, this whole process takes patience, persistence and of course a desire to make it work. If good communication can be established, cooperation and a good relationship will follow.

We all know that communicating with children from a young age until the preteen years can be difficult and if the individual has autistic spectrum disorder it will take a desire on the parent's part to work on developing communication skills with the individual. It should be noted

that the communication skills with the individual and understanding how the individual communicates would help them to develop adaptive skills that they can use throughout the rest of their life. Communication is not easy, but then again, it can be quite rewarding when you talk to an individual with autistic spectrum disorder because they do have something to offer. Working with them from childhood to early adolescence is very important, as it will help them to develop those adaptation skills that will be needed later on in life. If parents/teachers do not take the time to work with their children/students, they will end up in constant conflict with the child/student because they do not understand their child/student and their child/student does not understand them. Like any type of communication and cooperation, it takes a basis to start. The basis the parent may be using may be something they learned which is not applicable to their autistic spectrum disorder child. Henceforth, the old way of communicating with children, especially those with autistic spectrum disorder, does not work, will not work and will result in only disaster and constant conflict in the home/school. What I am proposing to all parents/teachers is to take the time, understand what your child/student likes, dislikes, and understands how they express themselves and what you can do to help them to express themselves better. Remember, children do not understand what you are trying to say until they learn what it is you are trying to say. An individual's autistic spectrum disorder may have several things going on at one time inside their head and in the process of interrupting them rather, than merging with them, will not lead to any progress. Professionally speaking, I have worked with some parents that have children with autistic spectrum disorder, and the hardest part is to teach the parents how to approach their child. Many parents believe that they can do the intimidation, loud voice, repeat the command repeatedly and get the desired response. This is an erroneous thought process, as it seems they complain that the constant outcome is some type of verbal confrontation or a temper tantrum. What they do not understand

is that their child had become frustrated with them because they did not understand what the parent really wanted and with the continued loud voice and posturing, the child was clueless and in throwing the temper tantrum or the meltdown is indicating that they are frustrated and want the parent to stop. They are trying to convey to the parent to stop what they are doing because they do not understand. Although this seems to be simple in theory, in practice, it takes a lot of work. One other issue, I would like to bring up at this time, is when I hear a parent saying to me that their child is mouthy to them. When I talk to the parent, they are frustrated, angry and very impatient with what the child has been saying to them. I usually have to bite my tongue because when the parent describes what the child is saying back to them, it is what the child has heard in the home setting. The child does not always understand what is being said in the home setting, but they do repeat what they hear and, in this case, the parent interpreted the child's responses, what they heard, as meaning that they understand and not what the child is trying to communicate. Remember parents, and these are children, that repeat what they hear and what they repeat they may not understand what they are saying. They may say it in such a way that is inappropriate for an adult to do but for the child, they are just repeating words they heard without attaching any meaning, understanding or inflection. The child is not mouthy, they are just repeating what they have heard, and they are doing so out of context. This is not what the parent wants to hear, but the child has no idea that what they are saying. It may be wrong, and the parent has allowed their emotions to take over rather than try to understand that the child is doing nothing more than repeating what they heard. In the case of a child with autistic spectrum disorder, they do repeat what they hear and when the parent gives them an emotional response, the child may interpret this as good, but it may be that the parent is becoming angry over what the child is saying. Of course, when this happens, the chain reaction starts in the child, as they do not understand why they are verbally reprimanded. The parent

who does this is reaping what they sowed because the child is just repeating what they have heard and have no idea what it really means or how they should be using those words. I have seen many frustrated parents because they refuse to think before they speak. When they are talking to their child, and the continuation of the frustration continues then the conflict in the home will continue until someone grows up.

So in summation to this section, I would be challenging parents to start to look at this thought process different than what they were taught because what they were taught was left over from the 20th century. We all know that what supposedly worked in the 20th century does not work in the 21st century. More intervention with autistic spectrum disorder is required. Teachers and parents, learning this type of communication skill can help those children/students with autistic spectrum disorder and can help them to succeed in some gainful and accomplished lifestyle. Without the ability to communicate at an early age, it possibly leads to many hospitalizations, a myriad of medications, all of which do nothing more than keeping the individual from communicating. They do not understand what is going on but are medicated and stare in one direction.

A final case study, which I will illustrate, involved a parent and their pre-teenaged autistic spectrum disorder child. The child was very intelligent, as was noted, but on the other hand, the parents were trying to mold the child into what they want, and this was remarkably unsuccessful, but they would not listen. One of the major issues was that the parent was having meltdowns because they did not get the response that they expected from the child. When you interrupt individuals with autistic spectrum disorder, especially if they are a preteen, they are thinking about many things at any given time. In interrupting them by trying to posture or yell or some act of wanting their attention now, you end up with a response that you do not want. In this specific case, the adult was asking for an affirmation of a question that they asked their child. The individual responded with a

grunt. The parents became enraged and felt that the child was disrespecting them and when it was explained to the adult that this was a simple response, they eased up. The child was probably thinking about many things while they were doing what they were doing, you interrupted them without any warning, and then you demanded an answer that you wanted that they did not give. Therefore, the adult started to scream at the individual, and thus they shut down. Shutting down is another response that can happen once a child gets into their late childhood to early adolescence. It seems for the most part that this behavior replaces the temper tantrum/meltdown. It is noted that sometimes when you interrupt the individual with autistic spectrum disorder when they are busy doing something you will not get the answer you want but accept the answer that you do get as an affirmation.

Therefore, you ask me what is next after childhood and these issues that can happen. Try to develop communication skills. What I can tell you very simply is this, if you have succeeded in developing some communication skills by the time adolescence starts, you as a parent will have a much better time in working with your autistic spectrum disorder teenager. If you have not succeeded in developing communication skills, you will have a much harder time. It is not impossible when puberty starts to set in to develop communication skills. Therefore, the next section is about the teenage through early adult communication issues.

Teenage through Early Adult

In this day and age, it is hard enough to communicate with teenagers through early adults. Their electronic devices such as their phones, tablets, laptops and any other electronic device that can take up copious amounts of time and use maximum concentration, constantly distract them. At this point sometimes, it is hard to distinguish between an individual with autistic spectrum disorder and someone with electronic gadget addictive disorder (EGAD-Future chapter on this). However, when a parent approaches individuals with electronic gadget addictive disorder, they usually get a verbal response which may include "in a minute," or a whiny verbal response or they will just look up at you. An individual with autistic spectrum disorder when interrupted like this will respond in the following ways: they will ignore you, they will grunt at you or make some type of guttural utterance, or they will respond with an angry outburst followed by a verbal tirade. As you can see the difference between these two responses and these are quite evident when it comes to dealing with adolescents through early adulthood.

Just as a reminder or as a footnote I would like to point out the following things that may be going on with your teenager through early adulthood. It should be noted that they all have a sensitivity to something. It may be sensitive to light, sound, smell, taste, texture and of course internal stimulation. It means you may be speaking to them they may be preoccupied with any the above mentioned along with the myriad of thoughts that they could be thinking of along with your approach to approaching them. Keep these items in mind when you attempt to talk to a teenager through young adult who has autistic spectrum disorder.

As hinted earlier, there is a difference in communication issues between the autistic spectrum disorder level I and level II. Level I may respond in such a way that it seems to be offensive or they have a tendency to overelaborate. Once they have spoken what is on their mind, they have a tendency just to walk away if there is no intelligent response to the comments and statements they had made. On the other hand, level II may stand his ground and overelaborate to the point where a verbal confrontation may then lead to the possibility of a physical altercation. It seems that the level IIs will continue to argue their point and it may be that somewhere during this verbal confrontation that they feel that you are no longer listening to them

and they will make you try to understand. However, for the most part, in this situation, the person that is listening quit listening at some time or had picked out certain parts of the conversation and was asking questions about the parts of the conversation that the person with autistic spectrum disorder level II was not talking about. Therefore, the misunderstanding led to a further conflict that, without outside intervention, would most likely end up in a physical altercation.

Another factor involved with all the internal and external issues that go on with inside a person with autistic spectrum disorder, during the discussed time frame, is the action of puberty starting. It seems that the outset of puberty during this time does not necessarily lead to the normal issues that individuals without autistic spectrum disorder may experience. Remember that a person with autistic spectrum disorder cannot necessarily describe how they were feeling or what they are feeling and in this sense, the action of hormones may cause other issues.

It was noted that talking with teens through early adults who have autistic spectrum disorder level II it seems that their maturity level, as described by outsiders, seems to be somewhat childish. However, it is noted that without interventions, their maturity level tends to stop somewhere in the mid to late teen's zone and not necessarily mature into what society considers an acceptable adult. Communication seems to revolve around what is most important to the individual with autistic spectrum disorder level II. Conversation can be directed away from this important topic. However, it will revert back to that topic as soon as the person with level II feels he has talked enough about the topic in which you had redirected them. At times conversation can continue to revolve back around towards whatever the individual with autistic spectrum disorder really wants to talk about. After all, I mentioned earlier that they have an answer; it is whether or not you come up with the right question as to how successful your

conversation may be. Therefore, if you come up with the right question, you may get the answer you are looking for.

One other area that needs to be talked about when dealing with communication with teens through young adults is what kind of parent you are? There are basically two parental types: the reactive and proactive. The reactive parent hears what is being said and reacts to it. The proactive parent listens to what is being said, translates what it means and tries to respond in the best way possible. Many times I've seen the reactive parent, and it seems that they do not listen to what is being said to them nor do they understand it and therefore they become angry because of either the tone of voice or specific words that are being used. They take action of a possible illogical and violent nature. This does not work with anyone who has autistic spectrum disorder. On the other hand, the proactive parent takes time and listens to what is being said, taking into account the wording, the tone of voice and also the body language of the individual. Then, tries to translate what is actually being communicated to them. What they understand that is being spoken to them and then respond in a positive manner such as asking the question for a better explanation. If this is done correctly, there will not be a meltdown. However, the best way to do this is such: after the parent listens, translates the response, ask: is this what you are trying to tell me? If this is different than what you are trying to tell me, please explain this to me further. If there is a positive and calm dialogue going on here, there would be a success in understanding what the autistic spectrum disorder individual is actually trying to communicate to you. Always remember, that they may say things that you do not understand or take offense. However, that is probably not what is being meant by the individual that is speaking but rather the only words that they know how to use to explain what they are trying to explain while they are trying to explain it to you. If patience is used here, in the translation and the response, there will be successful communication across this gap. If

not, such as in the reactive parent, this may turn into a screaming match whereby nothing is communicated other than a lot of loud noise. This is not impossible to do, but it does take some time, effort and patience on the part of the listener to try to comprehend what it is that the person with autistic spectrum disorder is trying to tell them. There may be times when the individual with autistic spectrum disorder is talking in such language, and it is English, that the words are not understood at all and asking for a simple explanation is not a bad idea.

It is essential to help the individual that has autistic spectrum disorder to be understood and that what you said is understood by them as well. Never hesitate to ask the question after you are done speaking to the autistic spectrum disorder individual, can you explain to me what you understood from what I just said? This will definitely be an asset in bridging communication issues now and in the near future.

A caution to people that interrupts an autistic spectrum disorder individual while they are working on something. Never ask a stupid question or one that involves lots of details. You will get a look of frustration if the question that is asked is obvious. For example, you enter a room, and the autistic person is on their phone. Don't ask the obvious question of: What are you doing? That is a dumb question that will result in frustration on the autistic person's part. However, if you ask a good question like; Do you see any difference in the reception in that part of the house? You will get a good answer. Ask specific questions not general or apparent ones, and you will get their attention and good answers. Once the first answer is given, then you can ask something else, but not before. There is a possibility that if you ask a dumb or obvious question that you will be ignored, growled at or even told off. Therefore, the question to get their attention should be somewhat technical in nature. Like if they are playing a game: What level are you on? Alternatively, did you see the new specs on a specific game? This will give you access to them through a door that

they will allow you to enter into their conscious world. In addition, this is an excellent place to be in such communication can go further. This is a bridge into speaking to them freely with some good exchange.

In a final note to communication issues with teenagers through young adults, the following should be noted: if you are talking to your autistic spectrum disorder individual and they are walking away from you, never assume they understood or even heard what you said. When an individual with autistic spectrum disorder is running away from you or walking away from you or has turned their back to you, they have stopped listening. If the message is that important, you need to get their attention and relay the message to them directly. Chances are after they have turned away from you they are thinking about whatever they are planning to do next or have some unwritten agenda going on inside their many thought processes. It is a good chance that if you assume, they heard what you were saying you are probably wrong. At the least, ask for an acknowledgment when they are walking away from you, and if they do not acknowledge, you approach them and get their attention. Then look at them straight in the eye and deliver your message and ask them if they understand. In addition, possibly even ask them to translate what they understand back to you. If this is done correctly, a communication bridge will have been built, and the message will be relayed. However if this is not done, chances are that the autistic spectrum disorder individual will not have a single clue about what you had told them, ask them or inform them of and they will go on to do whatever it was they were thinking about when you were talking to them while they were not actively engaged in listening. This usually could result in some type of verbal conflict afterward with the famous line of "you never told me that."

Communication in this age group can be difficult at times with the onset of hormonal issues, life issues, and in general the expectations of the parents that may not be plausible with their autistic individual. There is a possibility of good relationship building as well as

communication skills that can be accomplished during this time frame but, there needs to be patience and persistence on the part of the parent or caregiver. Otherwise, the possibility that the individual will start showing other mental health issues is possible. However, within the scope of this article, I am encouraging parents of individuals in this age group to not give up but to continue to work with them and seek outside interventions with a qualified professional. Remember parents/caregivers that it is never too late for you to learn new techniques as well as your autistic individual developing adaptation skills. This can only be done with patience, persistence, perseverance, and a dedication to helping them.

Adult Autism Communication Issues

At this point in the chapter, it is time to take a look at communication skills with adults who have autistic spectrum disorder. It should be noted at this point in history, 2015, since the adoption of the DSM 5, many people fell through the diagnostic criteria for autistic spectrum disorder due to the age limitations placed on the diagnostics from the DSM-IV and its predecessors. Although this was noted in a previous article, it should be brought up at this time when it comes to adults that were not diagnosed with autistic spectrum disorder due to the criteria or due to their ability to learn adaptive skills. They were not necessarily identified as having peculiarities in their behavior and function, but they were different. Some adults have autistic spectrum disorder that has survived life to the point where they are at today, but they do have some issues with their communication skills. Many of these adults were bullied in school and even over-disciplined in the home. Due to this negative stimulation, they developed adaptive skills to survive in that last century. Those that adapted have lived some interesting but productive lives. Their saga is one of learning through brutality and punishment. It would seem that in the 20th century if you

had autism of the first or second level, you were bullied, badgered and even punished severely by the caregivers to be forged into being the person that they wanted you to be. Any refusal in adapting by this methodology resulted in being beaten, whipped and made by severe consequence to adapt to what they wanted you to be or wanted from you. It is a wonder sometimes why these individuals even talk to anyone at all. However, they do find specific individuals that they will converse with at times, but that circle is limited and specific.

I have had the privilege of working with some adults who are diagnosed with autistic spectrum disorder, and they have adapted well to everyday life. They have incorporated their adaptive skills. However, their communication skills would be noted as being somewhat reserved if you were to try to carry on a conversation with them.

In my experience with dealing with adults with autistic spectrum disorder, when it comes to communication, they seem to be extremely reserved and tend to be very short with their answers. It seems that they have trust issues with whoever may be talking to them unless a specific topic of their interest is hit upon. In talking about everyday things, you will get one-maybe 2-word answers, but that is about it. This will happen until you hit a hot topic that they are either having issues with or have not been able to solve within their lifetime. At that point, you will get a very interesting conversation about some feelings, some conflict and possibly even some interesting behavior patterns that they have developed for themselves that seem to work for them. However, at this point in life, they are pretty much settled on what they're going to say and how they're going to say it to anyone they may come across if they come across people outside of their circle.

In my experience, adults with autistic spectrum disorder tend to only speak to those people who are closest to such as children, spouse, parents, and very close friends. In doing therapy with them, it took

several sessions to develop rapport because the therapist was not was in their circle of people that they would talk to. Therefore, it took a lot of effort on the part of the therapist to get the adult with autistic spectrum disorder to at least have a normal conversation. It should be noted that at this point in the life of an adult with autistic spectrum disorder they have daily activities down to a very specific pattern complete with details of everything they are going to do, how they're going to do it and how they're going to avoid other people. The adult autistic spectrum disorders speech is not spontaneous, and it seems to be calculated and measured, and therefore it appears that they do not want to engage in any spontaneous interactions when they are out in public. They will do what they came to do and get home as quickly as possible with as little contact as possible.

If an adult with autistic spectrum disorder does engage in any type of conversation outside of, what they consider necessary, it is usually short, to the point and they go on with what they were planning on doing. The stoppage of the thought process was not part of the process in which they put together to get the job done in which they were engaged in doing. Therefore, speech to them and communication with other people outside the circle is not essential and at times can be anxiety prone and thus they avoid it at all costs. It could also be noted that adults with autistic spectrum disorder have behavior patterns, have organizational patterns and have specific schedules in which they live by, and they do not feel that they have to talk about this organization and patterning as it works for them. They feel it would take too long to explain to anyone else why they do it so. Therefore, they avoid any type of conversation outside of those people who know them best. Fortunately, if you are a good therapist and pay close attention to an adult with autistic spectrum disorder, you will gain their trust, and they will have good intellectual conversations with you. However if you start making assumptions about them, and expressing it to them, they will shut down, they will not trust you, and

furthermore, they will not talk to you. Therefore, in this case, it takes a lot of patience, persistence and good listening skills on the part of the therapist to work with an adult with autistic spectrum disorder and to help them to communicate what they are feeling, what they are thinking and what they really want to accomplish through therapy. Communication skills and communication with adults with autistic spectrum disorder can be accomplished, but it is going to take time, patience and persistence on the part of the therapist or someone else who wants to engage with them in conversation. It could also be stated that to get past this door that they have developed, you need to find a key that will allow you into their circle.

Summary

In this chapter about communication skills with people who have autistic spectrum disorder, it should constantly be kept in mind that a good parent, caregiver, therapist, teacher and anyone else who engages in conversation or tries to engage in conversation with an individual with autistic spectrum disorder need to keep the lessons of this chapter in mind. Always be clear about what you are trying to convey to them and take the time to ask them to explain back to you what they understood. Do not be surprised when you are working with children that you may not get a verbal response but at least some type of guttural acknowledgment. Accept it and move on. When working with the teenage through young adults, this is the most difficult time, but it also can be the most rewarding, during this time the most progress can be made. With the adults that have autistic spectrum disorder, they have pretty much developed their own patterns for whom they will talk to and whom they will not talk to and how they may engage with people and how they may avoid them. Overall, it takes effort on the part of anyone who is trying to develop a

relationship with an autistic spectrum disorder individual especially when it comes to an understanding how they communicate, what they understand and how you are conveying the message to them. The outcome of this can be gratifying for yourself as well as the individual with autistic spectrum disorder.

CHAPTER 10

Autistic Spectrum Disorders

Social Issues

The Social Issues

The very fabric of society is in man's ability to develop, implement and perform social skills and appropriate and acceptable manner, which is deemed appropriate by social norms.

The previous statement has been one that has been accepted throughout the ages however since the advent of the cell phone, the computer and other devices of social media it has become lax to and at times undetermined. However, we still have to associate with people in the real environment that surrounds us. We associate with people in our jobs, in the marketplaces and at other events of the social nature. To the degree in which we associate is determined by a comfort level of the situation that exists in which we find ourselves. Social skills, for the most part, have been taught since childhood however people with autistic spectrum disorder have problems in learning the social skills due to several factors. In the following paragraphs, I will try to give a good representation of the social skills that someone with autistic spectrum disorder may develop, implement or even reject. However, they do have some ability to learn social skills implement them and use them, but other factors may come into play and prevent them from actually using them to the degree, which would be accepted by common social standards. The parents, teachers, employers may set those standards, and of course, to some degree, the world in which they engage in that surrounds us all. However, individuals with ASD cannot hold to that standard that was set for them by social norms and functions. They march to the beat of a different drum, or a horn or a kazoo.

Social skills since the advent of electronics and communication, (smartphones, social media, Internet), have delineated the ability of individuals to communicate and socialize on an interpersonal basis. Use of these devices was initially meant for individuals to learn social skills in the electronic media and then transfer that skill into the real

world, at least this was the intention. However, what has transpired was that these devices have caused us to lose our ability to be social in the real world on an interpersonal basis. Individuals with ASD, depending on how young they were diagnosed or how old they were when they were diagnosed, may not develop interpersonal skills to the extent in which they are expected to do so. The electronic gadgets that have been invented as a teaching tool may become a crutch for individuals with ASD and give them the ability not to have to learn social skills. On the other hand, average individuals who use these devices still have some social skill level and can interact interpersonally with other people. However, it seems as though the electronics have degraded the ability for people to interact interpersonally to a very high degree but that is not the crux of this article. The crux of this article is about people with autistic spectrum disorder and their ability or inability to learn social skills and social adaptive abilities.

One of the things that I have encountered over the course of the last 20+ years was a specific factor, which involves the age in which the diagnosis was made and how involved significant others become and what they are willing to do to help the individual with ASD learn/adapt/integrate social interactions. It would seem that the younger the diagnosis is made, the more open to social skills training the individual is. This is not to say that older individuals who are diagnosed with autistic spectrum disorder cannot learn social skills and adaptive abilities, but it is much harder to work with them on taking up new behaviors. Especially when there is no logical reason for them to do so as they seem to be happy with the way they are and adaption does not seem to be necessary for their point of view. However, younger an individual is, the better results can happen because their fluidity of thinking and habits are still in a fluid state rather than older individuals their thought process has become more crystalline and change is much more difficult.

Social behavior is somewhat easily observable at times when it comes to younger individuals with autistic spectrum disorder (early age through early teens). It seems that their playtime outside the home and without any first-degree relatives is observed as solo play near others however they do not enter act with the others but rather play by themselves. This changes if a first-degree relative, (sibling, parent, and involved adult) would enter into the situation. However, for the most part, an individual with ASD that is of early school age seems to focus more on individual play and ignores any other group around them. It has been observed that as this individual is engaged in solo play, and someone from another group decides they want to interact, there is somewhat of a meltdown, which usually results in the possibility of physical altercations. This is one of those instances where whoever the caregiver is for aid or supervisor, needs to interact rather quickly before this gets out of hand. An individual with ASD who is engaged in solo play does not want to be bothered by others. They seem to be very content with solo play. It should also be noted that the forcing of integration by an outside source on this individual with ASD would also result in a major meltdown and or verbal/violent altercation. Many caregivers see this as a problem and in the process of trying to help the individual with ASD integrate into a group causes more harm than good. The solution to this minor problem that could become a major problem is in building bridges. In addition, asked the individual engaged in solo play has their own thought processes going on and also their own goals to what they are doing while they are playing. Integration of this person into a group cannot be accomplished by pushing them into it. However, with the proper introduction by the caregivers/supervisor the individual may voluntarily get involved with the group. However, this must be done by explaining to the individual, without pushing them, and with some hands-on guidance by the supervisor/caregiver, the individual with ASD may engage without incident. However, if they refuse the supervisor/caregiver needs to allow them that space without pushing

the issue otherwise the meltdown will occur. There is another wrinkle in this as well; the individual with autistic spectrum disorder must have some working relationship with the character ever/supervisor for them to trust them to engage in social interactions with others or joining a group in the process. Without this relationship, the individual is autistic spectrum disorder may not engage but may have a meltdown. Techniques for doing this will be explained in future articles. For the most part, however, young children through early teens with autistic spectrum disorder do not see any reason why they need to engage with others since they seem to be perfectly happy doing what they are doing. The supervisor/caregiver/parent knows what the child likes and what their preferences are, (toys, electronics, activities, and games), can use these items to help their individual with ASD to build that bridge to develop social skills with others. This is where the involvement comes in helping the individual with ASD to develop these skills along with adapting them into their life. Without this attention to detail and the right communication skills to the individual with ASD, individuals with ASD may revert into their own world and only come out superficial at times. Their ability to socialize will be logically delineated because of other issues that may have been experienced by the individual with ASD over time. However, I will get to that later in this article. At this point, however, the discussion is about young children through early teens. Children at this point in their life, who do not have ASD, do go through an awkward phase where they are learning who they are, how to communicate and how to associate with others but, individuals with ASD have a more difficult time due to the issue of ASD. Children with ASD do not learn by observing others because they do not observe others. They may glance, take a quick look but it is only fleeting, and they will continue to do what they are comfortable doing rather than trying something new. The ability to learn socialization skills must be in fact spoon-fed by an adult. However, the adult should not force the issue. In trying to force social skills upon a child with ASD, it will cause them to go into

a meltdown. Any social skills that will be taught to children need to be taught slowly, with explanation and possibly a reward system. This does not mean that you pay the child for learning to be social but rather allow them to engage in those behaviors that they most enjoy. Apparent needs to know what those things are that their ASD child likes the most. They could be something as simple as being allowed to swing on a swing or as complicated is playing video games. However, in playing video games, they can be taught social skills when they are competing with somebody. However, it should not be the first and foremost way to get someone with ASD to engage in some socialization. Other items may be playing with Legos, model cars or even simple board games. However, this must be taken one step at a time as a child with ASD will be resistive at first until he sees that it is an enjoyable item to engage in and will find that others enjoy it as much as he does and therefore some socialization will take place. So it could be pointed out to parents have to be very observant of their children and use simple techniques in order to get them to engage in social skills training, and there should be a reward system involved. A caution the parents is very simply this if you promise something to deliver it or you will have the meltdown that you do not want to see. Therefore, building a bridge between the child with ASD and the parents, teachers and other caregivers is important and parents and those previously mentioned as taking the time to understand that yelling and screaming never will work. Those two types of frustration exhibited on the part of the adult will only cause the child with ASD to recoil deeper into their comfort zone. Comfort zone is what the child develops for themselves as a place where they feel comfortable and on threatened by the world around them. In addition, helping them to take steps out of this comfort zone a lot of patience, persistence and creative ideas will be needed on the part of the parents and caregivers. Just suggesting them to do something will not work. If a parent or caregiver takes time to get to know what the child likes and work slowly towards a socialization skill the success rate will be much

higher. If socialization skills are trying to be pushed on the child, they will 1st have a meltdown and then retreat into their comfort zone. One can see that dealing with children with ASD is something that takes a lot of patients. Many times when I observe is parents are trying to raise their child like they were raised and they have to be retrained on the fact that the way they were raised doesn't work and that they need to take time, patience and expend energy in order to work with their child instead of trying to mold them into what they want. A parent who takes the time to work with their child, understand ASD and use creative ideas to help them with their social skills will be much more successful. However, it takes parents patience, persistence and creative ideas to work with individuals with ASD. If you do not have the patience, the persistence or look for creative ideas the child will respond with some oppositional behavior and the pair will become frustrated and develop their own set of mental health issues. My caution to parents who don't have a lot of patients are persistence is to seek help as soon as possible and work with a professional who can help you to help yourself as you work with your child otherwise you'll end up with your own set of mental health issues and you will become very hostile toward your child and therefore they will build up a wall around them and not want to come out of their comfort zone.

I keep dropping this concept comfort zone, and I would like to explain it so all can understand. Individuals with ASD develop a world in the world in which they feel safe. It is usually an area in which they feel they will not be bothered along with a set of behaviors or protocols that they have developed over time. For the most part every individual I have worked with ASD level I into has developed these comfort zones. The goal of social skills training would be to help them to get out of the comfort zone and try something new. This is where the resistance will start, and without patience, anyone trying to help them out of their comfort zone will be met with resistance. This is where parents lose their patience and want to medicate their child. What is

happening is, in the situation, is that the parent is trying to push the idea upon the child and the child is resistive because either: the parents pushing too hard, there is no reward seen in the change or there is nothing comfortable about change itself. Parents and become exasperated and start to seek out medication for their child. It is not the child that is at fault here but the parent and their style of trying to teach social skills and socialization or in some cases boundaries. It is going to take time to work with the individual with ASD and helping them out of their comfort zone because it is a change to them and they do not like change. But, if the change appeals to them, the success of teaching the new skill or establishing a new boundary is much more successful. The unfortunate incident may be that the social skill or boundary is to change radically or uncomfortable for the individual, and they will recoil back into that comfort zone, and it will take more effort to convince them to come out. This is a lot easier to do with children and adolescents. When dealing with adults with ASD there wall that surrounds her comfort zone has become quite fortified, and a lot of explanations and pluses and minuses to the change must be explained and logically explained what the benefit to them is if they change or adopt a new behavior. This is where the patients on the part of the therapist, parents and other caregivers need to come into play. It could be said that teaching a child or adolescent a new behavior may be easier because they have not had the failures and disappointments that adult may have already experienced and therefore with patience, a child or adolescent will come out of their comfort zone to develop new behaviors. However, when dealing with adults a lot of explanation and reasoning must be used for them to even to think about attempting to try to do something that is outside of their comfort zone.

Therefore, working with children may take more time, more patients, and more energy, however, they may be more open to learning social skills and developing some socialization ability. Whereas on the other

hand adults who have experienced failure, discrimination or bullying may not be as willing to try new things. However, with the right help, they may try new socialization skills or change their protocol.

Being a teenager is a problematic time in the average individual's life. Being a teenager with ASD compounds the problem of social awkwardness. These individuals in the teenage years especially middle school through high school are usually the ones who are being picked on because of their social awkwardness and their lack of interest in the things that the average individual is interested in. They may develop their comfort zone and not associate with anybody, but they may be at the top of their class when it comes to their grade point average. For the most part, the word that gets to be used on them is called a nerd. A teenager with ASD has problems developing social skills because they are aware that people around them see them as being different and therefore they engage in a minimal amount of extracurricular activities. However, if the school has extracurricular activities that appeal to the teenager with ASD, they may engage in those behaviors and actually become part of a socialization process by which the organization functions. The most common of these is, of course, the band. Many teenagers with ASD are quite gifted when it comes to playing musical instruments, and therefore this is an excellent platform for them to actually learn some social skills even though their intent is just to play their instrument. They can actually be exposed to the possibility of social interactions and social involvement with a specialized group such as the band. The teenage group that has ASD may have the most opportunities to learn social skills and develop adaptive skills due to involvement with other individuals that they find that have a specific commonality such as in the band or possibly a club or organization that is very specific that they may want to engage in. Here's where the parents have to be very cautious as to not push the individual into trying something but to coax them into doing so and help them to realize that this is

something they really want, not what the parent wants but the individual with ASD wants. If they accomplish this and learn some social skills, this could then be identified as an adaptive skill, and hopefully, it is another stepping stone away from the comfort zone. However, if there is a bad experience, they may want to revert back to the comfort zone as it is a place of safety. This retreat into the comfort zone by a teenager needs to be addressed directly by the parent or by getting help to get the teenager with ASD back into the socialization process. The success of doing this depends upon the attitude and patience of the parent or caregiver or counselor to help the individual get out of the comfort zone and back into the activity. If the individual is pushed was threatened they will stay in the comfort zone and any adaptive skill at this time will be lost, and any social skills may be looked upon as "Bad for Me."

Since the change in the DSM 5, May 2012 and then adopted in September 2014, there have been adults that have been identified with ASD. What I will try to describe here is a group I call the under 30 years of age and the over 30 years of age adults.

Less than 30 years of age adults who have been recently diagnosed with ASD have adapted some adaptation skills, but their social skills are limited. It seems that their social skills would be limited to first-degree relatives and a few friends. They tend to not venture outside of their comfort zone, but when they do, they have a protocol that is wholly designed for maximum efficiency and minimum interaction. They have set up their life to eliminate socialization as much as possible. They tend to spend their free time on the computer or some activity around their residents. However, those in this age group who have been diagnosed with ASD long before they reach this time frame in their life may have developed social skills and social adaptation as well as other adaptive skills. It is the recently diagnosed individuals with ASD and this age bracket that have a lack of adaptive as well as social skills. Trying to teach them the need for any other social skills

or adaptive skills is nearly impossible because they have developed their comfort zone and their protocols to the point where changing them would take a significant occurrence in their life or a substantial need for some change. This group is not impossible to work with however it will take a lot of patience on the part of anyone who is trying to work with them to have them change. Individuals in this age bracket who were diagnosed earlier with ASD have similar traits however they still have some goals that they would like to accomplish whether they are implied or actually a necessity. The group that has been currently identified with ASD at this age has adapted their life to what they feel they need and nothing more. They are very rigid in their thinking and to change any of it will take a long time but it is not impossible, and it can be done.

The over 30 group that has been recently identified with autistic spectrum disorder are a fascinating group. They seem to have been able to adapt to things throughout their life, and they have been able to manage things efficiently. It appears that they have developed habits, protocols, and behavior that works for them and seems to be able to get them through their day-to-day activities. Two people that may know individuals in the above 30 group with ASD, their behaviors may look bizarre and at times seem to be non-purposeful but, to the individuals who have made it this far they seem to be doing well with most of the situations that normal life has brought them and they have adapted. Their socialization is minimal beyond those people that they have developed a relationship with over time. These would include first-degree relatives and possibly one female friend or one male friend but beyond that nothing else. They seem to avoid social interactions with anybody in the outside world and therefore their protocols: shopping, a type of errands needing to be run, are efficient and take a minimal amount of time and minimal contact with the outside world. They have problems talking with other people if they are stopped or if someone is trying to work with them therapeutically. These people

can be quite frustrating to talk to as it seems that they really don't want to communicate and they are looking forward to the end of the situation. They have reasonably good adaptive skills of changes to take place in their life, but when it comes to the socialization process, it has been pretty much eliminated down to those select few people.

As I've tried to explain to some extent in this article about the socialization or social issue when it comes to autistic spectrum disorder, there are a lot of factors involved with the success or failure of socialization and social skills adaption. Age is a significant factor, patients on the part of the caregivers, parents, teachers and anyone else involved with the individual is extremely important. The most important item is that the individual with autistic spectrum disorder is identified as having autistic spectrum disorder at a very early age and that steps are taken that help can be acquired to help this person to learn adaptive skills. At this point in history, the issue of autistic spectrum disorder is being identified more every day, and it takes a lot of patience, persistence and creative ideas to help them to identify their needs and what they can do to feel like they are more adapted to the social environment. It is also essential that parents take the time to work with their child and seek out help to get creative ideas to help them to help themselves, their child and work towards success in learning social and adaptive skills.

Social Relationships

Individuals with autistic spectrum disorder level I or level II, have specific limitations to some degree in their ability to form relationships. For the most part, the relationships revolve around immediate family members such as parents, brothers, and sisters, and to some extent grandparents. For the most part, this group of individuals is the whole world in the eyes of the individual. Going beyond these boundaries causes individuals with autism to become anxious and frustrated at times. It would seem that either they do not want to extend relationships outside of this group or they just do not know how or they are afraid to for fear of rejection or judgment. Regardless of the situation, there are possibilities for building relationships for individuals with autism. However, there needs to be some commonality. The commonality can be referred to as the key to individuals with autism building relationships.

By the time an autistic individual is in school, it seems they try to attempt to build relationships with other people, even though those relationships may be quite toxic in nature. It has been noted that any individual who pays any attention to an individual with autism will be considered the friend of that individual with autism in those early years. However, it has been noted, that certain individual will try to take advantage of the autistic, or they will pick on them and bully them. An individual with autism may take this attention as being something "good," but it is really quite toxic and possibly even harmful. It would seem, and after a while, that these people that the individual with autistic spectrum disorder calls their "friends" get tired of them. It seems that they are starting to do nothing more than cause them harm, such as pain, both physical and mental, and they seem to take this as a learning experience and become less trusting of anybody who pays attention to them. This type of encounter usually sets up a lifetime of a lot of mistrust and even bullying behavior towards others.

The question as it seems, is: "how do we help an individual with autistic spectrum disorder develop positive relationships?" It appears that the individual with autistic spectrum disorder to develop positive relationships with others. In the treatment plans at the back of the book will illustrate some of the items that parents can use as well as teachers and caregivers. This is not the only ways to help individuals

with autistic spectrum disorder develop positive social relationships, but it is a good start, and hopefully, the goal here is to help others to learn how to help individuals with autistic spectrum disorder develop good positive social relationships.

CHAPTER 11

Autistic Spectrum Disorders

The Autistic Perspective

The autistic perspective

The perspective of an individual with autism continues to be a topic that parents seem to have problems grasping as well as teachers and other people in society. It is noted through the continuous study on a case-by-case basis in the perspective of the person with autism seems to have some commonality as will be indicated in other parts of this document. The autistic individual is just looking for some understanding as well as respect, and sometimes it's hard for people who do not understand autism or the autistic mind, to give them enough of either one. What I will try to accomplish in this section is to talk about how the perspective of the autistic person needs to be understood by parents, educators and extended family members.

The average individual looks at things in the following format: A +B = C

This format has been taught to society for thousands of years and what it means very simply is this part plus this part equals this whole. This is the generalizing perspective, and this is the standard curriculum of learning as well as teaching. The individual with autism can learn to understand this over time if someone takes the time to explain it to them. However, what has been realized to some extent is that a person with autism does not think this way on a normal basis or with any regularity. They are willing to learn this but the educator, parent, extended family members or anyone else, need to learn how the person with autism thinks. To begin with, you cannot teach them this without understanding the way they see it. As noted, the way in which a learning perspective is taught, A+ B = C it has been discovered and realized on several occasions that the individual with autism usually sees things in the following perspective: C= B+A. I have approached most of my autistic individuals with this perspective, and they agree that this is the way they usually view things in the real world. This seems to translate out towards the whole equals the sum of the parts. If there is one thing that this reminds me of directly is an

old computer language called BASIC. The basic language seemed to have been written backward, and this is very similar to the autistic perspective of life especially in the level ones and twos. In explaining this perspective, parents do not quite get it right away, but you can see on the face of the autistic individual that they realize you finally realize how they see some things. This in and of itself is a therapeutic breakthrough because it does help the individual with autism to realize they are being understood and respected to some extent, and it also helps the parents to get a perspective of how the autistic individual thinks.

This type of thought process has been used in my clinic for several months now, and it seems to be able to bridge gaps between the autistic individual and at least the parents at this time. It appears that this is one way in which an autistic individual starts to realize that he has become understood and respected for who he is and especially in this case, the understanding of how thought process happens.

Along with using the Basic A (basica) program language from DOS in order to understand the thought process of the individual with autistic spectrum disorder, another tool has come into light that I have been using recently. This insight was brought about using an old model that dates back some 6000 years from ancient Mesopotamia. This model was taught to me back in 1984 by very well respected professor of education at Gannon University by the name of Dr. Paul K. Adams Ph.D. Dr. Adams stressed this in education because it was the basis for all education. (I had a very deep respected Dr. Adams. I am writing this in his memory for he has passed on at this time.) Dr. Adams taught about two aspects of education, and they were the following: the Trivium and the Quadrivium. The Trivium consists of the following subjects: grammar, rhetoric, and logic. The quadrivium consists of the following subjects: arithmetic, astrology, geometry, music. Although it has been over 30 years since I studied this, all of a sudden it came to mind in dealing with individuals with autistic spectrum disorder.

Individuals with autistic spectrum disorder, (level I and level II), have a dominant side of the brain and it seems to be somewhat related to the trivium and quadrivium.

The Trivium: rhetoric, logic, and grammar are related to the left side of the brain especially of a person who is left-brained dominant. An individual with autistic spectrum disorder can either be right brained or left brained dominant. It seems that the left-brained dominant individual with autistic spectrum disorder at both level I or level II can be quite verbal, and they do have some writing skills and can be very logical in their verbal explanations. In contrast, they seem to be somewhat less adept to the right brain functions such as in the Quadrivium: arithmetic, astronomy, geometry, music, but may have the ability to adapt and possibly build a bridge to at least have some skills in the right side of the brain. Their communication skills are extensive as they have lots of details and they are very verbally gifted. If you ask a left-brained dominant person a question, be prepared for a very long and detailed answer. They may distract easily as compared to the right-brained but, will have a hard time getting back on the task that you interrupted them from and they will not be satisfied in answering you or lecturing you till they are re-directed back to the task. This is where sometimes they are misdiagnosed with ADHD. The ASD individual may get distracted but whatever they are distracted by they will complete and return to what they were distracted from. In contrast, the ADHD person will be distracted and never complete anything without intervention because they will be distracted from their distraction and then on to the next distraction. Those with ASD may have some benefit from stimulus medication, but it may not be needed at a high dose unlike the ADHD person may need. But that is the topic of another article.

In contrast to the left-brained dominant person with autistic spectrum disorder, the individual that is dominant right brained with autistic spectrum disorder seems to be very good at mathematics: all math

which includes arithmetic and geometry, astronomy in regards to order and relationships between objects, and of course they have a very good ear for music. An individual with autistic spectrum disorder, right-brained dominant, has a way of expressing themselves in few words but mostly in symbols, mathematical expressions and also using rhythms like in music or grunts or growls. Most right-brained individuals of this nature have trouble writing more than a sentence and need remediation in order to master this skill. This can be accomplished but only if a program of writing skills remediation is done. Otherwise, this form of communication may continue to be problematic. The right-brained verbal presentation may also have some issues. One of the most unintelligent items that can be said to a right-brained individual is: "What are you doing?" when the individual is obviously doing a specific task, and they are fully focused on it. This will get a glare because it is obvious to the ASD person what they are doing and you should not ask such a dumb question. However, it takes an observant parent/caregiver/teacher/other to notice what is going on and not ask such a question. What I am inferring is simple: Pay close attention to what is going on and do not ask for an explanation of the obvious. Further, if you ask that obvious question, do not expect a response of more than a look or a grunt. If you persist, you are interrupting the focus, and you will see a meltdown followed by verbal confrontation. For the most part, Individuals with autistic spectrum disorder are not violent. There probably are some exceptions, however, what you will see is a combination of the following: loud verbal expletives followed by confrontational, in-your-face posturing. The wise person at this time will just back down and allow the person to de-escalate. If you are not a wise person and back down, be prepared for the unexpected. Remember this: if you start this and do not allow it to de-escalate, individuals with autistic spectrum disorder may overreact, and there can be a lot of avoidable consequences. Another caution is the following: do not triangulate other people into a conflict or a discussion or a disagreement in a one-on-one situation.

Individuals who will be triangulated in a confrontation cause a bigger problem and therefore the unexpected problems could happen. Try to understand what the person is actually trying to tell you and not assume you know what they are talking about. Individuals with autistic spectrum disorder do not always understand what you are trying to tell them and never assume they can understand what you are saying, especially if what you are telling them has many possible definitions. Do not expect them to know or understand what you are explaining. Just because you know, does not mean that they know what you are saying and the exact specifics of what you are trying to say. Be specific, no possibility of any other definition or meaning of what you are saying to them. Diffuse or general statements will lead to problems, consequences, and possible outbursts that could be avoided. At times, individuals with autistic spectrum disorder are very literal and cannot understand figurative language. Never assume they know what you are talking about, and never assume they understand what it is you're trying to say without some explanation of where the conversation should start and on a topic that you are not sure that the individual with autistic spectrum disorder understands. Keep your language simple. Old phraseologies, old terminologies, and innuendos do not register with the individual with autistic spectrum disorder. It may be that they have no clue about the wording you are using and therefore may not respond. If you persist with using old language, slang or innuendos, be prepared for a reaction at most or a blank stare at least. Mean what you say and say what you mean. No gaps or assumptions.

Individuals with autistic spectrum disorder do not understand emotion for the most part. They understand the following emotions to a point, but not necessarily the deeper meaning. They understand sadness when someone cries, but they identify the crying with sadness and not necessarily the emotion. They understand the anger with loud verbalizations followed by several words that they are not allowed to

use, but they understand the emotion by the outward signs of things that make their ears hurt, and also by the behaviors that are shown to them. An individual with autistic spectrum disorder displays the following behaviors: anxiety and frustration with some anger or nothing. For the most part, these are the emotions or emotional states that you will see an individual with autistic spectrum disorder display. It seems that due to their life experiences: being bullied, being yelled at and being told certain derogatory things, which they do not understand/display emotion, such as love, caring, kindness and following through on what they are supposed to follow through. These are adaptive skills that they need to learn and for the most part, can learn if a method to help them learn them is worked on, discovered and then used to the best of the individual's ability. I refer to this as finding the key. Each individual with autistic spectrum disorder has their own key that can help them move forward with their ability to achieve adaptive skills and therefore can function better in society. These adaptive skills need to be taught and then practiced. However, it takes a key to the individual that is of interest for them to start to practice and adopt these adaptive skills. Anyone who assumes they already understand certain positive emotions is wrong and be forewarned that they do not. These they have to learn, understand, and then they may assimilate them into their emotional construct.

Individuals with Autistic spectrum disorder just want a chance, but they need understanding and then guidance. Many just want to fit in the best they can, but they will be made fun of, bullied and taken advantage of. Parents have to be open-minded to techniques. They must be willing to understand, or the conflict in the home will escalate as the individual grows up. As they enter their school years, teenage years and early adulthood and into adulthood, they need help in learning the changes through those times. Remember, they do not learn by observation and yelling does not work.

Parents can have very unrealistic expectations of their individual with autistic spectrum disorder. It seems that these parents expect individuals with autism to pick up things the way they feel that they should pick up items such as tasks, common knowledge, and common sense and of course common practices. However, individuals with autistic spectrum disorder do not learn by observation, because they are usually in their own bubble and not paying attention because they feel what goes on around them may not be, or they are afraid of it. Individuals with autistic spectrum disorder are particular to their understanding of the spoken word. They know what they have been taught and what they have mastered, and that may be different from what the parent is actually expecting from them. There have been many examples whereby a parent has given a task to an individual with autistic spectrum disorder to do, and the task was not specific. The individual carried out the task to the best of their ability and knowledge, and the parent was displeased and started yelling at the individual calling them names and swearing at them. The individual did not understand why the parent became angered at them because they did what they were told to the best of their understanding. Parents need to be very specific and have the individual explain back to them what they have told them. This may take little extra time, but in the long run, the task will be completed to the best and most detailed result that could be achieved. However, if the explanation is not specific, and is in general terminology or slang, the individual with autistic spectrum disorder may look at them with a blank stare or may try to carry out the tasks the best of their ability and knowledge. A caution to parents is as follows: if you did not teach the task to your individual do not expect them to know what it is. A task that has been taught and has been mastered is very easy to be requested. However if you never taught the task, and expect them to perform the task to the greatest of your expectations, do not be surprised if something entirely different turns out altogether. Individuals with autistic spectrum disorder are very specific and very detailed. If you give

specific details, the task will be completed to the up most of their ability. This goes the same with teachers and other caregivers. If you are not specific, do not expect the task to be completed the way you expected it to be completed. All the autistic individual expects at this point is that you take time and explain to them exactly what you want them to do. It may be that you need to give it step-by-step and actually give it one-step at a time. When multi-step tasks are involved, give it one-step at a time. It has been known that if two tasks were assigned at the same time chances are neither one of them would be completed to the expectations of the parent. This happens because the individual cannot focus on the task because he has been given two of them and they may have trouble deciding which task is the more important.

The use of lists is a great idea. Have a parent take time and make up a list and go over the list with the individual. The task will be completed to the best of the individual's ability. In the use of lists, a parent has to explain their expectations and specifically the start with number one and work in the end. If a parent hands a list of the tasks to the individual, it is unknown what task will be completed if any, but at least one task will be completed, and that will be the task that the individual prefers most or has experience in.

Therefore, it is up to you the parent/teacher/caregiver to be very specific about your expectations of the individual with autistic spectrum disorder. If you are not specific, do not expect your expectations to be fulfilled but instead prepare to be disappointed. Do not, I repeat do not go off on the autistic individual with innuendos, cussing and swearing and screaming at them. This does not work as a type of disciplinary policy, and it may lead to an overall meltdown and possibly even long-term issues. Be specific and understanding and be prepared to teach a task from start to finish and work with the individual so they can master the task. Be understanding that your individual may not understand what you are saying. Ask them to repeat it back for you to understand what you just asked of them.

Communication issues are a huge problem in relationships between parents and children to start with, and when your individual has autism, it becomes even more of a challenge. However, that challenge can be overcome with some understanding, patience, and persistence. If you want your expectations to be fulfilled, take the time and explain. Never assume. The assumption is a fallacy. Individuals with autistic spectrum disorder become victims of that fallacy, and they usually bear the brunt of the consequences of the parent/teacher/caregivers lack understanding.

Up until this point we looked from the parent/teacher/caregivers viewpoint as to what their expectations and possible alternatives and of course consequences of expectations of an individual with autism. The following section will be presented from the perspective of the autistic individuals.

Individuals with autistic spectrum disorder need patience, and they need understanding. An issue that keeps coming up from the individual's perspective is "why are you yelling at me, and I don't understand." This seems to be quite common with parents who tend to yell a lot. All the individual wants to know is why you are yelling at them. They may not be sure about what they have just done but your yelling at them, cursing and swearing and calling them names, is not helping the situation. The individual is only a few moments from having a meltdown. What individuals usually do that are getting yelled at is they will stand there and listen for a few minutes and then they will put their hands over their ears. This is common, but it is not always done, but this is a sign that the parent should stop yelling. Another sign is a blank stare, possibly clenching of fists and of course, the serious facial distortion that comes from clenching one's teeth or whole body tension and stress. What the individual is trying to relate the parent is stop yelling at me, I do not understand why you are yelling at me, would you stop yelling at me, tell me what I did wrong. However, the parent is pulling a significant mistake at this time, and it

is a pretty good chance that a meltdown will occur. All the individual wants you to do is stop yelling at them, talk to them in a normal tone of voice or distract them away from the problem. Standing toe-to-toe and screaming at the individual with autism is not playing the parent role. The individual understands this, and since the playing field has now been leveled, they now have won. This may not be what they want, however, the parent has given them this level and normally a meltdown or conflict is about to happen. The individual wants to understand what they did wrong, and they want the parent to stop yelling.

Another issue that keeps coming up is the following: "why do you treat me like I'm stupid." Autistic individuals are very perceptive when they are being treated like they are dumb or stupid. Their reaction can be in a wide range of behaviors such as silence, a meltdown, or a remark that the parent may take in a very negative connotation. This is one of those situations where parents need to try to understand what is being said rather than to react to the tone or the wording. The individual just wants to be understood and does not want to be treated like they're stupid and they will let you know when they are offended. Some parents, caregivers, teachers use very negative words in this case such as idiot, retard, stupid and a whole host of others that have no purpose other than someone trying to dominate an individual with autistic spectrum disorder. Individuals just want to be respected. They are not dumb, they are not stupid, and they are not intellectually disabled. (This is the level I and II in ASD). Their IQs may range from borderline all the way up into the genius range, and they have intelligence and the ability to learn. They are very insulted by people who throw such negative innuendos at them especially if they are the parents. What the individual wants is to be recognized as a human being and recognized for their strengths and weaknesses. What they also need is someone to recognize their strength and help them to cultivate that strength in their life's work. The reason why people

disrespect them is that they have some problems with skills that everyone feels they should know. However, individuals will do some interesting things out of curiosity for the simple reason of seeing if it works or not. This is a sign of intelligence and not a sign of stupidity. However, parents see it as malicious mischief. Parents need to step back and take a look and ask questions rather than render judgment to the outcome of what had happened. For example, there was a specific scientific experiment that was performed, and the outcome resulted in a minor problem. It was noted that the supervising individual became angry with the autistic individual about what they had done. However, another adult sat down with the individual, went over what they did, asked them what they learned and explained to them a better way to do it. As illustrated, this became a learning experience rather than someone being demeaned for trying something new.

In a generic sense, the following has been noted: "you can't do this, you can't do that, and there are other things that you can't do." This overgeneralization by parents tends to limit the possible learning potential for an individual with autism. In the parent's mind, they believe that their individual cannot learn any of the items that the individual thinks they might be able to try. This demeans the individual, and they start to become angry and frustrated and may even have an outburst or meltdown. However, under the right circumstances, and with someone who is patient and understands how to work with people with autism, some of those ideas/tasks/aspirations may be possible. Individuals with autism can become depressed from the negative comments from parents, teachers, and caregivers. My warning to all those is straightforward: don't judge the individual by what you know they can and can't do but instead, get help from someone who works well with individuals with autism to help them find what their limits and restriction should be. Do not prejudge an individual with autism and tell them they cannot do something that they are thinking about. Instead, work with them on the idea and get

someone else to help you with that achievement of having them achieve some goals.

Another negative comment that has been thrown at individuals with autism is as follows: "you are an embarrassment to me because you do not know how to act in public." Individuals with autistic spectrum disorder can become overstimulated by many things in an environment. Putting them into an over stimulating environment may cause many different behaviors and adverse outcomes. If someone works with an individual with autistic spectrum disorder, they can help them overcome their problems in public. However, the problems need to be recognized and then worked with over a period of time and under special conditions that need to be planned out. The bottom line to this is straightforward; do not take an individual with autistic spectrum disorder into Walmart unless they have been there before when it was either less busy or less noisy. In addition, be there close to them to be supportive and to watch them for some of their possible behaviors. Putting an individual into an over stimulating environment may, of course, overstimulate his senses and he may lose control. Each individual with autistic spectrum disorder may have a sensitivity to any one of the five senses or a combination of them. It is has been shown, that with practice and supportive supervision an individual with autistic spectrum disorder will eventually be able to go into a busy, noisy place like a Walmart and complete the tasks in which they came there to do. This has been noted, and it has been achieved.

Social skills are something that needs to be taught (see autistic spectrum disorder-social skills chapter). Individuals with autism tend to be cautious when they are outside their familiar area, safe zone, bubble, home or familiar place. When they are out in public, they are usually reacting to the anxiety they feel of being in a place they are unfamiliar with or the overstimulation from the environment. With practice, these issues can be overcome. This is what is referred to as adaptive skills, and this is a topic for another chapter. Autistic

individuals can learn how to behave in public and how to ignore some of the overstimulation in their environment when they go out in public.

One of the major complaints that individuals with autistic spectrum disorder have expressed to me has to do with being abused. Individuals are only looking for an even break. They are not always looking for something extra unless it is help, encouragement or training. However, this expectation of being treated fairly does not happen. Individuals with autistic spectrum disorder can perceive when they are being singled out, criticized and of course maltreated in the home, school and in the public environment. They do not tend to fight back, yell and scream or necessarily become physical. However, if the emotional abuse continues over time, the individual will start to develop a form of posttraumatic stress disorder along with a separate kind of anxiety. They will begin to limit themselves to what they may and may not do, and you may find them alone a lot of the times engaged on the computer or video console. It seems that in that world of the computer or video console they find solace, equality, and peace. It is also a good sign for parents to do some intervention and try to help the individual understand that maybe you are not abusing them, but you may be trying to teach them something, and then you have to alter your ways of teaching what you are trying to teach them. Constant explanations do not work. Concrete examples that are brief may work much better than long drawn out explanations and lectures.

The physical abuse issue has been mentioned to some degree and can become quite dramatic to the autistic individual. Some individuals report that they tend to get loud in their explanations, which then may cause someone else in the environment to intervene in a very physical manner, which was unnecessary. This may lead to a struggle, hospitalization or even the possibility of arrest. If an autistic individual is stating their mind and they get loud all the person that they are talking to has to do is ask him to tone it down just a little bit. That usually resolves the situation. However, they may start to get loud

again but just ask them to tone it down. In certain situations, a third-party was observing this interaction and decided they needed to restrain the autistic individual. This led to several consequences along with the individual going into fight or flight mode and other consequences followed. All these consequences could have been prevented if the third party stayed out of the interaction. These types of events happen quite frequently when interventions by individuals who do not know anything about autism intervene in an interaction with an individual that has autism. An individual with autism tend to become sensitized, bitter and tends to start to hold in the negative emotions that they know so well: anger, frustration, depression, and anxiety. Individuals with autism are very intelligent and talking them down or using that key will de-escalate the situation. Simply getting their attention and talking to them works better than restraining and possible physical altercations and other consequences and issues.

Another abuse issue is a parent's assumption that their individual does not have any potential for growth or room for development or the ability to acquire adaptive skills. The parent tends to demean the individual by treating them like an infant, and individuals who have learned adaptive skills become very distrusting of those people who treat them like they don't know anything. Individuals in the ASD level I and II have talent, and it should never be assumed that they can't use that talent to learn new skills, education or any significant tasks. It is always possible that they will achieve something that the parent/teacher/caregiver would never comprehend that they could learn, master and then execute. Autistic individuals want a chance to learn adaptive skills and to try to fit in.

Another abuse issue comes from people and the environment. Individuals with autism do not always discriminate well when it comes to individuals who approached them and try to be their friends. Individuals have been taken advantage of monetarily and other ways by someone who has said all the right things and paid them attention.

The individual is used, abused and taken advantage of. Adaptive skills try to teach the individual to discriminate between someone who is really a friend and someone who acts like a friend who just wants to be their friend because you have something they want. This is an adaptive skill that needs to be taught because the individual with autism will be abused to some extent if they don't learn who the real friends are and who are the designing persons are.

From the Autistic point of view and expectations comes the following argument. How am I supposed to know what you know? Did you teach me? Was I supposed to learn from observation? You know I do not learn from observation unless it is pointed out to me and I am instructed on why I need to learn that. Do not yell at me, and you are only hurting my ears. I took care of my mess, why do I have to take care of others messes?

From the autistic perspective, the following dialogue seems to be quite common but it is relevant. How is it that I'm supposed to know what you know if you don't tell me what it is that I'm supposed to know that you think I should know. Why is it that you yell at me because I do not know what you know because I cannot think about what you thought because I do not know what you are thinking. Why is it that I am supposed to know something that I do not know that nobody ever taught me, but now being blamed for something I did or did not do because it should be something I should know that I do not know? Although this dialogue seems to be quite back and forth, it seems to be what is going on in the eyes of the individual with autism. Individuals have a tendency not to learn from experience unless it is pointed out to them the necessity of why they should learn that. Individuals who feel that people with autism should have common sense should think again. Common sense is not necessarily known to individuals with autism but instead needs to be taught and mastered before they can understand the necessity of knowing what it is they should know. Although this all seems to be quite scattered to the

average individual, the individual with autistic spectrum disorder, this is its own type of order. The bottom line is straightforward: if you did not take time to teach your individual what it is you want them to know they will not know it. They will not know what money is unless you sit down with them and go over what the coins are and what they mean, and how many coins to make a dollar and what is on the bills. These things are not crucial to an individual with autistic spectrum disorder until they are explained to them in such a way that they will assimilate the information. This is much like adding a program to your computer. For simplicity sake, working with autistic individuals in the first and second level, this seems to work well because they all seem to have some computer training and therefore there is a basis for a relationship here. If you are an old-school parent who has no understanding of computers or electronic devices, get help as soon as possible because you are going to make the situation worse. No matter how much you yell, how much you scream, how much you threaten you will get nowhere. However, if you start to understand that individuals with autism have an excellent understanding of electronics, you, therefore, can build that bridge and begin to learn what it is they do not know and help them to acquire that knowledge and fill in the deficit.

I mentioned earlier that individuals autistic spectrum disorder have an excellent ear for music. It seems that those that are left-brained dominant both in the level I and level II tend to be very acute to the words and specific types of rhythms in a song and can memorize them rather quickly. If they hear the song again and if it is not played correctly they will tell you exactly what is out of order. The right-brained dominant individual is attuned more to the rhythms and mechanics of music. They can tell when a note or a specific item is not in the right place, and they tend to be able to put together music quite easily because they understand its mechanics. These individuals are genuinely gifted and if they do show any passion towards music, parents, teachers, caregivers and anyone else, please, help them to either achieve this passion or help them to move onto something else. They are very gifted and deserve a chance at achieving their musical goals.

Adaptive Skills

Although I was going to reserve this for another article, I believe this fits quite well and should be mentioned at this time. I believe that the understanding of adaptive skills should be part of this chapter because of its usefulness in helping with the expectations of the autistic individual.

What is an adaptive skill? How can they be taught? How can they be identified? What is the importance of an adaptive skill? These questions will each be taken in turn, and hopefully, there will be an understanding of what it takes to teach someone with autism an adaptive skill.

An adaptive skill is any skill that is a necessity for a human being to know to survive in the world. Although this is a very generic definition, it has to be to be understood. Adaptive skills are unique to the survival of a human being in the world. Each human being learns adaptive skills through observation, through reading, and through contact with the outside world. However, Autistic people may not have picked up any of these adaptive skills in these ways. Adaptive skills can be as simple as taking a shower, brushing your teeth, changing your clothes, counting money, and understanding right from wrong. Although this seems to be quite simple, individuals with autism do not always pick these up by observation, by being yelled at or by being instructed by a teacher/caregiver/parent. These skills need to be put together in a functional protocol for an individual with autism to follow them. In other words, someone has to sit down with them, introduce these specific adaptive skills, help them to master those particular adaptive skills and then they may become part of the individual's protocol of life. However, this is all going to take work and effort on the part of someone who is willing to work with the autistic individual to help them to put this together in a protocol that works for the individual. In some cases, the use of electronic devices has been highly instrumental in helping the individual with autistic spectrum disorder to put adaptive skills into their life. Sometimes the use of alarms, smartphones, tablets and other handheld devices have been instrumental in reminding individuals with autism that there is something they are supposed to be doing at a specific time. In some cases, the electronics have become a very instrumental tool to help adaptive skills to become part of the autistic individual's life.

The next question was how adaptive skills are taught followed by the next question how are they identified. Although these two questions are reversed, they are both related. First off one must know what the problem is before one can come up with a game plan to fix it. Over the course of therapeutic interventions, lack of adaptive skills can become quite prevalent especially in problem-solving. Some of the simpler skills that have not been adopted are usually evident such as not showering, not changing their clothes, not brushing their teeth and not combing their hair. However, some of the more intricate adaptive skills that are lacking come from the parent, the school or another caregiver. Over the course of therapy, other adaptive skills that need to be taught will be identified through observation and interaction by the therapist, or the individual with autistic spectrum disorder will ask a precise question about how they can achieve something very specific that involves learning specific adaptive skills. Either way, the list of adaptive skills that may be needed to be taught will be presented through those means. The next step is how you teach the individual the adaptive skills they are looking for; they need or are requested by the school, parent or caregiver.

It is important to take excellent notes when it comes to the deficits that need to be worked on. The individual working with the autistic individual has to have an excellent rapport with them before they start working on the adaptive skills. Without this good rapport and trust, the individual will become frustrated and probably will stop the therapeutic interventions. But a good therapist will take the time and explain to the person why they need to know what it is they need to know to learn this adaptive skill and then to use it. Adaptive skills are specific to each individual because each individual's needs are different and the abilities that they have adapted to over the course of their life may not be working for them, and this is why the intervention of the adaptive skill is needed. This is especially required for the transitional period between childhood and teenage years and teenage years and adult years. As the demand of society changes during these times and expectations towards the individual changes during these times due to age as a defining factor by society, so does the adaptive skills need to become more complex and consistent. One can start to look at these as survival skills to a much higher level than just surviving. This type of survival skills is learning specific abilities to compete in the real world for things such as further education and employment. The successful ability to teach these adaptive skills helps the autistic individual to achieve higher levels and success rates in their life that would be expected if they do not learn these skills. Each autistic individual has qualities, talents, and ability, and for them to learn adaptive skills will help them to achieve the highest level of their ability.

In summation of adaptive skills, the autistic individual can learn to adapt to those things that he should know that he does not know and then master those things to use them for survival skills in the world. It also can help the individual with autistic spectrum disorder to achieve the highest level of their ability. It seems that the expectations of the autistic individual to know what other people know can only be a

fallacy, for the individual with autistic spectrum disorder learns differently, assimilates information differently and then decides what is important to them and what is not. With the teaching of adaptive skills, they may learn that something they did not feel was important is important and learn to master that skill. Therefore, expectations should be kept at a moderate level, but with the intervention and teaching of adaptive skills, expectations can be more promising for the autistic individual to learn how to adapt, survive and thrive in the world around them. This does take a lot of work but, when an autistic individual reaches a level of achievement that no one thought they could ever achieve, they have shown the world that they can adapt, thrive, and be part of society and not be considered someone that needs to be medicated and warehouse.

The Key

This was another topic I was going to save for a separate chapter; however, it is also instrumental that it fits in with expectations and adaptive skills. The key is the way to achieve those expectations and to learn the adaptive skills.

What is the key? How do we find it? How do we use it? What is it good for? The questions are very valid about what the "the key" is, so is its use and ultimately its value in the intervention process for the individual. As anyone who has ever worked with a lock, the essential part of the use of the lock is the key. As a metal key will open a metal lock so will the key work to open and redirect the individual with autistic spectrum disorder. The key is an essential part of working with individuals with autistic spectrum disorder, and it is the one thing that can help them to refocus from the focus that is currently the point of over focus. The key is unique to each and every individual with autistic spectrum disorder. The key may be any of the following and then possibly even something else: a preferred task, a preferred toy, a preferred gain. It is something they like very much which could be: food, clothing, a video game. The key will get their attention away from what they are currently talking about and what they are over-focused about. This is why the key is essential because when an individual with autistic spectrum disorder is over-focused; their entire focus such as their speech and attention is directed only at that item. It seems no matter what anyone else says they are either not listening or not paying attention because they are focused on that one item on which they are focused on. The key will get them defocused from that over focus, and then you have their attention and can work with them on something else, but they do not always use it. This is one of those issues whereby the parents may already have the key, but either doesn't understand that they have it or refuse to use it. They are around the individual the most, and they should have a possible list of keys that may help distract the person away from the over focus. This is especially useful if the individual is frustrated, angry or in the middle of the meltdown. The key can stop the negative behaviors from escalating. Any individual will have fewer problems as they become refocused on the item more pleasurable or interesting. This is why a good therapist will talk to the parents about how they have tried to intervene before possible meltdowns. Some parents do not pay attention to what the key could be, but they may have a list of things in which their individual likes very specifically. In therapy, the therapist can use the key to get the individual to refocus away from whatever their over focus is at the moment when the session starts. This is one way to make good progress and help the person to realize there are so many other things they need to learn such as adaptive skills, goals, and expectations. This is why the key is an essential part of learning adaptive skills and fulfilling expectations such as future goals and possible long-range objectives. Sometimes the key can be found just through normal conversation with individuals with autistic spectrum disorder. They may tell you about something they like or something they want to do. These things can become keys especially

to prevent frustration, anger and a meltdown. The key can prevent meltdowns; the key may deter the frustration from becoming anger or the anger from becoming a meltdown. However, it must be employed before the exacerbation of whatever topic the individuals are being overly focused on and is having an emotional reaction to that thought. This is why the key is useful to parents, teachers, caregivers and of course in the future possibly, employers and other individuals that may be significant to the autistic individual. The key can be used as a device to prevent behavioral outbursts but also as an item to work with an autistic individual to learn adaptive skills. It can be that an adaptive skill can become a key over time. This does take a lot of work and a lot of effort, but the outcome goal of working with an individual who has specific deficits in their behaviors and rational thought processes is quite successful. Helping an individual with autistic spectrum disorder to learn how to use his own keys for himself is the final goal. It is to get them to think about something else or to remove themselves from the situation and give themselves a timeout to avoid possible conflict and legal problems. This should be the goal of any therapist who works with individuals with autistic spectrum disorder. ASD individuals can learn these abilities such as their own keys, adaptive skills and to work on the expectations that the world has of them. However, this takes a dedicated professional who is willing to invest the time because it is not going to be an easy road. There will be setbacks, but there will be progress if the therapist is dedicated to helping people with autistic spectrum disorder.

Parents, teachers, and caregivers also have to be dedicated to helping the autistic individual to reach the highest level of their abilities. These endeavors will not be easy, however, for an individual with autistic spectrum disorder to achieve levels of academic performance, independence and some degree of normal living is the most important hope that could happen. It is a great achievement to help someone with autistic spectrum disorder to achieve their goals and to attain a

level of independence and satisfaction. People with autistic spectrum disorder have a lot to offer the world around them but only if society is willing to work with them to help them develop their talents and allow them to be a productive part of society. People with autistic spectrum disorder just want a chance to discover and achieve their goals, and it is only with the dedication of family, teachers, and other caregivers can this be possible. This is not an impossible task but is one it takes a lot of work and dedication. So go the extra mile, take the extra step but give the individual with autistic spectrum disorder chance and you will be surprised what they can achieve.

CHAPTER 12

Autistic Spectrum Disorders

What's It like to Have Autism?

Autistic spectrum disorder-What's It like to Have Autism?

I continuously feel misunderstood, all my actions seem to be misunderstood, and sometimes I feel so all alone even though I am in the company of family, friends, and others. Why do they look at me the way they do? Why do they point at me and laugh? Why do they insult me when I have the answer, and they do not? Why don't they ask me the right question because I have the correct answer? What else do they really want from me? What is it they expect of me that I am not doing to the best of their expectations? What is it that I should know that they expect me to know that I should be able to do without any knowledge of whether or not it is what they expect of me? Why do they interrupt me what I am busy doing other things that are more important than what it is they are interrupting me about? Why is it that when I am busy doing something, that I have to get done and I am interrupted by some minor detail that has no bearing on what I am currently trying to accomplish? Why is it that everyone treats me as if I am weird when I am as normal as they are that I see things differently than they do? I answered the request to the best of my ability why is it I am still getting yelled at? I am being yelled at for an unknown reason, and it's starting to hurt my ears, and they will not stop, and I'm on the verge of losing it due to the pain in my ears and the fact that this conversation is going nowhere, what are they expecting from me?

These are many of the questions which go through a person with autistic spectrum disorders head when they are interacting with other people. It seems that no one really pays attention to them and after a while, they continue to ask these questions which are not answered by anyone who is currently in their surrounding area. It is no wonder they always feel alone, and no one can relate to them. The result of this lack of understanding usually ends up in one of the two following outcomes: 1) a total meltdown which includes what looks like a

temper tantrum and of course some verbalization may not be understood as relevant to the current problem that is relevant to the temper tantrum/meltdown that has occurred. 2) Silence followed by a withdrawal to some other area which usually then results in a silence whereby the autistic individual will most likely withdraw to some electronic device whereby trying to refocus and forget the previous interaction. It is interesting how people with autism view the world and question what is going on around them. However, the tragedy begins when no one takes the time to try and understand the way they see the world around them and try and understand why it is the way they see it that way. Individuals with autistic spectrum disorder are not looking for your pity, your mercy or your sympathy; they only want to be respected for their abilities and understood the way they try to fit in. In other words, there just looking for an opportunity to fit in, make a living and have a life. The only way they can do that is if they are treated with some respect and not demeaned for their abilities and given an opportunity in which they can grow in whatever field that has been identified as their most significant strength and passion. Without the identification of where they are on the spectrum, there have been some who have been overmedicated to the point where they no longer have the ability to achieve the goals they once had. This is not only a tragedy it is also criminal, but we cannot restore what has been lost but what I have done is to help them find another way to continue in another direction. I have seen this abuse, this over medication and the lack of understanding and at times, it causes me to be very angry with the caretakers. It seems that they want things to be easy; however, working with someone with autistic spectrum disorder is not easy. It requires commitment on the parts of the caregiver to understand the individual, guide the individual and of course help others to understand the individual. Over the course of history, there has been a lot of abuse towards individuals with autistic spectrum disorder. There's been an overuse of medication due to the issue that no one has tried to understand the behaviors or what motivates the behaviors or

understand what it is that frustrates them and then triggers the meltdowns. Many statements I have heard that have caused me some form of anger towards the caregivers/parents and teachers will be illustrated in the following paragraphs. Please note carefully what the statements are and how they indicate illogical, irrational and incomplete thinking. Fallacies are quite common when dealing with individuals with ASD and it would be a start to learn to re-think those fallacies as they are illustrated in the following paragraphs. Parents/caregivers/teachers also make assumptions that are comparative to some other time in history or in their personal past, that worked somewhat then, but it is NOT APPLICABLE NOW.

<u>He should know</u>

This irrational statement and significant fallacy seem to be the hallmark of the unreasonable expectations of parents towards their child who has autism. As I picked this statement apart, please note that any parent is saying this is in for an argument with me and I will probably anger them because I will make them feel stupid.

Much of the social, emotional, and everyday day habits are assumed to be picked up through the observation of those behaviors. Individuals with autism do not pick up those behaviors because they are either: 1) distracted by some internal or external distraction, 2) they observe the behavior, do not understand it, feel it is illogical and disregarded or 3) it was noticed and felt to be insignificant and therefore not assimilated.

Individuals with autistic spectrum disorder may be thinking about many things at any given time. It is estimated that they think of anywhere between two and six different items at any given time, but they also may be distracted by any external stimulus as well. The internal thought process is a continuation that seems to be anywhere between problem-solving, entertainment, and these thoughts continue until one is focused upon and is worked on for a period of time. But, at

any time they can be possibly distracted by some external stimulus. That stimulus for the most part, on average, is noise. Most people are distracted by loud bangs, however; a person with autistic spectrum disorder may hear a sound that may not be detectable by the average person. This includes but not limited to: buzzing of lights, music, and bodily function noise and of course speech patterns. Other external stimuli that may cause them to be distracted are certain tactile senses such as: scratchy, soft, and hard and of course temperature. Other external stimuli that cause them to be distracted are different smells in the air, different consistencies in light and color. To a lesser degree, taste and texture can be a distraction. When it comes to speech around them, they may clue in on specific word patterns or phrases and be distracted by that. However, the bigger question is, how can you expect them to know what you feel they should know when there is no way they would have picked it up in their environment. Unless someone actually sat down and taught them and then practiced it and had them demonstrate those things that the parent/caregiver/teacher believes they should know. It is troubling to me when I talk to these people: parents/teachers/caregivers that assume that an individual with autistic spectrum disorder will pick up every day social skills, social practices and social etiquette from the environment without them taking time to teach them those skills that they feel they should know. I get incredibly frustrated with those individuals when I asked them the following question: "how is he supposed to know that if you don't teach him"? The look I usually get is one of anger followed by this statement: "well he should've learned." Once again, I find myself working with an individual with autistic spectrum disorder that is internally and possibly externally overstimulated at any given time and I have to teach them the social skills and how to focus. The idea I am trying to push at this time is that parents have to be patient because their individual with autistic spectrum disorder is not necessarily going to pick up any type of social cues or social skills from the environment. Skills have to be

taught and practiced and then have them demonstrate. This takes a lot of work and a lot of time, but it can be done successfully because individuals with autistic spectrum disorder can learn social skills, social etiquette and social cues in the environment. Level I and level II's want to understand what it is they should know that they have not picked up in the social environment and learn to live a productive social life. However, without the extra time, it takes for them to assimilate these practices they will not be successful. They have good logical sense and if instruction and if it is logically presented to them, they will pick it up easily. Statements I would like people to stay away from when addressing individuals with autistic spectrum disorder are as follows: "because I said so because I'm older than you are, because I'm your parent, because...". These statements make absolutely no sense to an individual with autistic spectrum disorder. If anything that you are doing is scaring them, and the next result will be a meltdown. An individual with autistic spectrum disorder wants to be treated like a person and not be treated any less.

In conclusion, this section never assumes that they should know because you do not know what they know and they do not know what you think they should know. Start at the beginning would be the best course of action because then you will know what they know and you can build from there. <u>Never assume</u> they know what you feel they should know because I would bet that they do not know what you think they should know.

<u>He is (X) number of years old he should know/understand this</u>

This is one of the most interesting statements that have ever been uttered this century. This is a common phrase from the 20th century, and it was not only illogical/irrational and just plain assumptive in its thought process, but it illustrates expectations that may or may not be achievable. When dealing with an individual with autistic spectrum disorder, expectations have to be kept practical in all senses. The

assumption that an autistic person is going to pick up things from their environment is illogical and irrational. This statement was quite popular in the 20th century and in some cases did make sense, but overall some expectations had no basis in logic or reason. In some cases, a person was expected to have achieved specific goals or behaviors by a particular age. To this day I have not found were that scale of age to meet expectations, is written. This century expectations for some reason continues to be illogical due to the inability of people to quote-unquote grow up. In the past, we had individuals to look up to and then set our sights on those goals. However, individuals with autistic spectrum disorder do not always have someone to look up to. It seems that there are a lot of expectations on the part of the parents for them to grow up with so-called normative behavior patterns and goal expectations and achievements by specific ages. As I stated earlier, I have never found this written scale of: reach this stage-achieve this goal. However, people seem to think one exists. I have never found this, and I believe that somewhere in past centuries this was all in the mind and goals of some type of parenting that pushed their child to achieve by specific ages. No matter where this had come from, it does not apply to individuals with autistic spectrum disorder. As I stated in the previous section individuals with autistic spectrum disorder, do not learn from the social environment or from observation. They need to be taught directly, explicitly and precisely what it is that they do not know that they may need to know and that they may use in the future. This must be done in logical steps and explanations, or this is never going to work. Setting an age standard and goal achievement list does not work for an individual with autistic spectrum disorder.

Maturity comes from experiences from the outside world as well as the home setting and of course school. However to pick up these behaviors and skills an individual must be paying attention. However, as stated in the previous section, an individual with autistic spectrum

disorder may observe these things but may dismiss them as some oddity or rarity or something that has no logical sense. This may also be said that they do not pick up on, what is called, normal social cues. They may not hear the entire conversation as they may have cut it off because it did not interest them or they felt that they should not get involved. Therefore, this being said it takes longer for an individual with autistic spectrum disorder to grow up to what someone would consider some standard adult behavior. It does not matter the age of an individual with autistic spectrum disorder, and they still may have deficits in their social skills, social etiquette, and social interaction ability. If they were not taught those skills or if they did not pick them up somehow, they do not know them. It is totally illogical and irrational for a parent/teacher/caregiver to assume that an individual that reaches a certain age or milestone should know what they know and assume that the individual with autistic spectrum disorder has picked up the skills, behaviors, and habits from the environment around them. It should be stated very simply that if they were not taught how to do certain things and given reasons why they are important, they do not know them no matter what age they are. From the standpoint of the autistic spectrum disorder individual, they look upon people who assume that they should know things by a certain age as abusing them. For all practical purposes, they are being abused by individuals who believe that by a certain age they should know certain things and be able to do certain things because some unwritten agenda that they believe is true. This should not be compared and contrasted to an individual with autistic spectrum disorder at any given age. It should also be noted that even though a person with autistic spectrum disorder has reached a certain age (chronologically), it does not mean that physiologically or psychologically, emotionally or responsibility wise, they have matured to that certain age or understand what the expectations of society are for an individual who reaches that age. Never assume that an individual with autistic spectrum disorder, when they reach the age of

21, know what the responsibilities and privileges are of someone who is 21 years of age. Chances are they had not thought about what the privileges and responsibilities are of an individual who reaches the age of 21. This is to be said because who is taking the time to explain to them and teach them about all the responsibilities and privileges when an individual reaches the age of 21? Even so, who is taking the time and responsibility to teach someone with autistic spectrum disorder as they reached the age of 18 what their responsibilities and privileges are? In addition, so goes it, on and on, with each passing decade and "so-called" responsibilities, privileges and obligations. If someone has not taken the time and explained these things to them, taught them and worked with them on; obligations and needs that need to be understood and followed through on, how is it at that age, they should know? The last thing an individual with autistic spectrum disorder needs to hear from a parent/caregiver/teacher is you are X number years old, and you should know this by now. Once again, I challenged back to the parent/teacher/caregiver about this expectation and asked them: who would have taught them this obligation, privilege, responsibility by this time in their life? It seems that the parent/teacher/caregivers do not get this, individuals with autistic spectrum disorder do not learn by specific age levels or by specific obligations, responsibilities, and privileges. Sometimes they do not understand what obligations are or what is expected of them or understand that by a certain age they should have achieved a certain level of something. It does not make any sense to them especially the expectations that have been set upon them by their parent/teacher/caregiver. This is where the counselor comes into play where he has to work with an individual on social skills, social etiquette, obligations, responsibilities and what privileges are. It seems that if there were a special curriculum in the school system for individuals with autistic spectrum disorder, it would help them to learn these items and there would be smoother transitions into adulthood. However, at this time we do not have this in any school system.

Individuals with autistic spectrum disorder that reach certain age milestones have to learn what is expected of them through an outside source that understands what it's like to not understand what is expected of them from the individuals who expect things from them that have not taught them. If this sounds like a lot of doublespeak that is because in the mind of the autistic individual this is what he is hearing. In addition, the question that is asked from the individual is "why is it they expect this from me when I don't know what it is that I am supposed to know that they expect me to know that I'm supposed to do that I don't know how to do and successfully do it to their expectations?" I believe this is a very valid question and it seems that counseling is the only way to help them to work through this. As a counselor, I will always do my best to help the individual with autistic spectrum disorder to try to learn what it is that they do not know and help them to use what it is they learned and then help them practice it in order to use it in an environment where these things are expected of them. Sometimes this can be a very daunting task and individuals with autistic spectrum disorder that have been rebuked by society because they don't fit the social standards and measures have a tendency to be very resistive to learning these behaviors that are needed for their survival in society. However, there is always hope, and with determination on the part of the counselor, individuals with autistic spectrum disorder may be very successful. Nevertheless, no time limit or time frame should ever be put on an individual with autistic spectrum disorder can learn and they will grow at a pace in which they are comfortable in and not to some scale of age to expectations and achievements timeline that is in people's minds.

In conclusion, in this chapter, it should be noted that age should never be a factor or never be a measurement of what a person should be able to achieve or how they should behave. Especially, individuals with autistic spectrum disorder that have their own timeline and time frame. This is going to take work on the part of those who are the

caregivers/teachers/parents. It is not going to be easy, but if the time is invested in this, there can be some very successful outcomes.

He should be looking for....

This thought process comes directly from the parent's perspective of the parent's thoughts. The parents, what they believe, what they assume, that their individual with autistic spectrum disorder should know. This illustrates once again how the parent continues to look for what they what to see that they believe that their individual with autistic spectrum disorder should know. It is a fallacy because the parent is not paying attention to what the individual is doing. The parent is trying to infuse their own thought processes into the assumption that the autistic person should be looking for what they believe they should be looking for. This fallacy is quite common, as it seems that individuals who have achieved something in their life think that their individual with autistic spectrum disorder should also be looking the same way, at the same things that they look at and understand them the way they understand them. However, this faulty thought process and fallacy of thought seems to frustrate the individual with autistic spectrum disorder because they have no clue what the parent has been through and what they know. Therefore how can they look for what they are assumed to be looking for when all these explanations and thoughts of the parent are not explained to the individual with autistic spectrum disorder. It is a mystery how parents are always in denial with the severity or the lack of learning process or adaptive skills that their individual with autistic spectrum disorder does not have. It seems that they assume that the individual with autistic spectrum disorder has the same wants, goals, dreams, and desires that the parent does. However, the individual with autistic spectrum disorder may not have picked up on any of what the parents' thoughts were because of the lack of communication. (the Previous chapter on "autistic spectrum disorder-communication issues," this chapter can be found on the following website:

www.drpaulbensurjrphdlpc). Along with the fallacy of thought process, the assumptions are also prevalent in the mind of the parent when it comes to their individual with autistic spectrum disorder. When it comes to dealing with the real world, individuals with autistic spectrum disorder, have problems sometimes in understanding the way the world works, and with this assumption of "he should be looking for...", The parent assumes that the individual with autistic spectrum disorder has a clue on how to achieve what it is the parent thinks they should be achieved when they have no clue how to start. If the parent does not intervene and try to help the person with autistic spectrum disorder to try to understand how things in the world work, there will be issues and connnsequences. This assumption becomes nothing more than a grandiose idealism, which will end up in the following problems: the parent will become completely angry and start to push away from their individual, and the individual will display signs of frustration, followed by anger and possibly even anxiety, depression, and maybe a meltdown. Take the time to understand where your individual with autistic spectrum disorder is before you start making assumptions about what they can do and what they should be looking for in life. Never assume that your individual with autistic spectrum disorder understands, or has the same thought processes that you have.

He should be more social.....

From the parent perspective, they feel that their individual with autistic spectrum disorder should be a more social person who should have no problems in public or in dealing with other people in general. This is incredibly far from the truth. Individuals with autistic spectrum disorder have social skills problems for several reasons, such as 1) they do not pick up on social cues from the environment as social skills from the environment may not interest them, may not get their attention, or they may see them as insignificant. 2) They may have misunderstood social cues as being nothing more than a distraction

and henceforth not given a time to either be assimilated into the possibility of something essential or just didn't think it was important. 3) Individuals with autistic spectrum disorder have not learned this adaptive skill at this time, and therefore it should not be assumed that they know what it is. Individuals with autistic spectrum disorder tend to have problems in public. Without someone guiding them along in dealing with being in social situations, they tend to withdraw or find a place that is quiet and are by themselves and more than likely engage in some activity with an electronic device. Since they do not have the social skills to strike up a conversation with the average individual, they tend to start to feel anxiety and some frustration, since they do not know what it is they are supposed to do, and avert themselves into the electronic world. Individuals with autistic spectrum disorder can learn social skills, but they need to understand the significance and importance of that social skill acquisition. Without their understanding of the importance of obtaining those social skills, they will not obtain them and find them to be nothing more than trivial with no satisfaction. However, if an individual with autistic spectrum disorder is instructed on social skills and social etiquette, they may become proficient in learning how to deal with people around them. It has been noted that when an individual with autistic spectrum disorder goes into a place with a lot of people, they tend to start to become anxious. This is because over time in their life, they have been ridiculed, bullied and treated very poorly by the public and therefore any type of social interactions with the public is always assumed to have negative outcomes and consequences. This type of anxiety due to past learning experiences and the anticipation of negative outcomes is a form of posttraumatic stress disorder. An individual with autistic spectrum disorder will not leave their comfort zone. Unless of course someone they trust is with them and works with them on how to get past their learned social stigma. This is not easy to do. However, with the right combination of therapy and social intervention, an individual with autistic spectrum disorder can become skilled in the social

environment. Many individuals with autistic spectrum disorder do not like to go into public or into any place that they must go to such as grocery stores. However, with the problem that they must go into these places for essential items such as food, and other essential items, most of them have a plan of action from the time they get out of the vehicle until the time they get back in the vehicle. In other words, they have a map routed out from the time they turn the key off to the time they turn the key to the on position. Although this is a control issue, it also keeps them within their comfort zone and will not cause anxiety or possibly an emotional meltdown. This is, of course, an adaptive skill and it can be learned.

One of the things that have come up over the past years has been how to introduce social skills to a person with autistic spectrum disorder. The answer to this question is not simple. If the individual with autistic spectrum disorder wants to learn social skills, a good parent/teacher/caregiver/therapist/other, will take the time and start slowly. First, they will begin at the office and explain the skills. Second: They will role play going both ways, and finally: take them into an environment and keep them close at hand and reassure them that nothing serious is going to happen. That guide will also help the person with autistic spectrum disorder to introduce themselves and of course talk about what their significant passion is in life. If they connect with someone who also has that significant passion in life, they will have taken the first step toward learning new social skills. If not, they may decide that this type of socialization is not for them and they will either retreat to a corner of the room and/or pull out their phone, or they will ask if they can leave. Either way, this is a chance, a gamble and a risk to some extent. However, if a person with autistic spectrum disorder can take that first step, and is encourage, promoted and complement, they will assimilate that adaptive skill. If they are complimented/praised and encourage, on what they have achieved and what they can achieve, they may want to learn more adaptive skills.

His Behavior is wrong

This statement is one I hear a lot of the time. It seems that parents/teachers/caregivers all tend to judge the behavior of an individual with autistic spectrum disorder very harshly. It appears that they will try to stop them in the middle behavior rather than cede to where the behavior leads, such as the final outcome. However, it goes deeper than that. It seems that parent/teacher/caregivers tend to judge behavior by their own standards rather than the uniqueness of the individual. It is a fallacy that everybody should behave the same. If everybody behaved the same, we would all be walking around like robots. The behaviors of individuals with autistic spectrum disorders are unique. There are many facets that I can only explain in brief over the next couple of paragraphs, but these are the most pronounced. Individuals with autistic spectrum disorder may show behavior that is very similar to attention-deficit/hyperactivity disorder. There are elements of going from task to task, multitasking, but there seems to be a direct goal in mind. Even if four or five things are going on at the same time, some of them will get done, and redirection will only cause a possible meltdown. So individuals with autistic spectrum disorder may resemble in certain aspects behaviors associated with Attention deficit hyperactivity disorder. Another behavior, oppositional defiant disorder, or aspects of it, may also be present. However, the reason for the oppositional defiance is that whatever was asked, task/statement/question did not make sense to the individual with autistic spectrum disorder. If the question is obvious, the statement is mundane or illogical; you will not get the individual with autistic spectrum disorder to listen/hear/follow through. Individuals with autistic spectrum disorder have logical thought processes that do not cater to the illogical. Henceforth you have someone who is not as flexible as you think they should be, but instead, are using logic and their own experience to make a decision not to cooperate. Another behavior that is the hallmark of autistic spectrum disorder is the

obsessive-compulsive disorder. Individuals with autistic spectrum disorder may be distracted by specific favorite things however they can be redirected back to those items in which they are currently working on. However, the competition between a current task and a preferred task is present; the preferred task will be chosen. Other items that come up are that people with autistic spectrum disorder like things in a specific order. That is why consistency is the hallmark of working with individuals with autistic spectrum disorder. They will arrange things in specific orders that make sense to them. If something is put out of place by another person, they will return it back to the way it was and possibly even make the change noted and caution others about touching their orderly items. Some other issues that come up may be an obsession with specific foods, specific sounds and of course specific visual and tactile stimulus that are either preferred or not preferred. Therefore, there are specifics that individuals with autistic spectrum disorder like to feel, touch, taste, smell and see and there are others they do not like.

Some of the negative behaviors that you may see have to do with specific events at specific times and in particular places. For the most part, individuals with autistic spectrum disorder tend to be standoffish from the crowd. It is noted that some of the emotions they do feel are as follows: anxiety, frustration, and anger. In regards to anxiety, an individual with autistic spectrum disorder will tend to withdraw from the environment or in the case of some, who have electronic devices, retreat into those devices. I will make it perfectly clear at this time that individuals with autistic spectrum disorder may look like they have some elements of electronic gadget addictive disorder. However, they are still aware of what is going on around them and are listening. The electronic gadget is just a way for them to feel less anxious because there is some comfort in being able to distract oneself from an environment that causes one to feel anxiety. In this case, the electronic gadget becomes a therapeutic device to help the autistic

individual relieve their anxiety to some degree and possibly even escape the anxiety-provoking situation. This phenomenon has been observed on many occasions, and it seems to work well when an autistic individual is feeling a lot of anxiety and has no clue on their recourse of action or speech. It appears that the use of electronic gadget is kind of like opening up the door so they can walk through it and removed themselves from the anxiety-ridden situation.

I have explained over and over again

This is one of those statements that I hear coming from both sides. It seems that the parents continue to say this about how their autistic individual does not understand what they are trying to tell them. On the other hand, individuals with autism tell me about how they explained to their parents over and over again what they are trying to do or say or accomplish. This seems to be one of the major conundrums with communication between parents and the autistic individual.

Parents indicate over and over again how they take the time in trying to explain over and over again what they expect, what they want and how they want the individual to behave but it seems that they meet with minimal success in doing this. What I try to explain to the parents is that they are overloading their individual with too many details to start with. If their tone of voice goes to a certain level, the individual already quit listening because they ears have been hurt and they stopped listening. When I tell parents to be very specific, be very direct, keep your tone of voice, consistent with a normal voice and tone inflection, and be very specific of what you expect and when exactly you want it done. Then there is excellent communication and an excellent possibility of success. When parents get into the bargaining where they start yelling at their autistic individual, there may be a meltdown because of sensory overload or possibly information overload and further explanation would do absolutely no

good. Be specific, concise, one step at a time and ask them to repeat the communication. When they repeat to you what it is you want, say a good job to them, and let them get it done. Reward them for their job well done.

From the autistic spectrum disorder side of this conversation, it seems that in the process of trying to explain oneself to one's parent/caregiver/teacher, the autistic individual loses the parent/teacher/caregiver because it seems that for a better word, a lack of patience comes into play and the individual quits listening to the individual with autistic individual. As this statement is quite prevalent, it needs a lot of work to make anything successful in this form of communication. Individuals with autistic spectrum disorder may tend to overelaborate or abbreviate, or they may tend to use the wrong words when explaining to a parent/caregiver/teacher. Chances are, in this over-elaboration, the individual listening, quits listening or takes a negative stance because the tone or the words are wrong, the words are wrong, or the wording is not correct, and usually, the individual with autistic individual is punished to one extent or another. It should be the duty of anybody working with individuals with autistic spectrum disorder to get to know them and to work on redirection if the explanation becomes overelaborate rather than to punish them. They have a gift and that gifts should be fostered, cultivated and encouraged rather than punished. The overelaboration is usually from an individual with autism that is left-brained dominant. On the other hand, the autistic individual that abbreviates is also misunderstood by a lack of wording and is ignored or punished due to a lack of clarity. This is a sign of someone with autism that is right-brained dominant. However, in either case, they know what they were trying to say, and it is up to the listener to be proactive and ask for clarity and try to understand. It seems; however that reactivity usually happens, and punishment and conflict continue due to this communication issue.

Parents, on the other hand, need to develop communication skills with their autistic individual. Yelling, screaming, cussing and swearing does not work and only result in a meltdown which then results in more yelling, screaming and cussing and swearing. Nobody wins the situations, and punishment for this situation is probably not going to be understood. As a parent, if you are not getting through to your individual with autistic spectrum disorder, give yourself a timeout, rethink what you want to say more concisely and then ask them if you can start again. Chances are this will be much more successful in developing communication skills and developing cooperation. The key to this is to be specific and not get into a lot of detail.

Frustration and anger seemed to be a good indication that the possibility of a meltdown is imminent. This can be averted if the people in the environment: parent/teacher/caregivers are paying attention and know what it is they are seeing and hearing and what it means. Otherwise, the frustration will lead to anger, which will lead to a behavioral outburst. At times, the behavioral outbursts have been categorized under a particular psychiatric diagnosis such as intermittent explosive disorder. However, if somebody was paying attention to the autistic individual before this significant blowup, they would've noted the stages that started with frustration and anger to the explosive behavior. For the most part, this behavior is mostly verbal with posturing, but on occasion ends up in a physical altercation. The physical altercation is not typical but could have been prevented if someone was watching the behaviors starting with frustration and anger to the behavioral outburst. At any time during the frustration or early anger periods, the entire situation can be resolved through direct intervention by an outside source. What I recommend is that an individual who is observing this behavior step in and talk to the autistic individual that is either frustrated or angry and walk them away from the situation and sit down and talk to them but something entirely benign that may be a preferred subject. The situation will de-escalate and therefore someone to work with the autistic individual on how the situation got to where it is and how they could resolve it prior to getting to that point. With some behavioral intervention, it seems that the possibility of an adaptive skill could be learned through this situation. However, it seems, for the most part, one situation may get to the anger and prior to the intermittent explosive disorder. There is a possibility that the wrong person intervenes and it ends up in a full-blown verbal to a physical altercation. This historically has led to the individual autism being removed from the household by the use of crisis workers or possibly even the police. In the past to deal with these behaviors, the individual was committed to a psychiatric ward and heavily medicated because the behavior described was such that the individual became explosive, threatening, and possibly even violent. Individuals who suffered at this irrational judgment seem to have lost something due to the many years of medication. Their behavior is quite controlled, and their abilities are diminished. However, they still have some ability, but they have no motivation, and most of them suffer from a form of posttraumatic stress disorder, abandonment issues, and significant trust issues. The question one would ask at this time was: "could this problem be averted, and what talent could this person have that can be applied to current society?" The answer is not simply because the previous diagnoses for autistic spectrum disorder were not as precise as it is today and there was a good possibility, at the time that some of these people were treated and diagnosed, they were misdiagnosed and medicated for the symptoms. This is a tragedy and some in cases a good therapist can try to work with what is left and try to help them have some type of a life that has some quality to it.

KEYS

When the word key is referred to, it is meant as a way to work with individuals with autistic spectrum disorder that may result in a very favorable outcome. Some of the major keys are listed below and hopefully, and in the near future, there may be more illustrated. At this time, the major ones will be discussed.

Consistency is a primary key to working with individuals with autistic spectrum disorder. Be consistent because they will keep track of what you are saying to the last syllable of what you uttered. If you are wrong and you mess up your consistency, be humble and listen to what they have to say. They will be very clear in pointing out your inconsistencies, and this can help you as a caregiver/teacher/parent to grow to help them. As you grow in understanding what it is they need, especially in the line of consistency, you will become a better parent/teacher/caregiver. Never be surprised at the intelligence and at times some wittiness of an autistic individual. Never be jealous and punish because your inconsistency was pointed out to you, but rather embrace consistency, and you will grow along with your autistic individual.

Patience is a key that is essential when working with individuals with autistic spectrum disorder. In working with autistic individuals, the caregiver/teacher/parent must take time to try to understand what it is that the individual is doing, saying and what they mean and possibly how they conduct themselves. If you are an individual who is prone to quick emotional anger, do not work with individuals with autistic spectrum disorder for you only get meltdowns and possibly worse. However, if you really want to work with individuals with autistic spectrum disorder, take the time to understand what they are saying, how they are saying it, their body language and posturing and of course know what to expect when they respond to you. This is an essential part of working with individuals with autistic spectrum

disorder. The reason is simple, if you do not understand what it is they are saying, what do they mean, why are they doing it, and what is meant by their response, you will get absently nowhere with them. That is why patience is an essential key to working with them and successful outcomes.

Always strive to find the key. In brief, the key is, in communication and other relationship building with an autistic individual, the item/thing/subject that is something that will get the attention of the autistic person. The key is essential to communication, redirection, and of course, opening any dialogue to have effective interpersonal as well as intervention success. Define the key a parent/teacher/caregiver must pay close attention to those things that are very near and dear and special to the autistic individual. Many individuals autism has more than one key, but it is important to find at least one key to have any successful relationship or intervention with them. This is where the parent/teacher/caregiver has to pay attention and note what that key is or they will never be effective in the relationship, or interventions with an individual with autistic spectrum disorder. That key is a difference between de-escalation, conversation, and even the learning of adaptive skills versus a total meltdown and negative outcomes. It is that important and foremost in successful relationships with individuals with autistic spectrum disorder.

Medication should never be thought of as a first line of helping individuals with autistic spectrum disorder, especially if they are a level I or a level II. The only exception would be a level III. Individuals with autistic spectrum disorder: level I and level II, for the most part, have excellent verbal skills, (there are some exceptions for level II), and respond well to sound verbal reasoning, logic, and explicit direction. There may be a need for medication for some of the behavioral symptoms (Attention Deficit Hyperactivity Disorder symptoms). However, it should be monitored closely for its need and

efficacy and should be discontinued or lowered as needed. Minimal medication of behaviors has been very common with autistic individuals and overall have had some good outcomes when appropriately monitored. However, some autistic individuals have been over medicated, and they have been diminished the ability to function as they want to. Proper monitoring of medication and behaviors is necessary to work on positive/productive autistic lives.

Conclusion

To wrap up this chapter, I would like to summarize the following key points:

If you are a parent/caregiver/teacher, do not judge individuals with autistic spectrum disorder as being what you expect them to be, but accept them for who they are and how they behave. You are not going to change these behaviors through strong-arm tactics such as threats, groundings and any physical punishment, which includes screaming, yelling and spankings. The behaviors will continue even though you feel that the behaviors change due to your intervention. What I am saying is, take a step back and take a look at the behavior in the possibility of what is motivating it at the moment. Then intervene and make it into an adaptive skills training time. Do not compare individuals with autistic spectrum disorder to those who do not have autistic spectrum disorder because the famous comparison of comparing apples and oranges applies at this point.

Do not, I repeat, do not, succumbed to the fallacy of "he should know." After all, how are they going to learn what it is you expect them to learn, what you believe they should have learned if someone has not taken the time and taught them precisely what it is you think they should know? Remember they do not learn from observation, but they do learn very well from direct intervention with patience and logical explanation. Take the time, be calm and explain what it is you expect them to know in clear and concise language and then have them

repeat it to you and then demonstrate. Take time and listen to what your individual is saying to you and if you don't understand explain to them what you understand and what else they mean by what they are saying. Do not jump to conclusions and do not let emotionality rule your relationship or for the most part, ruin your relationship. The more time and effort you put into understanding your autistic individual, the better your relationship is with them, and the better they will do in society.

Autism is here to stay, and without education, patience, persistence, and dedication to help those people who have autistic spectrum disorder, the situation will not improve. However, with further education, patience, persistence, and commitment to helping individuals with autistic spectrum disorder, they have an excellent chance of finding their niche in society and using their talents and experience and have the quality of life.

CHAPTER 13

Autistic Spectrum Disorders

Adaptive Skills

Adaptive Skills

Definition: The ability to learn a new technique, behavioral or methodical protocol/programs that helps the individual to move forward on to new endeavors and to employ those new abilities to better oneself in dealing with situations in the social, employment and family realms.

When it comes to autistic spectrum disorder, it seems that all levels (1, 2, and 3) can learn some form of adaptive skills. The ability to learn new skills may help an individual with autistic spectrum disorder diagnosis to actually be reevaluated (promoted in a sense) and possibly upgraded to the next level. Adaptive skills are those abilities that are learned and then employed to better a person's understanding, ability, and problem-solving skills. These abilities may be minor in some cases or can be significant changes in a lifestyle. They may be as simple as counting money to his complex as assessing one's response to a situation and choosing the right behavior to act upon rather than to be spontaneous. Every one of these adaptive skills has a possibility of being learned; however, one must first identify what skill is that is needed and then design a program for the individual with autism to learn that skill/behavior. After the skill/behavior is introduced to the individual, it must then be taught to them, and mastered by them, and then tested to see if it was mastered or there is more training needed. Until a thorough assessment is done, the adaptive skills needed are not necessarily identified. However, after a comprehensive evaluation, the skills/behaviors that need to be learned will be determined, and therefore a plan of action can be put together. This plan of action may vary depending upon the following factors: age, level of autism, previous issues, past problematic behavior and of course the rapport that is developed between the individual and the therapist. If there is a strong rapport between the

individual and the therapist, and a good treatment plan, adaptive skills can be learned at a more therapeutic rate.

The autistic spectrum disorder level III, some adaptive skills, even if they are minor can be achieved. My specialties are with the level I and II's. In the old definition of autism, back in the days of the DSM 3, 3R and in the DSM-IV, and IV-TR, individuals with autism were taught minor adaptive skills such as some social skills, eating with a utensil and possibly even toilet training. These may seem to be simple adaptive skills, however; they can be life-changing for this individual to some extent or another. Working with level III's takes a lot of patience, and a very detailed treatment plan was very small steps. Something can be achieved , but it takes the right type of person to help the individual to learn those skills. I do not work with level III's, and from the literature, past , and present, some skills can be learned and utilized , but I leave that to the people who work extensively with level III's. For the most part, adaptive skills to a significant degree are mostly seen in autistic spectrum disorder level I and II.

Autistic spectrum disorder level II seems to have some ability to learn adaptive skills to a significant degree. However, sometimes after learning the skill, they may revert back to the way they did things in the past. When this happens, it is usually caused by trying something new and failing and therefore it does not work for them but their old way of doing things did so they go back to it. This is where a good therapist will re-challenge them to do something different and try something a little more variable and with encouragement and a reward system in place a level II may learn adaptive skills. However, it seems after a time when new ideas are presented to them they may try them out but not adopt them into their lifestyle. It appears that they will retreat to what is referred to as their comfort zone, which consists of a certain amount of immaturity and behaviors that they are comfortable with. The problem here, to help them to adapt to new possible skills, specific therapeutic interventions may have to be employed to get

them past that wall that they seem to run into. When I talk about a wall, it is a behavior level, skill level or method level that they feel will not work with them. At this point, they will make very logical reasoning why it won't work for them , and they will revert back to their comfort zone where things work for them in their own logical manner , but when it comes to the larger world stage, they seem to be a little odd. However, in the mind of the individual with autistic spectrum disorder level II, they do develop defensive behaviors or logical defensive thought processes that keep them from gaining new adaptive skills. A good therapist will understand this, who understands people with autistic spectrum disorder level II, and will back away from that introduction to that skill because the individual will become frustrated with them and possibly even become argumentative and aggressive. However, when they do hit that wall, the individual should not be given up on because they cannot learn one specific skill, skill set, method or behavioral process. Instead, some modifications may be made for them to learn at least something new that they may be comfortable with. Even if only part of the skill or a minor part of the skill is learned, that may be the key to further acquiring skills related to the skill that they were able to acquire and master. This is where the treatment plan with a complete step-by-step process and individual goal levels is essential in the progress of the individual. For instance, if the individual is only comfortable with or achieved and mastered one skill out of a total skill set, through patience, persistence, and understanding, the therapist can work with them on other parts of the skill set, and this may work for them to achieve the entire skill set. However, it takes a dedicated therapist to understand that even though it is written one way, the goals; it might be more therapeutic if the goals are broken down into smaller steps. Therefore, the individual can learn no smaller steps, possibly, and achieve the entire skill set. This should be the goal of all therapists who work with individuals with autistic spectrum disorder.

It seems at least in my experience that age becomes a factor when it comes to dealing with people with autistic spectrum disorder level II. For the most part individuals with autistic spectrum disorder level II are somewhat adaptable (there are factors) and they do have reasonably useful abilities in the community such as grocery shopping, some money management skills, cooking skills and skills of daily living. Some modifications to each one of these skills are possible if it is taken on a step-by-step basis very slowly for the most part. However, if these modifications to any one of these items are pushed too hard, the individual will back off and go back into the comfort zone in which they are comfortable with.

In addition, some of the experiences that I have encountered it is noted that the older the person is with autistic spectrum disorder level II, the most considerable adaptive skill is to logically argue why they do not need to adapt to any further skills. As mentioned earlier, people with autistic spectrum disorder level II can be very intelligent and usually have an excellent left-brain function in the form of verbalizations. However, they tend to use his verbalizations to logically talk their way out of change and go back to their comfort zone. There have been cases of individuals with autistic spectrum disorder level II that have met with disappointment early in their life with regards to relationships, employment, and other outside encounters.   They have logically come up with a defense mechanism that states that the best thing for them is to avoid those: relationships, employment, and any other outside encounters. It seems that the autistic spectrum disorder level II may do their best to keep themselves from learning adaptive skills because of this defense mechanism that they seem to be able to master. However, if an adaptive skill that appears to be needed to be learned and the therapist help the individual to understand that they may need to learn it because it's something they want, this may be more successful. However, any adaptive skill to be successful should be planned right along with the individual. In younger individuals with autistic spectrum disorder level II, they seem to be more adaptable to some changes more readily than others, but they seem to be open to learning something new if they can see that they can gain something by adapting to it. That is why it appears that with autistic spectrum disorder level II individuals, the younger they are, the easier it is to work with them on adopting new skills. Whereas an older individual, who has already developed defense mechanisms and has run into the wall, may be much harder to work with and helping them to learn adaptive skills.

To help people with autistic spectrum disorder level II, the therapist must have the trust of the individual along with having a good working relationship. If these two components do not exist, the chances of any change will not happen. Instead, the individual's defenses will come up, and they will end up in a logical argument over why they should not learn anything more or try anything new. However, if the therapist is good at what they do, they can help the individual to develop a set of goals complete with simple steps. As this is a collaborative effort between the therapist and the individual, the possibility of a more prosperous outcome is more likely due to this collaborative effort. In this collaborative effort, the counselor will come up with goals but will also verify them with the individual and ask them for their opinion or give them choices. In this case, the collaboration seems possible on the part of the individual. If the individual were to throw up a defense about how they have tried that before, the therapist would logically argue back but that was then this is now, and this argument seems to encourage them at least to give it a try because things have changed in their life. It is important to encourage individuals with autistic spectrum disorder level II to try new things, possibly even keep a journal, and have them write down how it felt to do the different thing. In this way, the individual can self-monitor and then share the experience with the therapist and the therapist can give them the next step or have them continue with what they are doing until their comfortable for the next step. As this is a collaborative effort, if the individual wants to quit, the therapist can then point out to them that it was partially their idea to move forward. Therefore this knocks down some of that defense mechanism to the point where there could be a modification done on the goal, and consequently, the goal or part of the goal may be achieved.

The key to working with individuals with ASD II, is patience, persistence, and encouragement. The therapist should also be flexible to modify specific goals that may make it easier for the person to learn adaptive skills or to achieve an adaptive skill level or a new behavior or a new method. The therapist has to be patient with the individual but also must be firm at the same time to nudge them along. The individual may reach a very high level of achievement and in some cases may start to look more like an ASD level I, this has happened in some cases, but it does not occur in all cases. Some level II become very highly adaptive almost to the point of looking more like a level I., However, there could be some limitations to the adaptation skills, methods, and behaviors as it seems like there may be a natural wall that could occur which will be at the top of their ability to learn and assimilate adaptive skills. However, a good therapist will continue to work with them on coming up with new adaptive skills that they may indicate they want help. This does result in some problem-solving skills. There may be a limit to the adaptability skills of the individual (this is a case by case limit) may not be able to adapt any further.

The limits that an ASD II may experience are not fatal flaws. On the contrary, individuals with ASD II may live some very highly productive lives especially if they achieve some adaptive skills and work skills. However, there will be some deficits in their life skills needs that may need some supervision at times. Overall, the possibility of learning new adaptive skills is entirely possible in individuals with ASD II.

One such issue with level IIs may be noted with some behavioral control. Depending upon the age of the individual and the amount of trauma they may have suffered from (bullied, verbally abused, physically abused and mentally and emotionally abused) may determine their reaction to specific things in their environment. These may include a defensive posture or becoming verbally loud. Individuals are not known for assaultive behavior unless they are pushed beyond this point, and a noted regression will occur in their overall learning curve of how to handle situations. Those situations that may happen where the behavioral issues may arise should be noted and worked on to the resolution. Individuals can learn how to adapt and cope with specific situations in their environment that may in the past have caused them some traumatic memory. It would be to the best discretion of anyone having contact with someone with ASD level II, and witnessing some behavioral or emotional outburst. Remove the individual from the situation and take them to a quiet place where they can talk about what they are feeling. In this case, you are saving the individual from regression and possibly punishment as well as developing a solid rapport with them. If you can get them to the quiet place where they can talk, they will tell you how that situation they just experienced was similar to past situations that they did experience. This would be a key point for any individual working with individuals with ASD to work on choices and how they could respond to the situation differently. This could be a very positive learning experience if it is done correctly. Then that behavior would be expected to continue mainly in those similar circumstances.

The best way to handle this emotional control is by using role-play. In the course of role-playing, going through and demonstrating the situation, the individual can learn other possible choices or techniques for handling that situation in which they seem to have become quite traumatized in. It should be noted that their reaction to that situation came from experiencing that situation in the past without having a positive outcome or any choices to how they could control themselves and remove themselves from the situation rather than to become a victim of something they may not have started. In role-play, this would give the individual choices, and the therapist should take note of which choice they most easily adapt to. At this point, have them role-play that specific choice until it is mastered. If they master that particular behavioral skill, it then becomes an adaptive skill, and therefore there is a good possibility they will use it the next time they may be in a similar situation. It should be noted then that role-playing is one the more successful ways for teaching individuals with autism how to handle situations in their environment and give them choices, so they do not continue to repeat the same mistake with the same negative outcomes.

The overall goal of the emotional control which also leads to behavioral control is to help the individual to maintain a calm sense of being. It is also a good way for them to avoid any and all problems because it seems that once they have situations that have been noted such as in school society and work environments, they seem to be targeted as the person guilty of the situation. In addition, teaching them to keep a cool head, determine that they do not want to be part of that problem, since it is not theirs, and walk away. Teaching this adaptive skill will help the individual to be less of a target and more of an uninterested bystander. This could be one of the most significant adaptive skills they can ever learn is to stay out of situations that have absolutely nothing to do with them and walk away. As noted earlier, individuals with autistic spectrum disorder become targets of systems that they tend to be part of. However, if they learn the adaptive skills, especially the level IIs, they will be less of a target. They will be able to adapt to those systems that they are part of and be productive and live a pretty good life. However, the identification of adaptive skills and then the proper teaching of them is entirely the work of a skilled therapist, who really wants to see individuals with autism succeed and learn to deal with the world around them in such a way that they are no longer targeted but instead just function at a reasonable level where they have a good life and success.

Autistic spectrum disorder-level I-adaptive skills

Autistic spectrum disorder-level I have at least two levels within it and how will begin this by talking about one of the two levels which is the most adaptive yet most rigid.

The ASD-level I individual has learned a lot of adaptive skills and, at times, can be hard to identify. However, they do have deficits in specific adaptive skills that may not be readily noticed in any of the environments in which they may be part of. However, they do have deficits as they have problems that are the result of past traumatic experiences. The one issue that individuals at level one have is dealing with failure that has absolutely nothing to do with what they did. In other words, they did the assigned task to the best of their ability and probably above and beyond, and after it was over with, they were no longer needed and therefore dismissed. This emotional issue over the fact that they were dismissed because they did their job is something that they cannot logically put together and thus become depressed. In addition, even though they have the adaptive skills for living on their own and living in society, their depression may cause their adaptive skills to be diminished and, they may keep only adaptive skills needed to survive. For the most part, they may develop behavioral patterns that are very adaptive, and they are very specific, and this is to avoid contact with the outside world as much as possible. They may start to live their life in routines that they have put together as adaptive skills. This is highly functional, and it is precise and efficient. However, they tend to suffer from depression, anxiety, and posttraumatic stress disorder.

This type of level I is a challenge to any therapist. These individuals have adequate social skills and emotional control, but they do feel certain negativity in their lives but seem to have a level that they maintain. At times, they can be very rigid in their routines as these adaptive skills have become concrete in their lives and changes are not welcome. It is noted that they will try changes at times, but after they feel, they have given it enough time they will go back to their previous routine.

Age is a factor in this case as it seems that if there is a routine environment involved, then routines are quite common and followed quite rigidly. This is one of the other qualities of autistic spectrum disorder is the obsessive-compulsive disorder. Level ones are quite well known to have a process of compulsive disorder whereby they follow their routines quite rigidly, and any change in the routine may result in the event that may be as mild as someone just stopping and starting to someone who may start to argue why they have to change. However, given their intelligence and age, if a logical reason or reasons are given, they may try the chains with little to no resistance. However, if they see that the change is not beneficial to them, they will go back to the previous way of doing things. They tend to take advice and learning any new adaptive skills. For the most part, they are happy with their routines and adding any new adaptive skills may be met with resistance or acceptance and then later on rejection and back to the old way of doing things. For the most part, they are very adaptive, and they are happy with their routines.

On the other hand, there is another level of ASD-I, which seem to look at the possibility of what adaptive skills may benefit them. They seem to be less rigid in their routines and may be willing to add something to their routine or diminish something. Once again, this can be a factor of age, life experience and willingness to try new things. They seem to try and then incorporate or adjust to new adaptive skills as they see that it fits their needs. In addition, you seem to be very adaptable and

for the most part look entirely normal in their form and function. However, they will have some issues from time to time especially if it is something they have never seen or heard before and they may struggle for a reaction to whatever that instance may be. They may be slow to respond as they need time to think about how they're going to react to the situation. This type of level one may look and act like anyone, but they still have some issues that are not necessarily observable or detectable unless another individual is that close to them. Those type of adaptive skills that may never be learned may not even factor into their life as it seems that they have come up with many adaptive skills to overcome any deficits of the other adaptations they did not pick up. They are the highly adaptable individuals with autistic spectrum disorder that may not even be identified with autistic spectrum disorder, and less someone who specializes in autistic spectrum disorders works with them. Other professionals may give them some interesting diagnoses that may be part of specific symptoms that are observed, but overall a diagnosis will be very incorrect.

Adaptive skills can be learned to some extent in all levels of autistic spectrum disorder. However, each level has certain limitations as to what the overall ability of the individual is to learn, master and employ adaptive skills. Age, trauma and other life experiences may be all factor into the ability of the individual to learn adaptive skills. Adaptive skills will be learned if there are logical explanations and reason for them to learn them, master them, and then employ them. Any adaptive skill that is brought on by a whim will be discarded as quickly and easily by an individual rather than be employed. Adaptive skills can only be identified through a thorough assessment or spending several hours with an individual to find out what their needs are when it comes to adaptive skills. Adaptive skills can be taught, but it takes someone who has an excellent handle on how to teach adaptive skills to individuals with autistic spectrum disorder. People with autistic

spectrum disorder can learn, but it takes patience, persistence, and determination when you are working with someone with autism to help them understand, master and employ adaptive skills.

The most significant accomplishments any professional can do when helping someone with autism is to help them to achieve the employment of adaptive skills and to help them fit more into society and become less of a target. After all, if someone has the potential to be better why not help them achieve it by any and all means possible.

CHAPTER 14

Autistic Spectrum Disorders

Throughout life

Autistic spectrum disorders-throughout life

Throughout all these chapters on autistic spectrum disorder, I have handed and even suggested therapeutic interventions that may help individuals with autistic spectrum disorder throughout their life. There was always the possibility that an individual with autism can learn communication skills, social skills, and even academic skills. However, proper identification of the autism and the following systems must come into play.

The first system to help an individual with autistic spectrum disorder develop their adaptive skills is the parents. It has been my unfortunate experience to deal with parents who believe that their child is behaving the way they do because they want to. In a sense, individuals with autism behave the way they want to, but that is the only way they understand. They do not go out of their way to make trouble, anger other individuals or isolate themselves. They behave the way they do because that is the way they feel comfortable. They behave the way they do because they have not learned other behaviors or behavior patterns or social skills or communication skills. What they display is what they have learned, or their behavior is due to what they have failed to learn because it was assumed that they would learn a certain way by observation, example and through time. All these are very erroneous assumptions, and parents tend to be very tough on their autistic child. The parents have a certain expectation of their autistic child especially about the way they behave and the way they should communicate. These expectations are unrealistic. This type of parent tends to get very angry with her autistic child in maven become physically or verbally abusive but definitely emotionally abusive. This type of parent does not have a tendency to do well in trying to understand what is going on with their child, and further, they start the issues with trauma. The autistic child does not understand the expectations of the parent, but the parent expects the autistic individual to understand them. Another recipe for disaster is in the

making, which could lead to a lot more serious issues in the future if this is not corrected.

Another group of parents that I have had the experience with the ones that are in denial. This type of parent tends to become very hostile towards any interventions especially when it comes to the initial diagnosis. The first thing out of their mouth is "not my child." This is usually followed by: I have heard about autistic children before in my child does not fit that category. The most significant misnomer at this time is that the parent has probably read something written by a non-professional or someone who does not know what they are talking about and there is a lot of misinformation out there. The other possibility is that they read books from the past on autism which is based on what now would be called autistic spectrum disorder-level III. What the refusing to believe is her child has autism and may be either a level II or possibly a level I. This also may lead to time lost where possible interventions could help the autistic individual to learn adaptive skills along with other problem-solving skill sets.

Another group of parents that should be trying interventions to help their child is the ones that ignore it altogether. They categorize their child is being different and just let it go. This type of ignorance can only lead to a continuation and an escalation of problems over the course of a lifetime.

So the first group that could start interventions and helps the autistic individual to gain skills are the parents and seems to some point that there parents who don't want to be bothered with helping their autistic individual to possibly gain those skills are going to need for the rest of their lives. However, if parents will accept the diagnoses, except the advice from a qualified therapist and follow through with the suggestions, their individual may learn skill sets that will help them out through the rest of their lives.

The next group to get help out with intervention is extended family members. However, it seems that extended family members tend to either ignore the autistic individual or make fun of them. Instead of helping them out they start to add to the trauma factor in the individual's life. One never knows what could be gained by the autistic individual if their family and extended family accepted them. Throughout the process of life, the first teachers are the parents along with siblings and extended family members but, it seems when it comes to individuals with autism that group is the first one that can cause trauma along with the possibility of anxiety, depression and a myriad of other mental health issues. They could help if they wanted to but either they are ignoring the problem, in denial the problem, or want to punish the individual for their unique behavior patterns. Either way during this time individual with autism could learn skills and can also learn how to present themselves in public in an acceptable manner.

The next group that should be helping the autistic individual is the educational system. Due to the changes in autism and the lack of understanding of any educational system they autistic individual could gain a lot by being helped in the educational process. However, it seems that they are targeted, bullied and belittled by the educational system. In other words, this leads to more traumas and the lack of understanding and possible educational interventions, which could help an individual to learn what they may need to become a productive member of society. It was noted that most educational programs are lacking programming for individuals who are level I and level II but have a tendency to put autistic individuals in with special education classes. It seems that autistic individuals are not identified but rather categorized and put into educational programs that actually may cause further trauma and also a lack of gaining any type of educational or social skills. It seems that the educational system will not spend the time to identify individuals with autism and set up programs that would be geared directly to the needs of each autistic individual in the educational system. Instead, what seems to be happening is they continue to be traumatized, and at this point, they are not being taught any real skills that may be needed to function in the real world. Academically speaking, they may do well in some subjects and not as in other subjects and maybe put in some special education or learning support for those specific subjects they do not do well in. This can further lead to trauma along with a lack of being introduced to more advanced studies that they may understand but will not be able to participate in.

At this point, one may look at the fact that individuals with autistic spectrum disorder are not being handled well in the home or the educational system and they would be correct. It seems that outside intervention through a therapeutic component is the only support system they have. Outside interventions are only as good as the therapist who puts them together for the autistic individual and their family. The quality of the intervention is highly dependent upon the quality and dedication of the therapist involved. Good therapeutic interventions can lead to long-lasting skills and in the development of long-range goals. The only issue with this is, other than a therapist who is not that good, is the participation of the parents. Without the involvement of the parents, especially if the autistic individual is still living at home, no intervention will ever work until the individual is on their own or they get the help they need through individual therapy. Individual therapy with autistic individuals can be very productive but then becomes counterproductive without the cooperation of the parents involved. The individual may learn that dealing with his parents is best when they learn a skill of no longer listening to all the belittling but start to develop their own ego strength. It seems that the individual has gained specific skills to survive in the home and may begin to develop long-term goals for moving out on their own. This is

successful and can be done, but it takes patience on the part of the therapist and the willingness to work on the specific goal and skill set.

When we look at autism throughout the lifespan, it seems that the younger the individual that is identified with autism and with the cooperation of the parents and other ancillary individuals that are part of the autistic individual's life, the better the success of learning adaptive skills. The more adaptive skills that are learned the possibility of becoming more independent is possible. However, some intervention programs have to be specialized depending on the autistic individual and where they are at in life.

When it comes to autistic children under the age of five, the treatment planning goals have to be directly in response to children of that age. In addition, for the needs of the individual along with the understanding that the family will participate as well for them to understand what is going on and to carry on the treatment plan in the home setting. Good therapeutic intervention especially rapport and helping parents to understand what the child understands and how to communicate with them in a way that is therapeutic is vital at this step.

When it comes to children (ages 5 to 12), there are specific needs that need to be addressed along with skill sets that are specific to that age group. The treatment plan would be written directly to the needs of individuals for that age group. Parental involvement is essential in this age group. Since these are school-aged children trying to get the educational institution to understand and also make adjustments is necessary as well.

Dealing with adolescence (13 to 18) is also very specific at this point; the therapist needs to develop goals especially educational and career goals. Social skills are fundamental during this time along with socialization. Although the autistic teenager does view things differently, he does realize there is something is missing but does not

necessarily know how to ask for it. An attuned counselor along with asking the right questions at the parents can help this group immensely.

Adults can still make changes in their lives; however, it seems that they have developed behavior patterns by this time and held to those patterns very closely.

Can individuals with autism change? The answer is yes if for dealing with level I and level II individuals. There is a possibility that a level III can change if the therapeutic interventions are focused, and the individual does have some abilities. Individuals with autism can learn, and they will pick up different skill sets as well as adaptive skills throughout life. However, there may be some limitations depending on the individual's ability and willingness to learn. However, it is possible for individuals throughout their life to pick up new adaptive skills along with other skills and skill sets that will help them continue throughout life. It is possible.

With early diagnoses, good therapeutic interventions, and autistic individual may develop and adapt skills throughout their lifetime that will help them become independent and productive members of society. This is open to argument. However, I have seen changes. I have seen individuals make changes in their lives actually to give themselves opportunity and to some degree independence. It is possible with the right cooperation from everyone involved with the individual as well as the individual's cooperation changes, and adaptations are possible.

CHAPTER 15

Autistic Spectrum Disorders

Communication Issues Do's and Don'ts

Autistic Spectrum Disorder-Communication Skills

Do's and Don'ts

One of the keys to communicating with individuals with autistic spectrum disorder is to respect that person as an individual and talk to them in a calm, specific and direct manner. The following chapter is about the do's and don'ts in building communication skills with individuals with autistic spectrum disorder. For the most part. this has a lot of common sense, which does not seem too common anymore. They can be used in developing good working relationships with individuals along with helping them to understand your motivation for speaking to them. What I mean by motivation is that individuals with autistic spectrum disorder, once they start on a task or if they need to be redirected, need to be spoken to in such a way that does not lead to the following outcome: frustration-anger-meltdown. It should be the goal of all individuals: parents, teachers, caregivers and others who work with individuals with autistic spectrum disorder to master the skills so that your interaction with the individual can be more productive rather than reactive. Some of these examples will be taken from practical situations that may be of greater use than just giving do's and don'ts. If there are any questions after reading this, please feel free to call me, and I can further help you in working with your individual who has autistic spectrum disorder.

An individual with autistic spectrum disorder is working on something in the home setting. You the parent are coming up behind them. How do you handle the situation?

DO: make some type of noise that is not abrasive to the individual but will get their attention such as knocking on a countertop with a rhythm or calling their name in a calm and medium tone just loud

enough so they can hear it. This will get their attention, and you will be able to talk to them in a normal tone of voice and either direct them to something else or at least get their attention. In a cautionary note if you do not actually need them at this time just let them continue and do not bother them.

Don't: walk into the room where the autistic individual is working on something and start yelling. This is like lighting a fuse to dynamite. You will get an explosion of some kind or at least some negative reaction. Individuals with autistic spectrum disorder have a very low tolerance for startle and will respond in a manner that is appropriate to them but may be inappropriate to you. In this case, you just stepped into the minefield and good luck on what happens next. If you interrupt them by calling their name, for no obvious reason, and depending on the age of the individual, you may get any one of the following responses: ignored, growled at, talk back to in a loud and abrasive tone, possibly even sworn at.

In this previous example, it is obvious that the parent/caregiver/teacher went about this in a way that was going to fail from the beginning. Some of the things that I have written about over and over again is very simple: when the parent/teacher/caregiver starts to raise their voice, they have now lost control of the situation. The playing field has now been leveled, and the individual with autistic spectrum disorder may erupt. However, if they start to erupt, the parent/caregiver/teacher could apologize for interrupting them, and things may not proceed in a negative direction. After interrupting them and then apologizing to them, it is best to come up with a very good reason for interrupting them. Either way, handling things in a calm and controlled voice matters. What the individual says or how they say it, is the key to keeping control of the situation and trying to understand what is going on as well as trying to redirect them off to something else. Once you lose your cool, you have now lost and prepared for the worst.

An individual with autistic spectrum disorder is working on something and is fully concentrated on what they are doing. They see you coming towards them, and they look up to acknowledge you, what do you say?

DO: Comment on what a good job they're doing and ask them if they need any help. Tell them you are willing to help them if they need you or if they would like your help. Ask them if they ran into any problems while they were working on that specific job that they are performing. You will get a favorable response and probably a thank you or something very positive.

Don't: start off your conversation with a very stupid question that states the obvious like what are you doing. If you can see what they are doing, do not ask a stupid question because you will either be ignored or growled out. Do not start off the conversation with a superlative of very negative quality for the conversation will go in a very negative direction rather quickly.

If it is obvious what the person with autistic spectrum disorder is doing, do not ask a stupid question "what are you doing"?. This only annoys them, and any further conversation will be ignored or met with a certain superlative in return, depending on the age of the individual. Do give compliments whenever possible. Individuals need to hear compliments because most of their life or parts of their life they have either been bullied or traumatized in some way and rarely hear a compliment. A compliment may be the key to getting their attention if you want to redirect them from what they are doing at this time or even have a conversation separate from what they are doing.

An individual is playing a video game, and they are very much involved to the point where they are totally engaged with the characters in the video game, and they are actually yelling at the television. This behavior is becoming very loud and disturbing to the rest of the household. How do you handle the situation?

DO: go into the room in which the person is playing the video game and make sure they see you. You may have to come up on either left or right side but do not stand in front of them. Ask them who is winning or can you join in the game. Either question can then open up the door to you asking them to calm it down a little bit because you have Things in a very neutral position. If your goal is to get them to turn the game down or to calm down, do not ask them about the game but rather inquire as to how they are winning or if they are winning.

Don't: walk into the room and start to cuss and swear at them. Do not start yelling at them to turn it down or to calm down because yelling and autistic individual does not work. This approach will cause a meltdown, and in this situation, it is only going to get worse.

In this situation, and it can become quite common, the individual is in their comfort zone or their bubble. In the world of the video game, they find that they are in control and there are no judgmental or traumatic issues, and they are very comfortable in that environment. You as a parent/teacher/caregiver are invading that bubble or invading their space, and if it is done properly, the desired outcome in which you are seeking, (turning down the volume and calming down to some extent) can be achieved. However, if you enter the room cussing and swearing at them to tell them to turn the (superlative words) down, you have just leveled the playing field and be prepared for the same superlatives coming back at you whereby you the: parent/teacher/caregiver will have a meltdown as well. In this scenario if you both have meltdowns chances are things could get very ugly in a hurry and the possibility of outside intervention is very probable. Take your time in this situation, ask pertinent questions, remain calm, and things will go in a very positive direction. However, if you are going into the situation halfcocked, chances are you going to go to full cock and fire on this, and the outcome will not be anywhere close to what you really wanted before you went into that situation. Take your time, using common sense, and the situation can be rectified rather quickly.

You are having a conversation with an individual with autistic spectrum disorder. It seems they are starting to get a little loud and they seem to be becoming emotionally aroused. You are not sure of what the individual is getting aroused about, but you are concerned. You would like them to calm down and to turn their volume down and to slow down the rate of their speech. How are you going to go about doing this?

DO: listen to what they are talking about and ignore the volume and to an extent ignore the arousal and the possibility that their speech is becoming very rapid. Wave your hands in front of yourself to get their attention and then put your hands over your ears. This will get their attention because individuals with autism seem to be very perceptive to signs and this sign is a good indication for them to slow down or hold up for a moment. When they stop talking, tell them to turn it down a little bit slow down so you can understand them better. This will help them to slow down and speak at a better rate and rhythm that you can understand, and this will also delete some of the emotional arousals they may be verbalizing. Emotional arousal may not be about what the two of you were specifically talking about but may be of memory from a past experience that they are feeling at the moment but has nothing to do with the conversation. Getting their attention and being patient with them, asking them nicely to turn it down so you can understand and slow down so you can really comprehend will not lead to any further problems if it is done in this matter.

Don't: ever try to talk over them. They will just increase the volume, and emotional arousal may then be directed at the current situation rather than some memory that they may be having at the time during your conversation. Do not ever use superlatives at this time for it will just escalate the situation.

If you are a total rookie to dealing with individuals with autistic spectrum disorder, please take note of the situation because your lack

of understanding of autism could lead to your behavior being totally unacceptable, it also could lead to an outcome that could be totally avoidable. Also in this situation, do not let someone else into this conversation. They will not understand what is going on, and the possibility of an escalation in another direction or the misinterpretation of the conversation is possible, and the outcome of such could be very negative. If an individual happens upon a conversation going on between an autistic individual and another person, do not intervene unless it is totally necessary. What I mean by totally necessary is physical contact is already happening. Intervention is then authorized and encouraged but otherwise, if you come in the middle of a conversation where you have no clue whether or not this conversation is negative and threatening do not do anything. Rather stay out of the situation and if it escalates then intervene otherwise stay out of it. It may be that this conversation is not really escalating but is just loud. Intervention on a loud conversation can cause more problems and further intervention by outside authorities. If you are a rookie and have no clue about autistic spectrum disorder, I encourage you to read up on this matter and become fully aware of individuals who have autistic spectrum disorder level I and II. Otherwise, your assessment of the situation may be way off, and you may actually bring undue harm to the individual with autism.

You give instructions to an individual with autism. Instructions are very generalized and nonspecific. The individual carries out the task but is not to what you expect or want from them. How do you handle the situation?

DO: compliment them about the task they did perform in a normal tone of voice. If the task is not to the specifics, which you were expecting but did not make the specifics known, then ask the individual to try it again and give them the specifics of the task. The outcome goal of this is very possibly accomplished, but you may hear some complaining

from the autistic individual. You may hear the following statement "why didn't he tell me that to begin with." You have to expect this if you do not give specific instructions and have specific expectations. Make sure your instructions are, and there is no room for the possibility of a generalization. If you do not give specific instructions to the autistic individual, they will perform the task to the best of their ability. Complementing them on what they accomplished will avoid any problems other than maybe hearing a complaint. In addition, of course, if you wanted it done that way, to begin with, you should be very specific about what you wanted to be done.

Don't: start yelling at the individual because they did not complete the task to your specific standards which were only known to you and were not stated to them. Do not start off by calling them names or using superlatives which only tend to erode the ego of the autistic individual and may add to his history of traumatic events that seem to be part of their life. If you wanted it done a certain way, to begin with, be very specific about how you want it done and when you want it done by. Never assume that they know what you know and how you want something done. Unless you have taught them how to do it, do not expect them to know how to do it the way you know how to do it if you have never taught them how to do it. Using negative statements and superlatives may lead to frustration, anger, and a possible meltdown depending upon the age of the individual in which you are engaging.

As illustrated above, if you want something done a specific way to give specific instructions. Never assume that an individual with autism knows how to do things the way you want them done unless of course you have taken the time and taught them how to do it step by step. In this case, it seems that the individual did their best and should be complimented for doing what they did. If you want something done further be more specific and give them another task to do. However, compliment them on what they accomplished and give them words of

encouragement to go on to the next task. When someone starts to refer to individuals with autism with several negative remarks followed by several superlatives, you are hurting them both mentally and emotionally. This can be viewed as abuse. My advice is to follow this guideline and stop doing what you've been doing with them because all you've been doing to the individual is to demean them, traumatize them and have them question their self-worth, their ego strength, and their purpose. However, if this is what you are out to do, then beware that you will be reported for abuse and you can face the consequences of your negativism towards the individual.

As one can see through these various scenarios there is always going to be the possibility of two outcomes. 1) Start to build a better communication relationship with your individual with autism and work together to get something accomplished. Alternatively, 2) you end up in a shouting match which will continue to deteriorate, and the end will always be a negative outcome. My challenge to you the parent/caregiver/teacher or anyone else involved in working with individuals with autism, to develop good listening skills and keep your emotional issues in check. If you are an individual who has insecurities and issues with your authority and the fact that you need to be in control, do not work with individuals with autism. You will be very unsuccessful, and the individual with autism will suffer greatly from your egotism and a lack of compassion. There will be consequences to your inability to work with them and your mistreatment of them. On the other hand, if you are serious about working with individuals with autism, develop good listening skills. Listen to what is being said not to how it is being said or the tone of voice. In doing this and not taking their loud tone or body language as a threat, you will be more successful in helping them to achieve goals that you are both seeking for them to achieve. There is nothing more fulfilling in this world than to have someone with autism to achieve the highest level of their abilities and their goals and to see them become

as independent as possible. This can be done and in this case, following these simple guidelines can help them to achieve that level of skill.

Using these scenarios is a good start to helping individuals with autistic spectrum disorder. However, this is barely a thumbnail sketch, and I am sure other scenarios will come up over time. However, these are the most prevalent scenarios that I have come across in my practice and through contact with individuals outside of my practice. However, for the most part, the idea of listening and understanding what you are hearing should always supersede any emotional or egotistical influence in contact with individuals with autistic spectrum disorder. If you are an educator, being control does not mean screaming and yelling, but rather it means listening, trying to understand, keeping yourself calm and then in a calm voice speak or ask questions. As a parent, your emotion and egotism tend to be in a high state of authoritarian thought process. If you have individuals with autism, rethink who you are. You are a parent, but you also are the most significant guide the individual can ever have. If you do not establish communication skills, you will never be that great guide that you are supposed to become. Caregivers, you are the individuals who are supposed to be helping in this entire system to work with individuals with autism to help them to achieve specific goals that were developed for individuals with autism. If you are not dedicated to helping individuals with autism, then do something else because you are doing more harm than good. Anybody can help individuals with autism if they are committed to understanding what autism is and following through on a few simple guidelines. Individuals with autism have a lot to offer, communication skills following this DO and Don't article can be beneficial when it comes to helping them achieve goals and have a productive future.

CHAPTER 16

Autistic Spectrum Disorders

Legal Issues

Autistic Spectrum Disorders-Legal Issues

Individuals with autistic spectrum disorder are prone to get into trouble especially when it concerns legal problems. The crux of this issue will be examined in detail throughout this writing. It is my hope that individuals in the legal system: judges, magistrates, and law enforcement will take time to go over this document to help them with individuals who have autistic spectrum disorder and to look at them differently than just some common individual who through their own volition breaks the law.

Throughout this document, I will be looking more towards level I and level II individuals. However, level III individuals can get into some legal problems whether they are in an institution or in outside programming or even in the home. For the most part, it is a level II individuals who are most prone to get into legal problems and possibly also end up with prison sentences. This is due to the verbalizations of their thoughts in public places that may be considered threatening or even verbally aggressive that could lead to possible physical aggression. This will be explained in detail later on in the section on level II individuals. Level I individuals may have minor problems or they can have some very major issues depending upon what they are working on.

Before going any further on this specific topic of like to introduce a word that I formulated myself called "emotionality." Emotionality is a description and a realization that individuals with autistic spectrum disorder do have emotions and feelings but do not always express them in a socially appropriate manner. Emotionality has three parts: 1) the emotions and thought process is going on within the autistic individual, 2) the action, excitement, emotions going on in the environment around the autistic individual and 3) the interpretation and reaction to the combination of the individuals emotions and the

interpretation and reaction to those issues going on around them. In this case, the result will probably be some form of anger or possibly verbal or even physical aggression. Emotionality has a tendency to stop all rational thought and put in place emotion and behavior that can be considered inappropriate from the viewpoint of anybody observing this interaction between the autistic individual and his environment. Out of the three levels of autistic spectrum disorder, the individuals at the level to-middle level are the most prone to emotionality. More explanation will be done in the section on level II-middle level individuals.

Level III individuals

Level III individuals can be quite spontaneous, and they can become very physically aggressive and assaultive. For the most part, these individuals either are institutionalized or are in some type of supervised day programming. However, they can become assaulted in the home setting if that is where they are residing. As described in earlier chapters, it is unknown for the most part, what can set them off into their physically assaultive and aggressive behaviors. However, they can become very aggressive and very assaultive very quickly and may or may not be able to be calm down by their familiar individual.

Due to these behaviors, they could be charged with assault and could possibly be given a sentence. For the most part, they are put into a more secure environment, and their medication is usually adjusted. Bringing suit against individuals at this level are rarely prosecuted for the simple reason they can't be held responsible for what they are doing. This basically could be the primary defense for individuals at this level.

Emotionality on the level III individuals is well known to the caretakers who are consistently working with them. Those caretakers can pretty much predict when the individual will have a meltdown that could result in a physical altercation. Emotionality would not be known

to the casual observer or even someone who occasionally works with the individual. Emotionality can be predicted by those who are consistently working with the individual and have paid attention to their behaviors, their posturing and the precursors to the meltdown.

<u>Level II individuals</u>

For the level II individual, this section will be broken down into the three levels of the level II group.

Level II-high-level individuals, for the most part, do not cause any issues. They may tend to use any adaptive skill in which they have learned at this time to avoid trouble. They may even take the blame for certain things or also be utterly passive to the point of total shutdown and retreat into their safe zone. If they cannot retreat into their safe zone, they may tend to sit there and be quiet. This group may get into some type of trouble if they are with a group and the group as a whole gets into trouble. Level II-high-level individuals usually avoid trouble at all cost to the point of even being beaten up. It seems at this level they have learned enough adaptive skills, social skills and communication skills to think seriously about their behavior and do not go through the behavioral triad and end up in the possible altercation when they hit the meltdown level. However, it seems that they avoid the meltdown by shutting down and this could lead to other trouble especially if they are in a group that finds them in trouble.

Emotionality for them usually leads to a total shutdown whereby they quit talking altogether and stare off into space or stared people and they do not say anything. If there is an altercation with the law, they may be considered guilty because they quit talking. However, if this happens, it should be noted that they have nothing more to say and that further questioning will result in silence. They tend to keep their emotions in check to the point where it does not seem like they are showing any emotion. It has been observed with individuals at this level that they may be feeling some form of anxiety and feel that their

best option is not to say anything else. When they reach this point they do not express any words, and they show very little at all body language, and therefore their emotionality seems to be silence and sitting still.

Level II-middle level is the most common for showing high emotionality and getting in trouble with the law. At this level, it seems that they have a lot of raw emotion and the problem with expressing what they are feeling without using words that can cause further problems. Level II individual is still possibly learning communication skills as well as social skills. They do not always have a grasp of the situation around them, and therefore their emotionality may not be appropriate because of their misinterpretation of the issues in their environment and how they should feel about them. It seems whenever there is an issue in their environment level II middle-level individual will respond with some inappropriate angry outburst. Their words will be offensive such as swearing, cussing and possibly even threatening. However, they may also include specific words that may become misinterpreted or even offensive to the point of being considered terroristic threats. When an individual at this level gets to the point where they go into a verbal tirade where they may say things of an offensive nature and say things to the point of verbal threats with weapons, they are trying to push people away because something then their environment has triggered this outburst. For the most part, these individuals will not become physically aggressive until they are cornered but if they are cornered, touched, or pushed they will become physically aggressive. Due to their verbalizations and using such words is dying, knife or a phrase such as I'm going to shoot you I'm going to stab you I'm going to kill you, usually leads to the possibility of an arrest and possibly even some jail time. However, if this situation is examined to what is going on, it will be noted that the individual does not have any weapons on them as mainly using these verbalizations to punish other people out of their present environment.

This could be considered one way that may be used by the level to-middle level individuals to feel safe by pushing people away from them. This, however, may be regarded as terroristic threats, and the possibility of an encounter with law enforcement is entirely possible. However, this is an instance where their emotionality is misinterpreted as being a salt of an aggressive but rather is verbally aggressive only and is a means to help them get their space. It may also be that when this level of individual goes into a full-blown emotional event, they may feel they are helping the environment to restate the lives. However, if they are already noted as having emotional issues and possible violent outbursts, they would be targeted first as the guilty party rather than someone taking a step back and looking at the whole situation and trying to understand why the individual even got involved. In this case, lots of direct questioning will get the answer to this problem, and the situation may be that the individual felt that he was possibly protecting himself, protecting someone who is close to him or is trying to keep the peace between people. Although these are not good reasons for involvement, it is the emotionality factor that gets them involved. Situations like this should be examined closely for reasons why the autistic individual was even in the environment, got involved the environment, and finally had some sort of emotional meltdown in that environment in which they were entangled.

Level II-middle level also may have issues with law enforcement especially if they have not mastered any control of their emotionality or their verbalizations and social skills to being enabled to spend too much time in the digital world. There seems to be a group within this group that spends way too much time watching television, playing video games and being on their phone and therefore does not master any skills in the real world. They have a serious problem with relating to things outside their comfort zone and their understanding of their world, which is mostly entertainment, fantasy, and no human contact. It seems that their emotionality is based on what they have learned in

the storylines of the video games, television that they watch and communicate digitally. It appears that they are enabled to do this because as they spend their time and their safe zone engaging in these behaviors, there are no problem behaviors. However, when they do finally get out into the real world and have to deal with people and the environment in which they are mostly unfamiliar, their emotionality may lead to serious problems socially, emotionally, verbally and possibly even some form of physical altercation. These individuals may have serious problems with law enforcement because they have trouble separating what they should be doing from what they learned in their comfort zone. This group needs a lot of help and encouragement to get away from their fantasyland and get into the real world. They need to learn that real-world problems lead to real-world consequences and there is no reset button to start over.

Level II-low level individuals, for the most part, have issues with communication skills.

<u>Level I individuals</u>

Level I individuals are separated into two groups: the static and the dynamic.

Level I-static individuals, for the most part, may end up with legal problems by possibly speeding, a rare event that could happen, or perhaps becoming frustrated, due to somebody interrupting a process, and may say something inappropriate. For the most part, this group does their best to avoid any and all conflict. There is the possibility that they may get into a verbal confrontation with somebody and may not be able to walk away which would be their usual style. They may be cited for disorderly conduct or possibly even disturbing the peace. For the most part, this is the worst thing they may do. This is a course possibly a very rare occurrence, as this group tends to avoid all problems and follow the rules and regulations to the T. It would be a

very rare occurrence for an individual at this level to get into any serious problems.

Level I-dynamic may tend to push boundaries since they continue to expand their knowledge base along with their abilities and understanding and incorporating the world around them. They may end up with speeding tickets. They may find themselves in situations that either they cause by their own inability to understand what the situation is or they were associated with the problem by a designing individual which they felt was their friend. For the most part, the level I dynamic is a pretty conscientious individual, but there is a possibility they could become involved in some type of white-collar crime. Many of them are very good at working with computers and programs and may be given a task to do something which may be borderline legal possibly even illegal but, due to the fact the individual gave them the task to do and they trust this individual, they will perform the task to the best of their abilities. They may be held accountable for their actions as their part in this may lead to some more serious criminal activity. The question would be whether or not they knew this was right or wrong. There is a very good possibility they saw this is just another job and perform their tasks to the best of their abilities. It is not uncommon for individuals at this level to still tend to trust individuals that they should not trust and possibly do things that they may question but entrusting the individual, they follow through anyhow. The question is: are they guilty as an assessor to the crime? This will be one for the courts decide, but it should be brought to the attention of the judge and the judicial system that the individual has autism and may have been acting innocently and performing a job that he was paid to do. There is the possibility that the individual may have known what he was doing was wrong but did it anyhow under the circumstances that he was being paid for by someone who trusted. This will be a question that will continue on throughout history. For the most part, however, the level I-dynamic is one that follows all rules

and regulations and will become a little depressed if they make a mistake. They do not like to make mistakes, and they do not like to go outside the lines. This can be considered the type of individual who never colored outside the lines throughout their life, crossed all their T's, and dotted all their I's. They are very astute to detail and the parameters of rules and regulations.

CHAPTER 17

Autistic Spectrum Disorders

A Physics Model

Autistic Spectrum Disorder- A Physics Model

It would seem that trying to explain autistic spectrum disorder to anybody would be simplified if we can give a basic illustration. As in the case that I was a student (Bachelor of Science Degree in Chemistry/General Science and Secondary Education), it would be to the greater advantage of anybody who is trying to understand autistic spectrum disorder if it was explained in a more illustrative and scientific approach. The scientific approach I am proposing at this time has to do with the study of physics specifically, in the use of sound detection using an oscilloscope.

The oscilloscope is quite an interesting piece of equipment. Many people could sit there all day long and watch how different waves are illustrated in a digital format (mine, of course, were analog) and see how depending upon a frequency, how many times it crosses between two boundaries also referred to as cycles per second. It is also noted that there is a frequency factor, how many times the wave exhibits itself per second and even how high or low the wave goes. So at this point, if I haven't lost you, that is a good thing, but if I have, basically an oscilloscope measures the wave of a sound or impulse and how high or low it goes over a given a period of time. If you are still confused, the more modern uses of an oscilloscope or oscilloscope instrument are usually found in the doctor's office when they are monitoring heart rate, respirations and blood pressure. These are digital devices that you get hooked up to. However, these all go back to the beginning of an analog piece of machinery that measured sound waves and the frequency of the sound waves. What I'm going to do is use the oscilloscope type pattern to explain autistic spectrum disorder thought process to help people to understand better what is going on inside. For the most part, this type of thought process, to this extent is reserved for the group known as level II middle and high, and for the

level I. It is unknown about the thought processes of the level II low-level or about the level III. However the targeted levels: level II-M and H and the level I has thought processes can be illustrated through the oscilloscope model.

This first model illustrates the preferred and accepted thought process of a majority of human beings. This is believed to be the norm when it comes to thoughts and thought process.

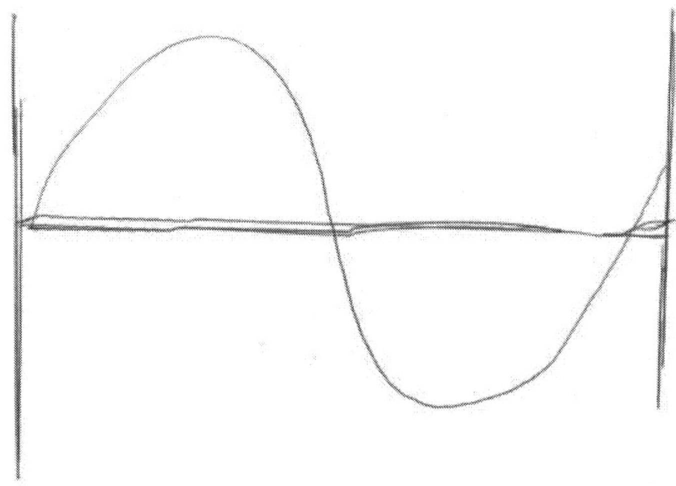

As one can see by the illustration, there is one cycle from start to finish. This represents the assumptions and expectations of the normal human being and the associated individuals around the individual. One thought from start to finish without exception. One thought or one task from the beginning to the end. One and only one and that is what is expected and accepted by most individuals.

However, the individuals with Autistic Spectrum Disorder (Level I and II) do not have just one thought on their mind or one task that they are working on unless the task is the preferred task and they will be focused on it. For the most part, they will still be thinking of other tasks and thoughts. The illustration looks like this:

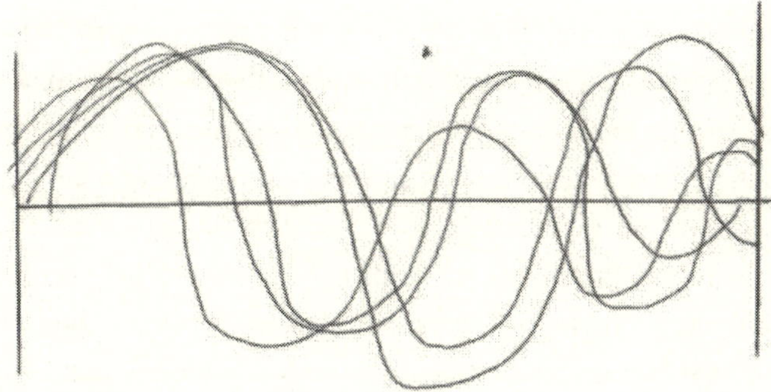

As one can see by this illustration, there are many thoughts in the mind of the Autistic individual, but they will finish the thought or task eventually. There may be some distractions, as illustrated by the crossing of the waves, but eventually, the task will be completed. The crossing of the waves may illustrate a distraction or a KEY (Mentioned in the article: The Autistic Perspective). Whether a KEY or a distraction, it is easy to see that even though there are many thoughts or tasks, there is a point of completion. The completion is on the part of the individual and not necessarily on the schedule of the requestor. However, the task will be completed. There also may be instances that they will stay on one task (The Preferred Task) to completion. It should be cautioned here that any Parent/Caregiver or teacher that interrupts this train of thought or tasks without using a key should be

prepared for the following response: Blank stare (you are interrupting me), a growl (can't you see I am busy), a verbal remark (back off I am busy) or if you really persist, and I caution you not to, a verbal tirade or an all-out meltdown. Know what the key is or another preferred task to direct them on to get their attention or to successfully have them change tasks. (This will be in the future article Autistic Spectrum Disorder- Do's and Don't's).

It is also illustrated that Autistic Individuals may jump from task to task as illustrated by the crossing waves but they will complete all the tasks that they start. They may complete them differently than what is expected of them, and they may do so in such a creative way that the people around them fail to see that they just showed an innovative way to start-complete a task. This is where many untrained professionals start to see them in another light. They may start to categorize them as having Attention Deficit Hyperactive Disorder (ADHD), and this is not the case. The way that they may switch from task to task and how they may focus on one task alone may look like ADHD to the untrained eye, but it is not. The next illustration will demonstrate the difference.

Attention Deficit/Hyperactivity Process (ADHD)

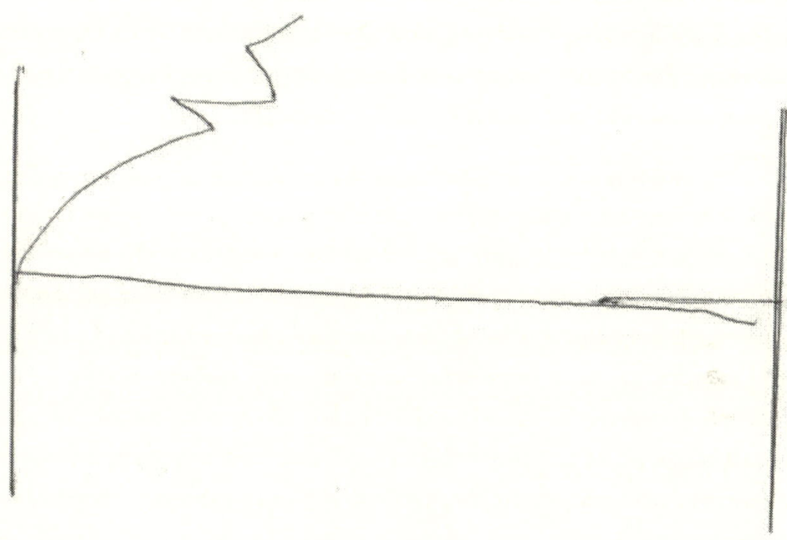

As noted in the above illustration, The Attention Deficit Hyperactive Disorder individual (ADHD) may start on a cycle but will be distracted and then distracted and then distracted again and never complete the task or cycle. If they are prompted, they may complete part of a task, but overall only the preferred task will be completed. They need help, direction, and supervision to get the task completed. In retrospect, the Autistic Individual (Level I and II) will complete the task or several tasks but it may be done differently, and they may only partially complete the task that was initially given them. Give them the opportunity to remember the task that they have only partially completed before the intervention, direction or counsel. The ADHD individual needs constant direction and will be distracted from the task given. They may however go and play a video game rather than to do their activities of daily living, but that is because they are

distracted by the opportunity for the preferred task, which is likely to be some type of video game. The autistic (ASD- I, II) individual may need direction on how the task is to be done because if they are given general instructions, they will perform the task the best way that they know how. If they are given too many tasks, they will get one or two done, but they will get them done completely.

In the use of physics to explain the Autistic Spectrum Disorder (Level I and II), it is obvious to see that with specific task parameters and time limits they will get the task done as you command. On the other hand, someone with Attention Deficit Hyperactivity Disorder (ADHD) will get sidetracked, and the task will not be completed without prompts and further direction. Also with ADHD, give them one-step at a time with directions on what to do after that step. They may get it done, but they may get sidetracked. They need supervision. On the other hand, the ASD person will complete the task and maybe even a few more.

Overall, if you are told that your child may have ADHD, look at this again, they may actually have Autism and not ADHD. Take your time and do observations before you have your child in the wrong diagnoses and consider a better life for your child with ASD.

CHAPTER 18

Autistic Spectrum Disorder

Possible Causes

Autistic Spectrum Disorders-Possible Causes

A long-term Proposal for the emergence of autistic spectrum disorder.

Over the course of the last 60 years or so, there has been an interesting story that keeps being told, not being told or modified to the point where it makes no sense to anyone and is not being paid attention to by the millennial group.

This proposition goes back to before the 1960s.

Some of the idealistic thought processes of the 50s seem that there was a lot of innocence, but still, there were certain factions of alcohol, drug use, and some minor gang activity. However, at the onset of the 1960s, it seemed that everything had taken a different direction. Some of the things that happen during this time were the full commitment to the war in Vietnam, the radical movement of the hippie organizations and there was a woman's movement that seemed to be minor and should have had a more significant outcome. However, no matter which one of these subjects is going to be looked at, there is a possibility that there may be some link to the outcome of autistic spectrum disorder.

Vietnam War was an unpopular war. However, those brave patriots put their lives on hold and either followed through with enlisting or honored the draft. It seems that they were subjected to specific toxins, both internally taken and externally exposed to. It was known that there were certain vaccines were given to them before their departure for Vietnam. It was also noted that after they were in Vietnam for a while, especially the infantry, and anyone who handled this toxin, Agent Orange, were susceptible to this externalized toxin, which was absorbed through the skin. It was also known and later

exposed that the veterans from the Viet Nam War were subjected to or were in direct contact with the spraying or sprayed areas where Agent Orange was used in. Recently it was uncovered that members of the armed forces in Thailand might have also been exposed to Agent Orange. Veterans were subject to the possibility of some toxic or toxin either ingested, injected or absorbed through the skin. I have every admiration for those brave men who fought in that war. It seems however that the government did not respect them and what appears in a long-term study did not respect their futures and their future families.

It seems there was a perpetuation of this, externalizing and internalizing toxins by the United States government on its military forces. There were a lot of experimental vaccines and oral medications that were administered to many of the servicemen who fought in the 1st Gulf War in 1990. There is a possibility that there have been some other experimental vaccines and medications that members of the armed forces after that time and possibly even currently have been subjugated to. The question is, however, what are the long-term effects of these vaccines and medications as well as any nerve agents or toxic agents that could be released? It seems that Agent Orange has definitely made its mark as many of the veterans who had been exposed to it are either now deceased or are dying slowly. There is also noted that many of their children had specific defects or deficits and now the children of the children of those who are exposed to Agent Orange are currently coming into their own. It seems from even a small study that there are some links to those individuals whose grandparents and parent who was exposed to Agent Orange have a long-term problem in the form of autistic spectrum disorder. The long-term effects of the experimental use of medications and vaccinations on the veterans of the 1st Gulf War of 1990, may also be emerging at this time in the forms of some mental health deficits. However, there is some evidence that the ancestors of the individuals

who were exposed to Agent Orange in Vietnam and other areas of South East Asia may have specific physical/emotional and mental health deficits. At this point, however, this author is examining these individuals from the aspect of having autistic spectrum disorder.

In doing some research on the Agent Orange issue, I talked to some veterans, and they had uncovered an interesting use of Agent Orange. It seems that Agent Orange was being used the United States before its use over in Southeast Asia. From first-hand information from individuals who worked on the railroad, Agent Orange was used as a defoliant along the railroad tracks. So Agent Orange has been around and used in the United States into the late 70s. This was also noted from a document that can be viewed online entitled the history of Agent Orange and can be found at the following web address http://www.11thcavnam.com/main/story_of_agent_orange.htm

This document confirmed with detail already discovered through discussion with people who worked on the railroad system and also Vietnam veterans. What is also interesting about this document is the fact that Agent Orange was being used heavily in a state of Oregon and some other selected states.

From my study of individuals with autistic spectrum disorder, there is a group that has lineage directly back to a direct blood relative who was affected by Agent Orange. It seems that first-generation individuals may have autism along with other physical health problems. It is noted that the second-generation has a high probability of having autistic spectrum disorder. This I have been keeping track of through my office and in working with individuals with autistic spectrum disorder. However, there may be other causes of autism besides Agent Orange.

Another issue that came to light the 1960s was the problems that resulted from a transition in the home life from being the innocent to be a more radical configuration. Before this time, the famous line of "if

you don't like it here move out" was quite prevalent. It was noted that the individuals, children, and young adults, shut their mouth and stayed under their parent's roof until they could afford to move out. During the 1960's a revolution started and individuals moved out of their parents' house and tried to make it on their own. It seems that the possibility of this behavior rather than the latter led to specific groups being formed for the simple reason of survival. The use of illicit drugs at this time seems to have been the next level of self-medicating behavior. Possibly, due to depression or another mental health issue the people who moved out when they decided to rebel left a very nice lifestyle to end up living on the streets or sleeping under a bridge. The typical human response would be to start to mourn the loss of a specific thing or miss individual family members or privileges that they knew well in their life led them into the self-medicating process. Drugs, alcohol, and associating with the new so-called family, the availability and the use of illicit drugs as well as sometimes prescription drugs to handle some of the depressive/other mental health problems or to just fit in, became widely used. At this point, the use of marijuana, heroin, LSD, and prescription medications such as barbiturates, amphetamines, and minor tranquilizers came into play. This was to alleviate some of the depression symptoms that people may have felt, but this led to the next problem of enjoying the altered experience rather than dealing with the actual problem. The use and overuse of these illicit drugs and medications may also be a long-term cause of the emergence of autistic spectrum disorder.

Use of illicit drugs especially: hallucinogens, amphetamines, barbiturates, and opiates may have caused some brain damage over the course of their use. It has also been proposed that these illicit drugs may also cause a change in the DNA of the user and therefore there is a possibility that this change will show up in their children. Therefore, this is also a possible cause of autism.

Also during this time and it continues into the day, are the use of prescription medication. If we go back towards the beginning of the 60s, there was very little medication available for people with mental health problems. It was also noted that many of these medications were only used under the supervision of doctors and mental health facilities. There are many people who had a residence in mental health hospitals and structured care facilities. There does not seem to have been many prescriptions written for mental health problems outside of those facilities. However, that changed during the time in the middle on into the late 60s when individuals were discharged from these institutions into a least restrictive environment, and along with them, their medications were also prescribed to their least restrictive environment. In a mental health facility, every medication, every pill is accounted for every single hour of every single day. In the community, this is not the case, and prescriptions can come up missing at any given time. As individuals continue to be treated in the community setting, there seems to be available for those medications that were used mostly in that facility to be then prescribed and used in the community. Therefore, not only are the residents being discharged to a least restrictive environment, but their medication is also no longer being monitored as well as it would have been in a closed environment. It seems as time continues during this era, the use of prescription medications that were more controlled in a controlled environment are now being prescribed in the community environment. This seems to have possibly opened up the door for not only individuals using medications they do not need but also in the abuse and illicit sales of those prescription medications. It seems over the course of the next 30 years after the 1960s, the use, and abuse of prescription medications has escalated. Therefore, the use of prescription medication and the possible addiction to these prescription medications have increased.

There does not seem to be any long-term studies on many of the prescription medication. It looks like the terms of long-term research and long-term effects, and possible side effects have never entered into discussions. It was popularized in the 1980s, and due to disciplinary changes, educational facilities were pushing parents to put their child on Ritalin or some derivative of a stimulant. This medication was very popular during this time frame and seems to continue to be popular for school-age children. To this day, I have never seen any long-term studies done on the possible side effects of using this medication over the course of the individual's lifespan. Due to its extensive use and in some cases overuse, there is a possibility that the long-term use of Ritalin and its derivatives may play a role as a cause for autistic spectrum disorder in their children.

Also during this time frame, there were other medications they were tried on children with behavioral problems that may not have been approved for use in children but, where used. There were no long-term studies on the use of these medications and therefore the possibility of a long-term outcome may be that their children may have autism.

At the beginning of the 1990s, there were several new medications introduced into the market. Some of those were antidepressants, and others were new antipsychotic medications. You medications had FDA approval, but there was no real long-term study on possible side effects to the individual taking medication or the possible side effects that could affect their children. This is also a potential cause of autism.

Since the end of the 1980s, there were new illicit drugs out there on the market. Some of these were the reemergence of old illegal drugs, and there were new designer drugs out there on the market. The use of any of these drugs and their effect on the brain and possible DNA damage may also have led to the children of these abusers having autism. The use of crystal meth became widespread and continued to

some degree in its manufacture and usage. It is unknown what long-term side effects this has to the user, but severe physical and mental health problems are noted to some degree, and there are no real studies on the impact from the use of these drugs on their children. This behavior possibly could lead to autism and or some other physical and mental health issues.

At this point in history, the emergence of the use of heroin has come back into society. There were no long-term studies done on this when it first emerged back in the 60s and at this point, there does not seem to be any long-term studies on the current users of heroin. However, this is a very toxic and addictive drug, and this could be another cause of autistic spectrum disorder.

Other possible causes that may lead to autism are as follows: radiation, contaminated groundwater, exposure to other chemicals in the environment and possibly even airborne contaminants. At this point, there is no research on any of these possible causes for autism. I am speculating on these at this time because I am, and always will be, a chemist. My bachelor's degree is in chemistry, and I worked in a research lab and in an analysis lab. I also taught chemistry at one time and therefore knowing chemistry as I do, I see that there are many possibilities of other contaminations to the human body that could lead to some change in the DNA. Some other chemical introduced into the human body that could lead to the possibility that the individual who was exposed/contaminated/radiated to these types of toxins may have children with autistic spectrum disorder. There needs to be more research on this, and as individuals identified with autistic spectrum disorder, complete family history should be taken to try to come up with possible causes of autism.

I take family histories and look for specifics that may cause autism. It was discovered that mothers who are pregnant that have been diagnosed with some form of cancer, and undergo chemotherapy;

there is a strong possibility that the child will be born with autism or possibly even intellectual disability. So word to the wise here if you find yourself pregnant, and you have some form of cancer that is being treated, make an informed decision on what to do overall for you and your child.

It seems those external toxins (agent orange, possible nerve gases, nerve agents, radiation), prescription medication, illicit drugs and the possibility of some other experimental medications, and possibly some other external and environmental issues, have led to the possibility of some relationship to the emergence of autistic spectrum disorder. If we take a look at the statistics and when the escalation of autism being diagnosed, it seems that people of this era, as they grew up, and as they had children appears that there is a possibility that there is a link between these behaviors and autistic spectrum disorder. This possibility is noted in several studies by different organizations.

In kind of a satirical format, this story would go like this. At the end of the 1950s, everything was beautiful kids went to school, they played sports, and they came home when they did their chores. They did their homework, and they studied they want to go on to college and become something. As the 1960s emerged, there was a rebellion going on between children and their parents and it seems that living at home was a drag. Two movements happen: 1) with those who continue to obey and then went off and fought in the Vietnam war and 2) there was a group who decided to rebel and go live out on the street, i.e., the hippie movement. Those soldiers were exposed Agent Orange and gave their all in that war, called Vietnam, came back and they started to have children. On the other hand, those who went into the hippie cult and started taking all kinds of interesting chemicals into their body for example hallucinogens, speed, downer, uppers, opiates, all had some physiological reaction to ingesting of these interesting organic compounds into their bodies. In some cases, there was a lot of toxicity. However, those that survived, no long-term study was done on

what could have happened to alter their genetic code and their children. There was no long-term study on their children's children as those individuals at this time are also having children. Therefore, there are issues with individuals who were into the drug scene and what may have come from their behavior that was passed on to their children and their children's children. On the other hand, those soldiers who went off to Vietnam were also injected with experimental vaccines along with being exposed to Agent Orange and other possible nerve agents. As time continued, it seems that people were discovering that if they felt they had a mental health problem, they would go to their doctor and were prescribed some legal medication. This can be used as well as abused, and in many cases, it seems it was overused, or it was prescribed for the wrong problem. People can be very manipulative, and doctors try to do their best, but some people will do whatever it takes to get that" high." What it is doing to their human physiology and the possibility of long-term side effects to their children is unknown. It seems that no one took the time to take a look at this whole picture from an objective viewpoint. It appears from the graphics that this is where some of the first significant identifications of autistic spectrum disorder started, and this is where some of the issues continue. We also have to mention a specific time in history. During the 1980s, where it seems there was quite a rise in the identification of autism, whereby many stimulants were being used on children. It does not look like there are any long-term studies done on the effects of using stimulants on children and at this time, those individuals who were children during the 1980s are now in their 30s and 40s and have children of their own.

There may be some connection to the events of the 1960s through the today, which possibly contributed to the increase of identified individuals with autistic spectrum disorder. Looking at various statistical analytical findings, there could be a correlation drawn from the use of illicit/prescription drugs and the exposure to a toxic

chemical that may have led to the increase in autistic individuals. There is an argument here that the use of toxic substances, illicit drug addictions, and the use of stimulants, may have caused autism. Working people during a specific time in history (the 70s through the 80s), were exposed to other chemical toxins that were in the working environment. This can also be to some extent about the asbestos problem but also in the fact that before OSHA was up and running. Many people were subjected to not using gloves when they were handling solvents or some chemical and there again what was absorbed through the hands into the body, which may have altered the genetic code of some kind, and could have at this point be a contributing factor to the autistic spectrum disorder.

As it is, I am a very busy person, and I cannot take this any further than what I am proposing at this time. What I am suggesting at this time is the following: There is a possibility that soldiers exposed to Agent Orange, injected with experimental vaccines, individuals who took prescription medication, and overused it or even just used it, could lead to autism. Individuals who took pharmaceutical medications and illicit drugs and the possibility of individuals being prescribed stimulants to help them to pay attention may have had children that have autism. No matter how you look at it, it is through the use of all this organic and synthetically derived chemicals, and there is a possibility that changes in the DNA and other structures within the human body may have led to the result of the increase in autistic spectrum disorder. I am leaving this opened up for discussion and debate, but there is some possibility here, and there is some direct linkage. Whoever takes this on and moves forward with it, I wish you the best of luck. As cases come through my office, I identify them in one of these categories, but at this time to continue further research it will be one case at a time.

There are several statistical analyses throughout the Internet on the prevalence of autistic spectrum disorder. In my presentation of the

statistical analysis what I did was take all the statistical analysis out there reanalyze them and come up with my own numbers in regards to all the available statistical charts graphs and current analysis. Some of the research agrees with each other, and some do not. I included all study and came up with my own statistical numbers in regards to all the differentiation between the charts and graphs presented by different organizations that have been tracking autism over the course of the last 47 years. The complete statistics are from the Center for Disease Control. The problem is with the statistic that was given in 1970 and 1975 was at the time of the DSM-II. The DSM II had no diagnosis of autism or an autistic spectrum disorder, and therefore the statistics given are in question. The figures presented are as follows: 1970:1 in 10,000, 1975:1 in 5000. I question the statistics because autism did not exist in the DSM-II, so I wonder the basis on which this was determined. The next statistical point was in 1985 and moving forward. 1985 time frame was during the time of the DSM-III which indicated: 1 in 2500 individuals had autism. It should be noted that during this time frame that an individual had to be diagnosed before the age of 30 months. The next statistic that appeared on the chart was in 1995. In 1995 the DSM-IV was in use, and the criterion for autistic spectrum disorder was 36 months of age. That statistic indicated that there were 1 in 500 individuals with autistic spectrum disorder. It was noted in that statistical chart that in 2001 (still under the DSM-4) the number of individuals diagnosed with autistic spectrum disorder was then 1 in 250. In 2004, this statistic went to 1 in 166. In 2007 statistic increased again to 1 in 150. In 2009, this statistic went to one in 110 people with autistic spectrum disorder. The figures were all done during the time that the DSM-IV was in use in the diagnostic criteria was still 36 months of age as the cut off for the determination of autism. The final statistic during the time of the DSM-IV was in 2012. In 2012, the incidents were 1 in 88, and another statistic indicated 1 and 68 people were diagnosed with autistic spectrum

disorder. Either statistic brings about the fact that there is a continuing rise in autism even with the cutoff date of 36 months.

The DSM 5 came into use in 2012. The criterion for autistic spectrum disorder was changed to eliminate this 36 months cutoff point. This then opened up the diagnoses of autistic spectrum disorder to individuals of all ages that may have the signs and symptoms of autism. In 2013, the statistics indicated that 1 in 50 people have autistic spectrum disorder. At this point, 2018, a statistic from (Autism Speaks.org) the prevalence is 1 in 45 individuals who are diagnosed with autism under the new DSM 5 criterion.

If we look across the history of autism, we can draw some parallels to incidents that were going on in the United States that may be possible causes of autistic spectrum disorder. As I stated the statistics that I found from 1970 and 1975 were interesting but the DSM at the time (DSM II) had no diagnoses of autism or autistic spectrum disorder. Therefore, those statistics can be questioned and will not be taken into account throughout the rest of this chapter.

The statistics are starting in 1985 under the DSM-III indicated that 1 in 2500 individuals (using the criterion of diagnoses before 30 months of age as a cutoff) indicate several possibilities when it comes to the cause of autism. During the time frame before 1985, and for years before 1985, there was a lot of pesticides being used that may have caused contaminated groundwater. Defoliants such as Agent Orange which was sprayed on members of the armed forces in Southeast Asia, Agent Orange was also used by specific companies to defoliate in places across the United States. There was extensive use of illicit drugs, there were several new medications introduced into the market, and there were some significant alcoholism problems during this time. It could be any one of these factors above that could contribute to the possibility of the development of autistic spectrum disorder. Anyone of these factors could alter the genetic code, which then would come out in their children. During this time, there also children were born addicted to certain illicit drugs, and this may be a possible cause of autistic spectrum disorder or some other developmental disorder. It was also noted that many school-age children were put on Ritalin at this time as they were diagnosed with attention deficit hyperactivity disorder but there is a possibility that they had autism. Even though they may have had autism the question is that nobody has ever answered was, what about the effects of them being on some stimulant for long periods of time on their children. Therefore, there is a possibility that children who were put on Ritalin during the 80s may have given birth to children with autistic spectrum disorder.

The statistics from 1995 through 2012 was under the criterion of the DSM-IV, which indicated that autism had to be diagnosed before the age of 36 months. During this time frame autism went from 1 in 500 to 1 in 88 or 1 in 68. Both statistics did come up during my search, and therefore they are both listed here. We look at what was going on during this timeframe as there seems to have been new illicit drugs on the market, new medications that were introduced to the market and individuals who may have been exposed to some form of the toxin as their children now have children. Speculation here is reasonable that there is a possibility that the behaviors during this time frame may have led to the increase in autism.

The first DSM-5 and only one at this time indicated that the rate of autism is now 1 in 50. It is possible that individuals who had been into the illicit drugs, current medications and past medications, exposure to toxins, possibly even exposure to radiation, have caused this increase in the statistic of autistic spectrum disorder. The other possibility for this rise in autistic spectrum disorder statistic is that the 36-month time frame for diagnoses was removed and anyone can be diagnosed with autistic spectrum disorder. It will be interesting to see what the next statistical analysis reveals.

It seems there are parallels to drug abuse, drug use, medication use, exposure to environmental toxins, the possibility of worksite contamination, radiation and the fetus being exposed to toxins while in development. There is a wide array of possibilities that has led to this increase in the number of autistic individuals from the statistics that were given.

In current practice, one group seems to stand out at this time. However, this is from my practice, and this could be different in other places, but with my analysis of the current situation, there are two specific causes that I see in my office. The first one being, individuals whose direct relative had been exposed to Agent Orange in Southeast Asia. There are first-generation second-generation cases of autistic spectrum disorder. So at least from my experience, there is a direct link from Agent Orange to autistic spectrum disorder. I will continue research on this as time goes on, but there is a direct link from my practice. The second interesting finding for my practice is individuals who were into illicit drugs and medications that were prescribed and treatments that were prescribed during the time before and during the gestation of the child. There seems to be a parallel with the parents (especially the mother) if illicit drugs were used before fertilization and then during pregnancy. This may also produce an individual with autistic spectrum disorder. The other side of this issue, that a mother using particular medication, which was prescribed or prescriptive procedures due to her own health issues, resulting in the child being born with deficits and possibly even autistic spectrum disorder. Both of these issues should be researched further.

One last area that I see very infrequently has to do with the mother having some forms of physical disability or ongoing disease process. There is a possibility that due to this condition, their children may be born with those diseases and possibly even autistic spectrum disorder.

As time goes on autistic spectrum disorder is not going away. It may be hard to ever find the etiology behind autistic spectrum disorder as it may be a combination of many things or just one thing but it continues. As an individual who has been designated as an autism expert, (I take this complement humbly), I will continue to work with as many individuals who come to see me with autistic spectrum disorder. I continue to put together tailor-made treatment plans for each individual to work with them on reaching the highest level of their abilities. I will continue to keep working with parents on understanding the behavior of their individual and how they can help them as well to reach the highest level of the possibilities in their life. I encourage others to the use this book and do the best they can in helping individuals with autistic spectrum disorder because each individual has something to contribute to society and only with the dedication of the caregiver/parent/therapist will they be able to reach that ability. I leave it to anyone reading this to continue and try new things with individuals with autistic spectrum disorder and see what they can do and not just put them away in some asylum or some close workshop where they just put in their time. Work with them to help them find and use the specific talent that they have. Individuals with autism have a place in society and only through diligence and hard work on the part of those who work with them will help them to reach that goal.

CHAPTER 19

Autistic Spectrum Disorder And Electronic Gadget Addictive Disorder

EGAD- Electronic Gadget Addictive Disorder- The inability to function, exist or breathe without the possession of an electronic device. This includes cell phones, tablets, iPod, etc. or any portable device that a person feels that they have to have on their person to become complete. An electronic device that a person believes that they have to be connected to at all times or most of the time to be connected to the digital world around them or to be distracted from the real world around them. An addiction that was stated as " I can't live without my electronics."

EGAD and Autism

The most profound question that can be asked about someone with autism is: Do individuals with autism have EGAD?

The answer to that question may surprise many people is the answer is no. Unlike the average individual who has EGAD, and is drawn to their electrical device at every possible moment because they have become so addicted to them, a person with autistic spectrum disorder retreats to their electronic device to avoid situations by which they do not have the skills to handle or to avoid possible anxiety. It seems that they do so to refocus. Then they get away from the electronic device when they have refocused enough to engage in a more comfortable manner. In contrast, the average person who has electronic addiction continually delves into their electronic device, as it seems, to avoid any and all contact with the outside world to purely entertain/distract themselves from the possibility of any social engagement that requires any social skills. A person with autism uses their electronic device, especially when the environment in which they are in and that they are actively engaged in, becomes too emotional for them to handle. They use the electronic device as a timeout to refocus, think about what's going on and possibly come up with a strategy (protocol) in which to deal with the situation. They are not avoiding the situation, but instead, they are trying to understand the situation through stepping out of the situation into the electronic device and then, after refocusing, possibly re-engaging in that environment. This may take a

little time, or this may take a lot of time as it seems, it depends on their ability to come up with a strategy in which to deal with the situation. It would be said that an individual with autistic spectrum disorder will use the electronic device to give themselves a timeout, think about the situation, refocus on the situation and then leave the electronic device and then re-engage in the situation around them. If the situation around them cannot be solved, they may stay in the electronic world for a period of time. It should be said that they can leave that electronic world at any time because they voluntarily entered into it, unlike the addict who jumps into it as by habit and an unconscious need to be engaged in the electronic device. People with autistic spectrum disorder can disengage at any time unlike the addict, and once they engage, they are engaged until some natural barrier occurs and they have to stop. The addict becomes angry when he has to stop engaging with his electronic device. In contrast to an individual with autism willingly disengages when they have solved the problem that seems to be bothering them which was the reason why they went into the electronic device to solve that problem or to refocus so then they can think about how they can solve the problem.

Individuals with autistic spectrum disorder can master the electronic world, and they can do things inside that electronic world that are quite amazing. It seems that the reason why the individual likes to engage in the electronic world to refocus is simply that the electronic world has logic behind it. The real world has a lot of illogic, and sometimes an individual with autism cannot figure out what a solution is to an illogical problem because the logical problem has no logic in it and therefore it is hard to come up with a logical solution. However, if they give themselves a timeout and go into the electronic world, they tend to figure out what the answer is in the real world by use of coming up with a logical solution that they may have figured out while engaging in the electronic world. Individuals with EGAD do not solve problems but rather cause more problems due to their addiction to electronics. It seems that people with EGAD entertain themselves with the electronics rather than learn from them or gain any knowledge from them in. An individual with autistic spectrum disorder has a tendency to go into the electronic world to seek answers or possible solutions for their situations in the real world and therefore learn from

their experience within the electronic world and bring it out into the real world.

Working with individuals with autistic spectrum disorder at all levels results in the following observations of electronics when it comes to its relationship with the individual. Each level will be described, and hopefully, this will help some parents gain insight into either individual spends, what can be considered a great deal of time, in the electronic world.

Level I

Level I individuals whether they be static, or dynamic, seem to be very masterful in the use of electronics. They do use electronics to develop their safe zone/bubble/comfort zone, but they also can use this as a portable bubble as well. They seem to be able to take a step out of a situation and try to come up with an answer by the use of an electronic device. They do seem to spend a lot of time in the electronic world, but it also seems they are trying to figure out problems that many individuals who do not have autism would never understand. They are continually trying to solve problems they continue to circulate throughout their conscious mind, and their relationship with the electronic device seems to be a way to solve those problems. Many of those problems are usually of design in nature, a creative nature or an artistic nature. It seems that they utilize the electronic device for what it was meant to be rather than use it is someplace to hide. They do at times hide in his electronic environment, but this comes from being jaded by life and having issues with social skills.

Level I individuals do understand that the electronic devices are devices and represent a world that can be real to an extent, but it is not the total reality. They do understand there is a reality around them beyond the electronic world and they have explored it from time to time. Some individuals may even have jobs, engage in the real world on a regular basis and have friends and hobbies outside of the electronic world. If they become disenchanted with the real world, they may retreat into this electronic world, which is part of their

comfort zone/bubble/safety zone and may seem to be spending a lot of time there. However, is usually productive and they are coming up with answers to issues that may be unknown to the world around them however it does exist. These people are deep thinkers and do have a lot of satisfaction in life. Some parental figures do not understand this behavior, as they have not opened their mind to the fact that their individual may be much smarter than they will ever be. It is also known individuals at this level have a very high IQ and are looking for ways to utilize their ability with this electronic world. They also seem to have the understanding that this electronic environment is not going away because it is sold a lot of problems were created more problems and it will continue.

On occasion, a level one individual may engage in playing certain video games or some types of online entertainment. This is not typical for them, but it is something they do on occasion. For the most part, they are trying to come up with answers to questions as well as developing new ideas. A level one individual will not over engage in the electronic world unless of course, they have no clue on how to handle their current situation in the real world. At that point, they may retreat into the electronic world and try to come up with answers will they try and calm himself down. It seems that they have developed their own method of over focus, defocused, refocus that utilizes whatever electronic device they have or would ever electronic system they are engaged in. It seems that they can solve a lot of their own problems and move forward.

A cautionary statement to any and all parents with a level one individual that seem to be spending a lot of time working on their computers or engaging in activities on their smartphone. They are not lost in that electronic world of ones and zeros. They are trying to develop a new strategy for whatever situation is going on or whatever problem they cannot seem to solve. It is true, on occasion that they will engage in specific entertainment but, for the most part, they're either trying to solve the problem, come up with an idea for development or they are bored and need to defocus their thought process. Either way, do not throw out at them "you are spending came much time on your electronic device." It is only your perception and

lack of understanding of what they are doing which causes you to say this and you should never say this to them because now they are trying to figure out what is wrong with you. For the most part, there is a lot wrong with parental figures who do not take time to figure out what is going on with their individual. Denial is not an answer to this problem. Social engagement on a very easy-going level will produce answers that you will never understand, but the individual does their best to explain it to you in their own language. As a parent, you need to take time, understand your individuals thought processes to appoint and then allow them to come up with the solutions to the problems on which they are focused on.

Level II

Level II designation is divided up into three generalized divisions: high, middle and low. Each one of these will be described in detail.

Level II-high level

These groups of individuals are very similar in scope to the level 1's in regards to their use of electronic devices. The similarities are striking in regards to the safe zone/bubble/comfort zone and electronic devices that may be found in this environment. The difference is that they are a little more attuned to their electronic devices outside their comfort zone/bubble/safety zone and they may be more dependent on the use of those electronic devices to accomplish specific tasks in which they are engaging. This is why they are level II because they have not mastered the adaptive skills needed to accomplish those tasks that they are somewhat dependent on the electronic device to accomplish. There is a possibility that they could achieve a level I status but it depends on their ability to learn, master and utilize adaptive skills that they may learn. Moreover, it seems that as long as they have their electronic device, which they are more dependent upon, they can figure out the problem and not learn from the solution. This group does engage in electronic play as well as problem-solving, but it seems that they do not learn from solving the problems or at least learn, remember and use. They are little more dependent upon their electronic devices to figure out situations in which they may be in that

they do not quite understand and have not come up with an adaptive skill to deal with. It seems that part of their protocols has to do with an electronic device. They are somewhat dependent upon them to figure out or to keep notes or to deal with situations. This group tends to utilize the electronic device for what it was meant for more than play with it. They seem to understand that electronic device may be for learning or for getting answers. They do not necessarily spend a significant amount of time playing electronic games, but instead, they seem to be engaging in some social programming as well as doing some creative work. They are not addicted to their electronic devices, but instead, they can become dependent upon them due to their utilization.

Level II-middle level

This group splits into two different directions when it comes to electronic gadgets. One group actually will spend more time in activities that have nothing to do with electronics. They do seem to carry their phone everywhere they go, but it is more for some socialization or communication. They do not know how to utilize the smartphone for what it was meant for but instead use it for communication purposes and some gaming programs. This group does understand the real world and they do seem to be able to hold down jobs and understand the need for and value of money. At times conversations can go back into some video game world in which they have been working on, and it may become the entire topic conversation. They are usually refocused when the mention of something in the real world, especially when it has to do with work and money, is mentioned. They will get out of the electronic world and come back to reality immediately. It seems that they use the electronic world to feel good about themselves in the downtime when they are not working. This gives them a sense of control and accomplishment as well as a means to unwind from a hard day at work. They usually develop limits on how long they will allow themselves into the electronic world, but they do need some supervision to set up protocols and adaptive skill such as bedtime, wake time, work time and time to engage in the electronic world. They can self-regulate to appoint when it comes to the needs of the outside

world in comparison to their want to be in the electronic world. They can learn the protocols of bedtime, wake time, work time and then game time. They can adapt, but for the most part, they are not addicted but Instead seem to utilize the electronic world for something positive. They do know the difference between the electronic world and the real world.

The other side of the level II tends to have a problem with dealing with reality. It seems that reality has been very cruel to them or, their interpretation or they seem to have trouble engaging in a positive way in the world around them. This group does have a problem with reality testing to the point that the electronic world has become the reality and they may engage in specific behaviors in the real world as they did in the electronic world. This group can be very dangerous as they may engage in some problem solving that they carry over from the electronic world into the real world. It is speculated that most of the individuals who have had experience with the criminal justice system are from this group. They tend to hide inside the electronic world because they cannot figure out why the real world is being so mean to them. This group can still learn adaptive skills; however, it seems that the older they get, the harder it is to teach them any adaptive skill because the engagement with the electronic world has become their reality. There was a time that when an individual could not determine between reality and fantasy, they were called schizophrenic. However in this day and age, and given the autism level, they are individuals with either an inability to or resistance to learning new adaptive skills and mastering them. This group can be very dangerous because their problem-solving skills, solution sets, may include some violent behavior that they have mastered in the electronic world. It seems that they have mastered it in the electronic world are going to try to utilize it in the real world. This is where the trouble starts, as they tend to have a problem with the reality of life as it is. This group is somewhat addicted to the electronic gadgets as is their reality. However, with the proper interventions and program, they can be rehabilitated from being an electronic gadget addict to having some position in the real world where they can be a productive member of society. If they are working a job, and with the proper intervention and supervision, they can be rehabilitated away from this electronic

addiction and earn a living. Without this type of intervention, what you have on your hands is a ninja warrior with a short fuse that may become dangerous in a minor conflict. It is essential to identify these individuals and start them on a rehabilitation program away from electronics and into the real world. This can be done, but it will take time, patience, and effort.

Level II-low level

This level is the closest thing to having an electronic gadget addictive disorder. Due to their limitations, they may become easily addicted to the electronic systems. However, they use the systems they do not understand them. This level can determine the difference between reality and fantasy to some degree. However, this group needs constant supervision, and the degree and frequency of their engagement with electronics can be determined by those people who supervise them. It is very easy for this group to become addicted if there is no supervision and limitations. It should be noted, and when it comes to the use of the Kindle or some reading device, this group may be very interested in utilization when it comes to reading. The other usage would be for games and of course watching of some video. It is unknown the capacity of these individuals as my experiences with them have been limited to some degree. It is known they can utilize some skills depending on which side of their brain is underdeveloped a compromise. The individuals may use the dominance either brain to develop it, learn or even be entertained. The use of electronics with this group can be educational as well as entertaining. They may use electronics to get out of certain situations that they cannot emotionally handle, have no skill set for or do not want to engage. They may use the electronics as a means to excuse themselves from the situation they are not comfortable in. Electronics may also be used as a means for this group to get them to engage in certain conditions and follow through on requests. In this group, electronic seems to be used in both directions, for education and recreation as well as motivation.

Level III

Individuals at this level can be quite amused by electronic gadgets. Depending on the device and the utilization of the device, these individuals can be distracted and possibly be brought out of a meltdown by using some electronic device. In addition, experiencing individuals from this level, it was found out in the office that they respond to music and visual stimulus. It seems that more testing would need to be done to determine each, individual likes and dislikes when it comes to the utilization of an electronic device with this group. It seems that there is a possibility it electronics can be used for them to refocus, regroup and calm down. Each individual in this group needs to be thoroughly tested for what stimuli helps them to refrain and even stop their meltdowns along with what device may provide that stimulus for them to defocus and refocus from the situation in which they are in. There is a possibility that they can become dependent or even addicted to some electronic device but this type of addiction or dependency would help them with their behavioral problems. In this case, the electronic device becomes an electronic intervention that could be extremely therapeutic for this group. I hope that someone will take these findings and possibly utilize this to help this level of individuals that seem to be difficult to work with.

A simple conclusion can be drawn from the following statements: an individual with EGAD engages in the electronic world because they choose not to engage in the real world. They are not looking for solutions to their problems but rather a place to hide and hope the problem will go away by itself. Individuals with EGAD cannot live without their electronic devices. EGAD seems to be eroding at the very fabric of social skills and social society as it continues to become more important than any personal interaction or any activities in the real world. Individuals with EGAD seem to be losing sight of the real world and are more engaged in the man-made world.
An individual with autistic spectrum disorder who engages in the electronic world is using it for their own type of timeout. They can focus on whatever they are doing with the electronic device, refocus on the problem or situation at hand and come up with a solution. Individuals with autism appreciate the logic that surrounds the

electronic world because it has a linear flow of existence where logic is pure. This is why individuals with autistic spectrum disorder can use their gift and master electronic devices to solve problems and come up with solutions whereas. The average individual with electronic gadget addictive disorder (EGAD) creates problems in their real world as they tried to hide or avoid. They can become so addicted that they neglect the needs, necessities, and responsibilities that they have in the real world. If you were to ask someone with autism why they engage in the electronic world, they will give you a good logical situation and a solution and probably even a very sound logical reason. A person with electronic gadget addictive disorder will only look up at you from their screen and say" what"? What do you want? In addition, usually ends with the following statement of "you're interrupting me."

When it comes to electronic addictive disorder and autism, the level of autism should be examined first before a declaration of the electronic addictive disorder is given. It is possible for individuals with autism to become addicted to electronics. For the most part, an individual with autism, depending upon what level, can utilize electronics to solve problems, utilize them for their safe zone, or become somewhat dependent on them for communications. There is a group that could be addicted to electronics. However, with the proper interventions, supervision, and cooperation any group that becomes addicted to electronics can be rehabilitated to some extent. Nevertheless, for the most part, individuals with autistic spectrum disorder do not have electronic gadget addictive disorder.

GLOSSARY

Adaptive skill: The skills needed for activities of daily living, work, communication, social skills and any other skill that individual may need and utilize in order to live their life to the best of their ability.

ANGER: The second phase in the behavioral triad. Manifested by the clenching of fists, louder responses, aggressive posturing, foot stomping, arms flapping, etc. Resulting from lack of intervention during the Frustration phase of the behavioral triad misinterpreted as the possibility of physical aggression.

The Autistic Perspective: The way that the Autistic Individual perceives the world around them through the interpretation of the five senses and insight.

Awareness: The ability to understand, adapt and live in the world around you as safe as possible. This includes understanding safety and practice of caution and developing behaviors to avoid dangers in the real world. The understanding of the real world and the consequences of not practicing safety and discretionary behavior.

Behavioral Triad: The three escalating behavior that results from the parent/teacher/caregiver failing to acknowledge the individuals present, meaning or verbalizations. It starts with FRUSTRATION- usually, body language, raising voice or clenching or unclenching hands. Followed by ANGER- agitation noted in voice, body posturing and tone and volume and pressure of speaking, resulting in a MELT-DOWN. Meltdown is the final part of this Behavioral Triad. If this is reached, there could be a serious physical altercation and outside intervention. This is typical of males. Females may combine Frustration and Anger as one-step and proceed to the Melt Down.

Brain-behavior and thought process: The ability for a person to use both sides their brain congruently and in conjunction with thought processes in decision-making and activities.

Comfort zone: Also known as The Bubble, Safe Zone: That environment or environments in which the individual prefers to be or seems to be most comfortable. For example home, bedroom, school, friend's home.

Consequences: The final outcomes of one's actions or behaviors as dictated by society.

Discrimination and Discretion: An adaptive skill by which the individual learns to discriminate between those people who are their friends and those who want to be their friends and can start to develop a sense that people want something from them and they have developed methods to avoid those type of individuals. This is awareness. This seems to be a very specific characteristic to some degree of self-survival and also to personal and emotional survival. This ability seems to be very specific to the level I autistic spectrum disorder. This is a learnable adaptive skill that can be well learned depending on the individual and their intellectual level. However, individuals at the level I status usually have a very good working ability of this characteristic. Level II varies in this ability.

Dynamic: Term associated with Level I Autistic Disorder, indicating that the individual is still learning and mastering adaptive skills.

Extension Bubble/Safe Zone/Comfort Zone: Those places and environments that the individual has added to his initial comfort zone. This could be places, places with specific people, items, and areas. This can vary with age and acquisition of adaptive skills.

Familiar individuals: Those individuals that the person is most comfortable being around. For the most part, this is first-degree relatives and extended family. However, there are friends who have common interests that the individual will have comfort being around.

Individuals with autism can to some degree notice other autistic individuals and may actually become familiar with them.

Fixation: The item, thought or person that becomes repeated by the autistic individual even though another answer is expected. This will be verbally repeated until it is: 1) Satisfied to some degree, 2) substituted for by another preferred item or 3) Placated completely.

Focus-De-focus-Re-focus: The technique utilized with the Key to stop the Obsessive Verbalization. The Focus is on an obsession. Utilizing the Key is De-Focusing the individual from the obsession and then the Re-Focus of the individual on a substitution for the obsession.

FRUSTRATION: The first observable behavior in the behavioral triad. Usually manifested due to the individual interpreting that the parent/caregiver/ teacher is not listening or understanding what is being stated or inferred by them. Manifested by body posturing, sighing, pacing or shifting side to side, repetition of verbalizations, escalation of the volume of speech, etc., tension is building up in the individual. Intervention here can prevent further escalation in the behavior triad. Use of the KEY or focus-de-focus-re-focus can prevent the next step-ANGER

Jaded by Life: Bad experiences, failures, and disappointments either by their own doing, trusting others or just did not succeed due to not following through or trusting that something should happen that did not: causes them to give up easily, rationalize why they should not try again. This is a form of Conative Dissonance where their learning process and experiences cause them to choose to avoid similar situations for fear that the same outcome will happen and cause them to feel the following: Anxiety followed by depression and hopelessness. This becomes their parameter for not moving forward and the "What If" thought process becomes the logic.

The Key: This is a person, place, thing, a word, or a sentence spoken that de-focuses the individual from the obsessive thought manifested by repeated verbalizations. The Key de-focuses the individual and the individual re-focuses on the Key that is spoken or presented. The Key can be considered a substitution for the obsession that the individual is verbalizing repeatedly. It may be a preferred item, activity or some privilege.

Left-brain dominance: Thought process that is dominated by the left side of the brain to include verbalization, verbalize logic and reasoning. This includes abilities as described in the Trivium, which includes: rhetoric, logic, and reading. Music on this side is not the tone and rhythm but rather only the words are heard.

Meltdown: The behavioral result when an individual with autistic spectrum disorder is pushed to their maximum limit of keeping their behavior under control. These can be as simple as shouting matches to the point of it all out temper tantrum. The last phase of the Behavioral Triad can result in police involvement, hospitalization and a physical altercation. A good intervention plan can de-escalate the individual if it is applied and avoid consequences.

Obsession: A thought that the individual verbalizes over and over again. It may be a preferred activity, food or some item or even a person. The Key will stop this obsession.

Progressive: Characterization of the subgroup of the Level II-Middle-Middle level. Making progress into being a part of society and spending less time in the fantasy world of the comfort zone. This group will work and hold a job.

Regressive: Characterization of the sub-group of the Level II-Middle-Middle level. Preference to spend time in the fantasy world of the comfort zone rather to become part of the real world and deal with real life.

Right brain dominance: Thought processes that are dominated by the right side of the brain to include the following: mathematics, logic, and reasoning as dictated by mathematical and science, practical knowledge and the ability to use said qualities. This is modeled after the Quadrivium, which was a collection of academic studies to include the following: arithmetic, astronomy, geometry, music and to some extent logic that applies to mathematics. Music as it applies to the rhythms, and sounds of the music.

Skill Set: The set of skills needed to accomplish a task. The skill set may have more than one way to accomplish the task. The skill set can be part of an adapted skill. The skill set will be used to perform and master the adapted skill or another task that may be mastered.

Skills SET: The sum total of all skills that have been mastered and utilized by any individual. This would include the mastery of adapted skills and other tasks.

Sensory Overload: The event that occurs when the individual is affected by an external stimulus from the environment around them. This could be one or a combination of sensory perceptions from the environment in which they are in. The sensory receptors are the five senses. Hearing, Touch, Taste, Smell, and Sight.

Shut Down: An event that happens when an individual may have an overload of either: sensory, emotional or situational events. This is usually resulting in withdrawal, looking away, and no verbal communication from the individual. They may sit there and distract themselves with anything in the environment but not respond to any verbal interactions.

Social awareness: the awareness that a person is expected to understand in modern society: this would include any and all systems

that exist in the world. For example banking and money, the legal and judicial system, rights and responsibilities and social boundary issues.

Social etiquette: accepted or allowed social behavior in society by any person.

SSET: Acronym for the following: Symptoms: Reported behaviors, psychometric results, and observations. Syndrome: Diagnosis of the noted behaviors and results. Etiology: the cause of the Symptoms. Treatment: treatment of the Symptoms and Syndrome.

Solution Set: The thought process that proposes that there is more than one right answer. Instead of a single answer, there are at least two or more correct answers to any specific problem. Also can be part of the skill set.

Static: Term associated with Level I Autism. The individual is not acquiring any more adaptive skills and seems to be set in their ways. They do have the potential to change and adapt.

4-P's: The organizational construct of behaviors, activities, and methodology by which individuals carry out tasks. PROTOCOL-The methodology to deal with the current situation. This is followed by the PROCESS- skills to be used in the PROCEDURE to end up with the final outcome finally- PRODUCT. Depending on the individual and his adaptive skill level, learning process and intelligence level, They may have many different ways to achieve the final PRODUCT, or they may only have one. Depending again on the previously mentioned parameters, any interruption during the process may cause a slight re-thinking time out for the more adept to an incident whereby a Behavioral Triad may be experienced. Bottom line is simple when it comes to this. If an individual is involved in completing a task, leave them to finish it. The only exception to this is if they are actually in danger during the task or they are being impulsive and not using caution.

Autistic Spectrum Disorder-Statistical Analysis

(Circle all that apply)

Coding:

Category:

Emotional Behavior.

1) frustration.

2) anger.

3) anxiety

4) intermittent explosive disorder.

5) over focus

Emotional, behavioral outbursts.

6) Depression

Observable behaviors:

1) Attention deficit/hyperactivity disorder symptoms.

2) Intermittent explosive disorder-provoked.

Intermittent explosive disorder-unprovoked.

3) Separating self from others.

4) Over focused-

5) No emotional

6) Staring behaviors.

7) Tremors

8) Tics

9) Weakness in:

- **a) Hands**
- **b) Arms**
- **c) Upper body**
- **d) Legs**
- **e) Abdomen**

Other deformities or physical issues: (eyesight, bowel or bladder control, bed wetting, etc.)

Sensory Sensitivity:

1) Hearing.

2) Vision.

3) Taste.

4) Touch.

5) Smell.

6) Insight

Birth Order:

1) Oldest child.

2) Youngest child.

3) Only child.

4) number/total number of children.

Mother's Age at Birth:

Mother's Health:

1) Healthy-no history of health problems.

2) Mother on medication prior to conception.

3) Mother on medication during pregnancy.

4) Mother's use of substances prior to pregnancy.

5) Mother's use of substances during pregnancy

Define: Alcohol, tobacco, prescription medication: opiates, antidepressants, antipsychotics, anti-anxiolytics, illegal substances: Marijuana, crystal meth, LSD, hypnotics, amphetamines, crack, heroin.

List each medication:

Father's Health: Circle all that apply

- **healthy, no vices, normal childhood illnesses**
- **health issues,**
- **smoker**
- **drinker**
- **illicit drug use**
- **legal drug abuse**
- **combination of vices as previous listed**
- **history of mental illness**
- **history of legal offenses(prison time) misdemeanors and felonies**
- **possible exposure to toxins-Agent Orange-direct descendent of someone exposed to Agent Orange.**
- **Exposure to radiation or radioactive substances**
- **exposure to experimental chemicals**

- **exposure to asbestos or direct descendant of someone who was exposed to asbestos**

Father's education:

- **no education**
- **high school graduate**
- **GED**
- **college graduate**
- **graduate school graduate**
- **professional school graduate**
- **trade school graduate**

Child's Birth:

1) Normal birth-vaginal delivery.

2) Normal birth-complications. List complications

3) Cesarean section birth.

Child's Health:

1) Normal development-hits all milestones within normal range.

2) Minimal issues-still meets all milestones within normal range.

3) Issues in meeting developmental milestones.

Child's Development:

1) **Starts talking between 1 and three years depending on the birth order.**
2) **Toilet Trained on time: between 2 and 3 years: y or n**
3) **Can feed self by age 3: y or n**
4) **Can sit still for meals: y or n**
5) **Can't sit still for meals: y or n**
6) **Gets along with siblings: y or n**
7) **Gets along with others: y or n**

Child's School Years:

Attention Problems

Getting along with other students

Gets bullied

Gets bullied and defends bully and indicates it is their friend.

<u>Problems with specific subjects</u>:

Math

Science

Social Studies

Reading

English

Music

Writing

Social Problems:

1) Gets into trouble easily
2) Spends too much time with electronics
3) Carries electronics everywhere
4) No real friends but usually people that use them

Family history:

This questioning deals directly with biological parents, grandparents and possibly great-grandparents of the individual with autistic spectrum disorder.

1) Did a parent, grandparent or great-grandparent ever experienced the following items:

Vietnam War: Agent Orange

Farming: Pesticides

DDT

Malathion

Parathion

Work-Related Chemicals:

Benzene and its relative chemicals: xylene and toluene

Acetone and its relative chemicals: methyl ethyl ketone and any other ketone compound.

Ether and its relative compounds

Other organic compounds: gasoline, kerosene, jet fuel, turpentine, paint thinner and other straight-chain/organic compounds.

Acetates: any compound made from acetate

Other work related issues:

Exposure to the following:

Asbestos

Metallic Oxides to include: iron oxide (rust) and other metallic dust

Exposure to nonmetallic dust: cement, gypsum, and other earthly elements: sodium, chlorine or any chloride compound, or any light metal.

Radiation or radioactive substances

Home-related issues:

Lead, lead paint

Coal mining areas, run-off from the mines

Toxic Waste dumping areas

Landfill areas

Medical issues:

Chemotherapy for cancer

Radiation therapy

Thalidomide

Any type of psychiatric interventions: Electroconvulsive Therapy, Insulin Shock Treatment, Medication. This would be in a direct bloodline history. (Parent, Grandparent, great-grandparent)

Child:

Intelligence Quotient:_______________

What IQ Test:____________________

Current Grade:____________________

Current Grade Average: Each Subject:

Math:_________

Science:_______

English:____________

Spelling:____________

History/Social Studies: ________________

Hand Writing;_________________

Reading: ____________________

Any Special Education Programs/Subjects:___________________

Please List:

Any Standardized Testing:

List results or attach a copy:

Treatment Program

FOR

ASD I and II

Treatment program-General Goals

1) work on rapport-build rapport and trust
2) assess autistic spectrum disorder level
3) after assessing autistic spectrum disorder level begin to work on identification of behavioral, emotional, educational and family problems
4) work with the individual in communication skills
5) work with individual and social skills
6) work with family members on understanding autistic spectrum disorder, the behaviors, and strategies for working with individuals with autistic spectrum disorder.
7) Work with an individual on their individual goals in life and also identify the specific behaviors that are unique to them
8) work with those specific behaviors towards achieving individual goals such as school, relationships, emotions and future endeavors.
9) Determine what ancillary services may be needed and help the family to achieve the acquisition of those ancillary services.
10) Determine what other needs may be needed and refer out as necessary.
11) Work with individual and family on a transition towards discharge planning.

Social Skills Training Program

ASD levels 1 and 2

- **individual demonstrate personal space concept**
- **the individual will demonstrate how to acknowledge another person's presence**
- **individual demonstrate how to greet another person**
- **the individual will demonstrate competence self-introduction to another person**
- **individual demonstrate one way to start a conversation**
- **individual demonstrate one way of ending the conversation**
- **the individual will demonstrate at least one way to accept can give a compliment**
- **individual demonstrate how to acknowledge and apologize for a mistake**
- **the individual will demonstrate an assertive way to say no**
- **the individual will demonstrate an assertive way to refuse to hand over their personal property**

Communication Skills Training Program

ASD levels 1 and 2

1) The individual will work on speaking in a normal tone of voice
2) The individual will make a statement and ask if there are any questions
3) The individual will learn to ask questions if they do not understand the statement
4) The individual will repeat the statement back to the person and ask a question.
5) The individual will learn how to start a conversation about a common topic
6) The individual will learn to say that they are not interested or do not understand the topic being discussed.
7) The individual will learn to end a conversation if they are not following and the person will not answer the questions.
8) The person will learn to communicate their feelings in a manner that is understood by others.
9) The person will learn to communicate how they feel in social situations.
10) The person will learn to communicate verbally and in gestures what they understand of other's feelings
11) The individual will learn how to communicate effectively in various situations.

Emotional Control Program

ASD level I and II

1) The individual will explain their frustration

2) The individual will explain ways they become frustrated

3) The individual will demonstrate the ability to ask a question prior to becoming frustrated

4) The individual will describe alternatives to becoming frustrated

5) Individual world role-play becoming frustrated and developing an alternative to emotional outbursts

6) The individual will demonstrate the ability to speak in a calm manner when they become frustrated

7) The individual will not be allowed to say the words "I don't know."

8) The individual will use simple words to describe what they are thinking/feeling.

9) The individual will do their best to calm down with prompts and encouragement by the therapist.

Parental Training Program

1) Parents will learn to understand what ASD is all about

2) Parents will develop options for dealing with individuals with ASD

3) Parents will learn to understand their child's way of thinking

4) Parents will learn communication skills with their child

5) Parents will role-play situation with their child

6) Parents will learn alternative communication skills with their child

7) Parents will develop and organize methods of completing tasks

8) Parents will acknowledge the fact that their child may not understand what they are saying

9) Parents will learn to ask questions of their child as to what they understand

10) Parents will learn to keep their calm while their child is having an emotional meltdown and determine alternatives to yelling and screaming

11) Parents will develop alternatives to being reactive towards emotional meltdowns or a lack of expected responses

12) Parents will learn to understand the different ways in which their child communicates with them

13) Parents will develop their specific communication abilities with their child.

BIBLIOGRAPHY

DSM-II, DIAGNOSTIC AND STATISTICAL MANUAL OF MENTAL DISORDERS, SECOND EDITION. COPYRIGHT, AMERICAN PSYCHIATRIC ASSOCIATION, 1700 EIGHTEENTH STREET
WASHINGTON, D.C. 2009
PUBLISHED, 1952

DSM-III, DIAGNOSTIC AND STATISTICAL MANUAL OF MENTAL DISORDERS, THIRD EDITION. COPYRIGHT, AMERICAN PSYCHIATRIC ASSOCIATION, 1700 EIGHTEENTH STREET
WASHINGTON, D.C. 2009
PUBLISHED, 1980

DSM-III-R, DIAGNOSTIC AND STATISTICAL MANUAL OF MENTAL DISORDERS, THIRD EDITION-REVISED. COPYRIGHT, AMERICAN PSYCHIATRIC ASSOCIATION, 1700 EIGHTEENTH STREET
WASHINGTON, D.C. 2009
PUBLISHED, 1987

DSM-IV, DIAGNOSTIC AND STATISTICAL MANUAL OF MENTAL DISORDERS, FOURTH EDITION. COPYRIGHT, AMERICAN PSYCHIATRIC ASSOCIATION, 1700 EIGHTEENTH STREET
WASHINGTON, D.C. 2009
PUBLISHED, 1994

DSM-IV-TR, DIAGNOSTIC AND STATISTICAL MANUAL OF MENTAL DISORDERS, FOURTH EDITION-TEXT REVISION. COPYRIGHT, AMERICAN PSYCHIATRIC ASSOCIATION, 1700 EIGHTEENTH STREET
WASHINGTON, D.C. 2009
PUBLISHED, 2000

**DSM-5, DIAGNOSTIC AND STATISTICAL MANUAL OF MENTAL DISORDERS, FIFTH EDITION. COPYRIGHT, AMERICAN PSYCHIATRIC ASSOCIATION, 1700 EIGHTEENTH STREET
WASHINGTON, D.C. 2009
PUBLISHED, 2013**

Agent Orange reference
http://www.11thcavnam.com/main/story_of_agent_orange.htm

Psychological Dictionary
https://psychologydictionary.org/

Merriam-Webster Dictionary
https://www.merriam-webster.com/

Center for Disease Control
https://www.cdc.gov/ncbddd/autism/data.html

https://www.cdc.gov/media/releases/2016/p0331-children-autism.html

Made in the USA
Middletown, DE
12 January 2020

83068177R00231